KU-736-037

Summary of Contents

THE WORDPRESS ANTHOLOGY

BY **MICK OLINIK**
& **RAENA JACKSON ARMITAGE**

The WordPress Anthology

by Mick Olinik and Raena Jackson Armitage

Copyright © 2011 SitePoint Pty. Ltd.

Product Manager: Simon Mackie
Technical Editor: Tom Museth
Expert Reviewer: Brad Williams
Indexer: Michele Combs
Editor: Kelly Steele
Cover Designer: Alex Walker

Notice of Rights

Notice of Liability

Trademark Notice

Published by SitePoint Pty. Ltd.

48 Cambridge Street, Collingwood
VIC 3066 Australia
Web: www.sitepoint.com
Email: business@sitepoint.com

ISBN 978-0-9871530-0-5 (print)

ISBN 978-0-9871530-5-0 (ebook)
Printed and bound in the United States of America

About Mick Olinik

Mick Olinik is a web developer and business model expert who's had the luxury and pleasure of watching the Web grow up over the past 15 years. A partner at Superfast Websites and NinjaDesk Elite Technical Support & Training, Mick is a WordPress expert who specializes in graphic design, WordPress theme skinning, and organic search engine optimization. He's the go-to web development guru for several of the top internet marketing specialists in the world, and a regular contributor to sitepoint.com. A graduate of Michigan State University and member of Phi Gamma Delta, Mick spends his time evenly between Asheville, North Carolina and Traverse City, Michigan. Aside from an obsessive passion for the ever-evolving technologies that bring the Web to your local internet browser or phone, Mick enjoys music, outdoor activities, photography, playing with his dog Lacie, spending time with family, and observing different business models in action. Come and say hi at his personal site at http://www.mickolinik.com, or follow him on Facebook at http://www.fbmick.com.

About Raena Jackson Armitage

Raena Jackson Armitage is a web developer, trainer, and content management geek. In 2010, Raena co-authored SitePoint's *Build Your Own Wicked WordPress Themes,* and has contributed to the SitePoint blogs and newsletters. When she's not pushing bytes around the Internet, you'll find her on her bike, watching Australian Rules football, gaming, or tracking down the perfect all-day breakfast.

About Brad Williams

Brad Williams is the co-founder of WebDevStudios.com and the co-author of *Professional WordPress* (2010) and *Professional WordPress Plugin Development* (2011), both published by Wiley. Brad has been developing websites for more than 15 years, recently focusing on open-source technologies such as WordPress. He is also one of the organizers of the Philadelphia WordPress Meetup Group and WordCamp Philly. You can find Brad on Twitter at @williamsba and at his blog at http://strangework.com.

About Tom Museth

Tom Museth first fell in love with code while creating scrolling adventure games in BASIC on his Commodore 64, and usability testing them on reluctant family members. He then spent 16 years as a journalist and production editor before deciding web development would be more rewarding. He has a passion for jQuery, PHP, HTML5, and CSS3, is eagerly eyeing the world of mobile dev, and likes to de-stress via a book, a beach, and a fishing rod.

Table of Contents

Chapter 3   The Loop and WordPress File System 55

Chapter 4   Post Types 79

Preface

WordPress is the most widely used website platform and content management system on the Web today, running on approximately 15% of websites. It is open source and, hence, free, released under the GNU Public License version 2, or GPL2 for short. Its permissive use and development license, combined with its ease of use from both a website user's and developer's perspective, has helped WordPress rapidly gain global market share for the past several years. It continues to grow each month, outpacing other content management systems at a rate of more than two to one. Indeed, in the eight years since Matt Mullenweg and Mike Little created WordPress as a branch of another open-source project, WordPress has become big business … and business is good.

Today, WordPress has become something of a hot topic making its way from the sphere of designers and programmers into the corporate world. Business owners seeking a website often look to build a WordPress site because they hear that it's a great platform, and while some of them might be unsure why WordPress is superior, their intuition is correct: WordPress is an excellent, flexible content management system with which to build a website. And that means whether you're a web designer or web developer (and regardless of your experience), learning to develop websites with WordPress and bend the platform to your will is a potentially lucrative proposition. Luckily, it's quite easy to learn too, and we're here to help you with that.

So pull up a chair, grab a beverage and a highlighter, and dig in while we show you how this powerful, flexible, extensively developed, and ever-popular content management system works!

Who Should Read This Book

This book is aimed at beginner to intermediate-level web developers seeking to work with WordPress on a fundamental level, so as to develop effective websites for clients in the real world. The book begins by explaining fundamental concepts, and then extends to intermediate and even advanced-level topics.

While noncoders will be able to glean some useful information from this book, you should at least have a ground-level knowledge of HTML and PHP to gain the most out of it. There's certainly no requirement to be a coding guru, but understanding integral concepts such as if statements, loops, functions, variables, and the manner in which PHP creates HTML for screen output will go a long way in helping you comprehend how WordPress does its thing. Solid conceptual appreciation of functionality are more important than memorizing specific functions and syntax—you can always look those up easily enough. Other languages and abilities that are useful to have when broadening your WordPress knowhow include CSS, JavaScript, and web server configuration skills via interfaces such as cPanel.

What's in This Book

This book could be divided into three sections. Chapters 1 and 2 serve as a thorough introduction to WordPress and are appropriate for beginner-level web developers who are just getting their feet wet with WordPress, as well as experienced developers who are new to the WordPress world and are looking for a solid primer. While a deep understanding of coding is unnecessary when reading the opening chapters, it is absolutely recommended for the rest of the book. Chapters 3 to 6 discuss in detail some of the fundamental aspects of WordPress's functionality, and how you can manipulate each one to build a successful WordPress site. Finally, Chapters 7 to 12 cover specific WordPress topics that are useful for gaining an intricate comprehension of the platform.

Because each chapter builds upon the information presented in previous chapters, you'll benefit the most by reading through from start to finish. However, if you're looking to simply further your knowledge on a certain concept, the book can also accommodate you. By reading the entire book, you'll have a thorough understanding of WordPress's strengths, weaknesses, and capabilities as a complete CMS solution as of WordPress version 3.2.

Chapter 1: *Hello World*

WordPress is really cool. Want to know why? We'll start with a brief history of the platform, before introducing you to WordPress 3.2. You'll also learn which types of projects are appropriate for WordPress, and which aren't. And of course, we'll introduce you to WordPress's famous five-minute installation.

Chapter 2: *WordPress 101*

Before we dig too deeply into how you can make WordPress do handstands at your beck and call, you'll want to become acquainted with the core platform. This chapter is your black-tie guided tour that introduces you to all the menus, functionality, and basic concepts about core WordPress you'll need to have down pat before you tackle the code underpinning WordPress.

Chapter 3: *The Loop and WordPress File System*

The Loop is the beating heart of WordPress, as it controls how content is displayed in any given installation. In truth, The Loop rules everything in WordPress; it is a fairly simple concept, but without having a firm understanding of it, you'll struggle when taking on any sort of serious development. So we'll break it down for you right here, along with a solid overview of the file and folder structure you'll need to be familiar with when manipulating and writing code for WordPress.

Chapter 4: *Post Types*

Creating pages or blog posts is great and all, but sometimes you need the ability to format elements so that they appear uniform; for instance, items such as recipes, staff listings, or the product details page in a shopping cart. WordPress offers custom post types to meet this need,

and in this chapter we'll explain what they are, how they work, and how you can create your own.

Chapter 5: *Plugins*

One of the primary reasons WordPress has become a content management powerhouse is due to its plugins system, allowing web developers to easily extend functionality beyond core. We'll explain everything you need to know about plugins, and how you can quickly and easily install them. We'll also create and analyze our own plugin so that you can understand how every line of code works.

Chapter 6: *Themes*

Themes make things look awesome—it's as simple as that. In any modern content management system there's a separation of content and design, so you can easily make changes to how a website looks, and themes are how WordPress addresses this. We'll talk about the components of a theme, as well as how you can use the nomenclature hierarchy and page template systems WordPress provides to create rich visual experiences. We'll also discuss the difference between display logic and site functionality.

Chapter 7: *Taxonomies*

Modern, robust content management systems provide methods to group pieces of similar content together in meaningful ways; these methods are referred to as taxonomies. In this chapter, we'll discuss taxonomies in detail and show you how to create them. We'll also introduce the notions of information hierarchy and content wireframes, important tools that help facilitate intelligent website development.

Chapter 8: *Image Galleries and Featured Images*

WordPress provides a host of low-level and high-level functions for manipulating images, ranging from the ability to insert prebuilt galleries into any page or post with ease and flexibility, to creating custom preset image sizes for use in commercial theme development. Whatever your skill level, you're bound to find something in this chapter for you.

Chapter 9: *The WordPress API*

Knowing the ways of the various application programming interfaces (APIs) made available within WordPress will lead you to truly mastering the platform. We'll cover the Plugins and Shortcode APIs that handle surface functionality, and more fundamental processes found in the HTTP and Database APIs. We'll also talk about the best ways to use JavaScript libraries throughout your themes and plugins, and discuss BackPress, an open-source PHP library that provides much of the core functionality available in WordPress. This is probably the most advanced chapter of the book.

Chapter 10: *Multisite: Rolling Your Own Network*

In addition to being configured for standalone websites, WordPress can be used to run a network supporting many individual websites off a single installation; this is the Multisite feature. We'll

explain how to set Multisite up, and take you through a guided tour so that you can try it yourself.

Chapter 11: *Going Global with Themes and Plugins*

As WordPress gains global market share, it follows that developers around the world would be interested in translating it into their native languages. Here we'll cover the distinction between internationalization and localization, and explain why you owe it to yourself to ensure your themes and plugins are properly localized. We'll finish the chapter by showing you how to install WordPress in a different language.

Chapter 12: *SEO, Marketing, and Goal Conversion*

While it's fun to play with WordPress, the real reason any business owner builds a website revolves around making money—and this is where search engines come into play. We'll conclude by explaining to you why search engine optimization (SEO) has always been so hard to master, and explain the difference between search engine optimization and search engine marketing. We'll investigate the three most vital SEO components, and introduce you to the importance of goal conversion.

Where to Find Help

SitePoint has a thriving community of web designers and developers ready and waiting to help you out if you run into trouble. We also maintain a list of known errata for the book, which you can consult for the latest updates.

The SitePoint Forums

The SitePoint Forums[1] are discussion forums where you can ask questions about anything related to web development. You may, of course, answer questions too. That's how a forum site works—some people ask, some people answer, and most people do a bit of both. Sharing your knowledge benefits others and strengthens the community. A lot of interesting and experienced web designers and developers hang out there. It's a good way to learn new stuff, have questions answered in a hurry, and generally have a blast.

The Book's Website

Located at http://www.sitepoint.com/books/wpant1/, the website that supports this book will give you access to the following facilities:

---

[1] http://www.sitepoint.com/forums/

The Code Archive

As you progress through this book, you'll note a number of references to the code archive. This is a downloadable ZIP archive that contains the example source code printed in this book. If you want to cheat (or save yourself from carpal tunnel syndrome), go ahead and download the archive.[2]

Updates and Errata

No book is perfect, and we expect that watchful readers will be able to spot at least one or two mistakes before the end of this one. The Errata page[3] on the book's website will always have the latest information about known typographical and code errors.

The SitePoint Network

The SitePoint network now features a host of sites dedicated to the latest hot topics in web development and design: RubySource[4], DesignFestival[5], BuildMobile[6], PHPMaster[7], and CloudSpring[8]. In addition, SitePoint publishes free email newsletters that feature the latest news, product releases, trends, tips, and techniques for all aspects of web development and design. You can sign up to one or more SitePoint newsletters at http://www.sitepoint.com/newsletter/.

The SitePoint Podcast

Join the SitePoint Podcast team for news, interviews, opinion, and fresh thinking for web developers and designers. We discuss the latest web industry topics, present guest speakers, and interview some of the best minds in the industry. You can catch up on the latest and previous podcasts at http://www.sitepoint.com/category/podcast/, or subscribe via iTunes.

Your Feedback

If you're unable to find an answer through the forums, or if you wish to contact us for any other reason, the best place to write is books@sitepoint.com. We have a well-staffed email support system set up to track your inquiries, and if our support team members can't answer your question, they'll send it straight to us. Suggestions for improvements, as well as notices of any mistakes you may find, are especially welcome.

---

[2] http://www.sitepoint.com/books/wpant1/code.php

[3] http://www.sitepoint.com/books/wpant1/errata.php

[4] http://rubysource.com

[5] http://designfestival.com

[6] http://buildmobile.com

[7] http://phpmaster.com

[8] http://cloudspring.com

Acknowledgments

Mick Olinik

First, I'd like to thank everyone at SitePoint for their help and support on this project—especially Tom, Kelly, Lisa, and Brad. You guys were all fabulous, and I enjoyed working with you on the project. I'd also like to especially thank Jen Sheahan for introducing me to this group in the first place, and Mark Harbottle for asking me to work on this project; it was truly an honor. Special mention goes to Jeremy Ferguson for his assistance with some of the code and general research throughout the book—you saved me a lot of time. Thanks to my wife, Claire, for her initial edits that made me look good in front of the SitePoint team, and for putting up with me as I wrote it. My team at Rockstar, especially Zack Fretty, kept all my ducks in a row as we went through this process. Thanks to James Schramko and Nic Lucas for giving me so many opportunities in Australia; I appreciate working with both of you more than you'll ever know. Thanks to Jason Silverman, for giving me that initial kick in the behind to begin writing, and to my father, John Olinik, for giving me the initial push into both web development and entrepreneurship. And finally, thanks to Trey, Mike, Page, and Jon for almost 20 years of perpetual inspiration, creativity, and energy … I'm forever indebted to you. Cheesecake.

Raena Jackson Armitage

Thanks first of all to everyone at SitePoint whose task is to crack the whip and polish my words into something approximating cleverness—but especially to Louis, Tom, Lisa, Simon, and to Kelly most of all. A big thanks to Mick, whose enthusiasm and immense knowledge of everything WordPress is, frankly, kind of staggering. Thanks to my family and friends all over the world. Finally, thanks to the WordPress community, for being kind and sharing people who make this product great.

Conventions Used in This Book

You'll notice that we've used certain typographic and layout styles throughout the book to signify different types of information. Look out for the following items:

Code Samples

Code in this book will be displayed using a fixed-width font, like so:

```
if (have_posts()) : while (have_posts()) : the_post();
        the_content(); endwhile; endif;
```

If the code is to be found in the book's code archive, the name of the file will appear at the top of the program listing, like this:

example.php

```
add_action('save_post',
           'save_conference_speaker_attributes');
```

If only part of the file is displayed, this is indicated by the word *excerpt*:

example.php (excerpt)

```
function check_current_screen() { if(!is_admin())
           return; global $current_screen; print_r($current_screen);
           }
```

If additional code is to be inserted into an existing example, the new code will be displayed in bold:

```
function the_author() { new_variable =
       "Hello"; }
```

Where existing code is required for context, rather than repeat all the code, a vertical ellipsis will be displayed:

```
function the_author() { ⋮ return new_variable;
       }
```

Some lines of code are intended to be entered on one line, but we've had to wrap them because of page constraints. A ➥ indicates a line break that exists for formatting purposes only, and should be ignored:

```
URL.open("http://www.sitepoint.com/blogs/2007/05/28/user-style-she
       ➥ets-come-of-age/");
```

Tips, Notes, and Warnings

Hey, You!

Tips will give you helpful little pointers.

Ahem, Excuse Me ...

Notes are useful asides that are related—but not critical—to the topic at hand. Think of them as extra tidbits of information.

Make Sure You Always ...

... pay attention to these important points.

 Watch Out!

Warnings will highlight any gotchas that are likely to trip you up along the way.

Hello World

We're glad you've picked this book up, and want to learn about one of the most increasingly popular pieces of web software on the Internet today: WordPress. WordPress is incredibly simple to install and use, but it's a lot like an iceberg; the stuff the vast majority of people will ever see or use represents just the tip of what's possible. True WordPress rock stars understand that it's actually an elegantly crafted content management system that goes much further below the surface. Our aim is to show you the fundamentals so that you can harness it to build almost anything you want online.

As you'll soon see, the power to do whatever you like already exists within WordPress's core installation. All you need to do is shape your application to look the way you want it to with a few simple tools. Let's dig in, starting with a short history lesson.

In the Beginning ...

When the World Wide Web was born and began to become populated with early websites in the mid-to-late 1990s, website developers used What You See Is What You Get (WYSIWYG) programs like Microsoft FrontPage and Macromedia Dreamweaver (later purchased by Adobe), or minimalist hand-coding tools like Notepad to create their HTML files and upload them directly to web servers via FTP clients. Web pages were generally created and maintained individually, which led to a whole host of problems (looking back with the benefit of hindsight!). For instance, if you wanted to change the same item on several web pages in the same website, you typically had to update each of those pages separately. It was also common for pages to differ slightly from one another on the same site because of a stray image or some slightly different code, resulting in a hodgepodge collection of pages that lacked uniformity and appeared rather amateur. Worse yet—and maybe

even worst of all—there was no clear separation of design, functionality, and content. This made web developers the only people qualified to make content changes to just about any website; additionally, it often proved to be a tedious, time-consuming process. The result was that building a website tended to be a high-cost, low return-on-investment proposition that produced mostly frustration for web developers, business owners, and website users alike—not to mention stagnant websites.

In response to these issues, web developers began to create web-based software that attempted to allow users to systematically manage content. While rudimentary at first, these **content management systems** (or CMSs) developed and became more widespread. However, while new features were always being introduced and added, they all had their limitations, most notably usability for the non-technical, content-oriented administrative user.

Over time, three general types of content management systems evolved:

- commercial
- open source, or free
- homegrown (defined as a set of programs developed by a particular web developer or web shop for their clients' exclusive use)

While the individualistic, hero mentality of the common coder dictated that homegrown systems were initially the most common, commercial and open-source CMSs gained momentum. Many developers found (and continue to find) the open-source world a useful and satisfying way to collaborate and build better systems than they'd otherwise create on their own; hence, open-source projects began to take off like wildfire.

A Brief History of WordPress

Now enters a developer named Michel Valdrini. In 2001, Valdrini added to the open-source community by launching the b2/cafelog project, an open-source content management system written in PHP[1] and utilizing MySQL[2] as its database. While b2/cafelog met with limited success, 2003 saw two new developers, Matt Mullenweg and Mike Little, step in and create a **fork** of the project—a legal copy of a piece of software developed to create a distinctly new product, with a different purpose and direction. The software created as a result of the fork became WordPress.

While b2/cafelog is recognized as the official predecessor to WordPress, it's still in active development itself under the name b2evolution[3]. In forking b2/cafelog to create WordPress, Mullenweg and Little sought to develop a blogging system that was more focused on the user experience as well as web standards, topics that at the time were still very much in flux. Over time, major features

---

[1] http://php.net/
[2] http://www.mysql.com/
[3] http://b2evolution.net

including plugins, themes, post types, and custom navigation have been added and improved upon, resulting in an extremely robust web publishing system that continues to evolve.

WordPress itself is actively developed and supported by several core developers—including Mullenweg, Little, and Valdrini—as well as a volunteer team of about 100 key contributors who work diligently to make it a better piece of software to use. About half of the core contributors work for Mullenweg's company Automattic, while the others are from all walks of the WordPress community. Furthermore, developers around the world continue to build and support new plugins and themes that are useful for a whole range of purposes, and translators abound to voluntarily interpret plugins, themes, and WordPress itself into additional languages where demand exists, further increasing the scope and reach of the project.

Despite coming into the world as blogging software, today WordPress is a full-fledged CMS with page navigation, user management, blog creation, and management tools. Whilst the word **blog** is shorthand for a combination of two words: "web" and "log," it's best defined as a collection of information that you want to categorize. For instance, if you're a photographer and you want to showcase your images, you could do so by putting together a blog for your photos. Each post could comprise one photo, which in turn would combine to create a collection of photos. Similar examples can be found in a range of topics, from current news and happenings to an online recipe collection. For this reason, you can view WordPress as both a blog and a full-featured CMS. It's a piece of web-based software that lets you create pages, categories, and posts and associate posts with different categories.

WordPress.com versus WordPress.org

WordPress comes in two flavors: wordpress.com[4], and self-hosted WordPress that's available for download at wordpress.org[5]. Wordpress.com is a network of websites supported and hosted by Automattic. Users can visit wordpress.com, sign up for a free account, and create as many blogs as they like in a similar fashion to other popular hosted blogging services like typepad.com.[6] Each of the blogs that a user signs up for will have its own URL, and will employ many popular features, such as the ability to add pages and basic design elements like backgrounds and colors. While a solid service, this is all we'll cover on wordpress.com in this book.

On the other hand, self-hosted WordPress is free to download, but no hosting is provided—you actually need to secure hosting separately. The advantages of self-hosted WordPress are numerous, including the ability to customize every aspect of your site's visual appearance through themes, add additional functionality via plugins, have custom permalink URL structures, and of course have full access to the source code. In fact, self-hosted WordPress includes an option that enables multisite functionality, essentially allowing you to create blog networks similar to the one employed

---

[4] http://wordpress.com

[5] http://wordpress.org

[6] http://typepad.com

at wordpress.com (for more information on multisite, flip over to Chapter 10). From here on out, when we talk about WordPress in this book, we'll mean self-hosted WordPress unless specifically otherwise stated.

Core WordPress

When you download WordPress from wordpress.org, you are downloading what is referred to as **core WordPress**, or sometimes just *core*. Core WordPress includes all the fundamental functionality maintained and honed by the core developers and contributors, and each successive WordPress release is the next iteration of this primary functionality. Minor releases tend to be security patches and bug fixes, while major releases introduce new functionality and occasional design changes. This book is based on the WordPress 3.2 major release, nicknamed Gershwin.

WordPress and its License, the GPL

WordPress is an open-source content management system licensed under the Gnu Public License (GPL), version 2. The license itself can be found in the **license.txt** file delivered in every WordPress installation; however, most people usually ignore it, because they just think of WordPress as open source, or free. That's really all you need to know, but if you are interested in how the GPL works, here's the deal in a nutshell.

The primary assertion made by the GPL is that all source code for any GPL-licensed software must be made openly available for anybody to use on any basis, including those with commercial intent. Furthermore, any modifications made to the GPL-licensed source code must be made freely available if that software is to be redistributed in any way. For example, if you were going to make a whole bunch of changes to WordPress's core code and then use it to run a profitable business selling oversized lawn darts to outdoor gaming enthusiasts, that's perfectly fine … and you wouldn't need to redistribute your code to do so. However, if you made changes to the core code, renamed it PhrasePress, and began to distribute it, you'd be required to make your source code freely available and release your new software under the GPL.

It's necessary to note that the GPL license employed by WordPress in no way involves content, because content isn't derived from the WordPress core. Instead, the content housed on a WordPress site is distinct from WordPress. This is an important distinction to understand, specifically for legal professionals concerned about the security and integrity of their client's intellectual property rights.

The Main Ingredients: HTML, CSS, JavaScript, PHP, and MySQL

WordPress's power comes from the simplicity of its system. Its standardized file hierarchy is intuitive and easy to understand, and keeps a clean separation between commonly modified components and the core installation. Additionally, for all but the most novice of developers just starting out, it's likely to be unnecessary to learn any new languages or technologies to effectively work with

WordPress. Instead, WordPress accepts any flavor of CSS and HTML that you're comfortable with, and PHP 5 & MySQL 5 when you need to perform some heavy lifting.

WordPress is truly an easy-entry piece of software, and if you're intending to just set up a site and go, there's no requirement to understand any code at all. As we'll see in a moment, installing WordPress is a piece of cake, and from there you can use a free theme or purchase a commercial one to make your site look awesome. After that, it's really all about understanding the controls and figuratively driving the car, and we'll cover a lot of this functional usage in Chapter 2. Beginner WordPress developers will need a working knowledge of HTML and CSS to do simple modifications. Still, there's no getting around it … if you want to really get your hands dirty and bend WordPress to your will, you'll need to be comfortable with PHP, and if you really want to get fancy, some JavaScript experience will come in handy too. This book is not designed to teach you either of those things, but if you'd like to broaden your repertoire, there are a number of books from SitePoint that we can recommend. *Build Your Own Website the Right Way Using HTML & CSS*[7] is a great place to start in the world of client-side development, while *Build Your Own Database Driven Website*[8] provides a wonderful introduction to PHP, MySQL, and server-side coding. If you're keen to dive into more client-side stuff and tackle JavaScript, you could look into Kevin Yank's excellent Learnable course, JavaScript Programming for the Web[9]. Without a functional understanding of these technologies, you may become a bit confused once you get past Chapter 2.

Why WordPress?

Let's be honest: as much as anything else, WordPress has become a popular buzzword in the past few years. Many newbie web developers flock to it immediately without much thought as to why they might want to use the platform. Experienced web project managers will tell you that there's a direct correlation between the ultimate success of a project and your reasons for why you're selecting a particular CMS platform, as well as how you intend to utilize it within the scope of the project. Luckily, WordPress is an exceptionally flexible platform that serves as a fabulous choice for most applications—but not necessarily all.

Which applications are appropriate for WordPress? Let's have a look:

Blogs
WordPress started its life as a blogging platform, and it's arguably the best currently available. Whether you're looking to create a topical hobby blog or an authority blog, WordPress is an excellent selection.

---

[7] http://www.sitepoint.com/books/html3/
[8] http://www.sitepoint.com/books/phpmysql4/
[9] https://learnable.com/courses/javascript-programming-for-the-web-40

Information-rich websites

Flexibility in handling simple content types like fairly static pages, combined with the custom menu options and robust blogging capabilities, makes WordPress an awesome platform for small, mid-sized, or large businesses alike. It's suitable for just about any informational purpose.

Information marketing and affiliate marketing websites

An industry that exploded in the latter half of the '00s, information and affiliate marketing has special needs that blur the line between blogging and ecommerce. Having been banned by most free blogging platforms, this type of site can find a home with WordPress, offering all of the required customization, sales functionality, and token passing and tracking in a format that allows marketers to own their space instead of renting or potentially breaching terms of service elsewhere.

Light to medium-level ecommerce

Combined with one of several supported plugins, WordPress can be an extremely robust ecommerce platform for physical and digital products, all while offering a simplified, easy-to-use interface.

Membership sites

Whether you're seeking a simple membership wall, or selling access to a multiple-tiered membership program on a single site, there are myriad plugins available that provide solid functionality.

Intranets

Core WordPress includes most of the fundamental functionality that IT managers look for in an intranet. Combine that with WordPress's standard privacy options, as well as a well-placed plugin or two that provides solutions to each corporation's unique needs, and WordPress is appropriate for many corporate intranets.

Social media

A set of plugins and themes exist that are collectively referred to as **BuddyPress**. BuddyPress extends WordPress's standard functionality to allow registered users to message and interact with one another, as commonly seen on social media networks. While there are certainly other options available in this particular area, WordPress is, at a minimum, a viable choice.

Light to medium-level forums

WordPress can also be extended to serve as a forum (also referred to as a bulletin board). There are several plugin-based solutions that introduce this functionality, the most lauded of which is bbPress.[10] It's useful to note that while you can technically add forum functionality to a WordPress installation, it's typically done as an addendum to other functionality on the same

---

[10] http://bbpress.org/

site. Sites that are fully dedicated to forums often find more fleshed-out functionality in other solutions.

Blog networks

We've already alluded to WordPress providing for what's called multisite capability, allowing you to manage either a few websites or thousands of them from a single installation. Multisite also centralizes the management of network-wide plugin additions, and introduces more sophisticated, layered user and roll support. For more on multisite, have a look at Chapter 10.

You might think this preceding list covers just about everything, but it really doesn't. There are a few more specialized types of sites that the current core release, combined with the selection of widely available plugins, simply fails to offer a commercially viable solution. Many of these types of sites are either extremely specialized or incur enterprise-level traffic. Of course, this isn't to say that there are no WordPress solutions available for these types of sites; certainly, new plugins are developed daily that may not have existed or had wide release at the time of writing. Please take the following list with a grain of salt—but here are a few examples of the kinds of sites we're talking about:

Large-scale, specialized forums

Businesses and organizations whose entire business model revolves around extremely large, robust, and secure forums often opt for more specialized commercial software to suit their purposes.

Large-scale ecommerce sites

While WordPress does offer excellent ecommerce platforms to work with via premium plugins, there are still several types of ecommerce functionality you commonly won't find. In such instances, there are specialized commercial options that can prove to be better solutions for the high-volume retailer with specific needs. Some functionality that's currently lacking includes customized visual product configurations, support for multiple shipping centers based on factors such as proximity to the purchaser or type of merchandise stocked, or automated RMA (return merchandise authorization) support.

Photography sales and gallery management

This is a fairly specific one. While there are plenty of WordPress themes and plugins that manage images and galleries in various ways, there continues to be a gaping hole in the market for photography professionals who seek to present public and private, password-protected photo galleries that have full ecommerce integration. These types of sites are usually sought out by event photography professionals and portrait photography studios. Currently, better options are found with commercial and **SaaS** (software as a service; typically cloud-based and on-demand) solutions.

Customer Relationship Management

CRM solutions do exist for WordPress, but most organizations find that the feature set they require is better served by one of several popular SaaS CRM solutions.

Web-based project management

Similar to CRMs, solutions do exist for WordPress, but more widely accepted and utilized project management solutions can be found through popular SaaS options.

Now that we have a good idea of what WordPress is mostly used for, and what you can use it for (and what you probably shouldn't use it for), you should now have a better sense of how you'll implement it within the context of your project. With all that said, let's start playing with WordPress a bit.

Installing WordPress

One of the biggest reasons for WordPress's mad popularity is its ease of use, beginning with the famous five-minute installation process it touts … and five minutes is fairly accurate. There are two primary ways to install WordPress, but before we check them out, let's take a moment to talk about your server's operating system.

Choose Your Operating System Wisely

In very general terms, there are two flavors of web servers commercially available:

- Linux servers
- Windows servers

Officially, WordPress runs on both server types, but it runs **natively** on a Linux server, not a Windows server. This means that not all of WordPress's awesome functionality works as intended on a Windows server. For instance, it's extremely difficult to properly activate **Pretty Permalinks** (see the section called "Permalinks" in Chapter 2) on a Windows server (and next to impossible to do without full root access)—Windows forces the insertion of **index.php** to make it function. In pragmatic terms, instead of a precise link like http://www.esquandolas.com/footwear/shoes/running, you are forced to have the more ponderous http://www.esquandolas.com/index.php/footwear/shoes/running.

While this technically works, it's a bad solution for a variety of reasons, not the least of which is search engine optimization. So while you can technically run WordPress on a Windows server, it doesn't mean that you should. It is best practice to run your WordPress sites on Linux servers.

Now that we have operating systems covered, let's jump into the installation process.

Installing WordPress through the Web-Based User Interface

There are two accepted ways that most professionals prefer to install WordPress: manually, or via the web-based interface that WordPress provides. You can use whichever method you like, and we'll detail both here, beginning with the web-based interface.

1. Download the current version of WordPress.

   Start out by visiting wordpress.org[11] and downloading the current version of WordPress. You'll end up with a single compression file, either a **.zip** file or a tarball,[12] depending on which version you choose to download.

2. Upload and extract WordPress.

   Upload WordPress to your web server using either your FTP client or the control panel running on your server, as shown in Figure 1.1.

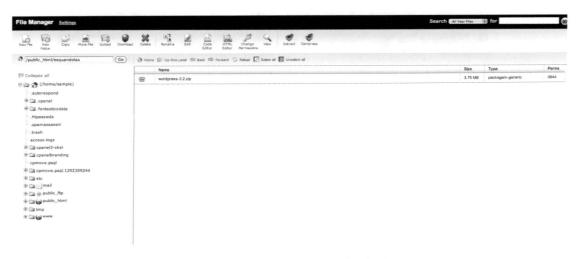

Figure 1.1. Zipped WordPress package on a cPanel web server

Note that you can extract the WordPress files locally and then upload them to the server individually, or you can upload the compressed WordPress file and then extract the files directly onto the server. The latter method is the way to go if you can do it, because it's typically faster, and it minimizes the risk of a corrupted or incomplete upload. You'll also remove the chance of an upload timeout that causes some files to not be uploaded at all.

---

[11] http://wordpress.org
[12] http://searchenterpriselinux.techtarget.com/definition/tarball

The Right Place

Once you extract the files on your server, take care to place the files where you want to install WordPress. By default, WordPress will extract all its files into a single directory called **/wordpress/**. If you want to install WordPress in the root directory that your URL is mapped to, you'll probably need to move the files down one directory, out of the **/wordpress/** directory.

3. Create your MySQL database

WordPress requires a MySQL database to store essential data, and you'll have to create it manually. If you use a hosting control panel like cPanel, you can do this very easily through a visual interface. Create your database, database user, and password, and then add your user to your database as shown in Figure 1.2. Be sure to write down all of this information and keep it in a safe place.

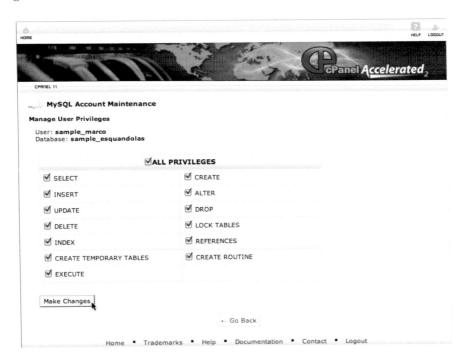

Figure 1.2. Add the database user to your new database

4. Point your web browser to your installation.

Now that your files are in place, navigate to where you expect to see your website. You'll be greeted by a screen that looks like Figure 1.3, and it will ask you to create a configuration file by clicking the button. Go ahead and do so.

There doesn't seem to be a `wp-config.php` file. I need this before we can get started. Need more help? We got it. You can create a `wp-config.php` file through a web interface, but this doesn't work for all server setups. The safest way is to manually create the file.

Create a Configuration File

Figure 1.3. The screen you'll see when pointing your browser to the install location

5. Get your information ready.

Next, WordPress is going to give you a little reminder as to the information it's about to ask you for (how thoughtful, eh?), as shown in Figure 1.4. Nothing to be concerned about here; make sure that you have the database information you just set up, and then click the **Let's go!** button to keep moving.

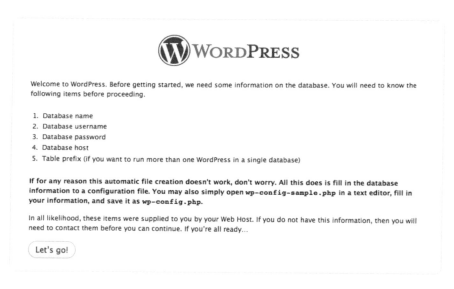

WORDPRESS

Welcome to WordPress. Before getting started, we need some information on the database. You will need to know the following items before proceeding.

1. Database name
2. Database username
3. Database password
4. Database host
5. Table prefix (if you want to run more than one WordPress in a single database)

If for any reason this automatic file creation doesn't work, don't worry. All this does is fill in the database information to a configuration file. You may also simply open `wp-config-sample.php` in a text editor, fill in your information, and save it as `wp-config.php`.

In all likelihood, these items were supplied to you by your Web Host. If you do not have this information, then you will need to contact them before you can continue. If you're all ready...

Let's go!

Figure 1.4. WordPress prompts you for the information you'll ultimately need

6. Enter your database information.

Now just follow the instructions and enter your database information as per Figure 1.5. Remember, it's case-sensitive, so capitalization matters.

WordPress

Below you should enter your database connection details. If you're not sure about these, contact your host.

Database Name	sample_esquandolas	The name of the database you want to run WP in.
User Name	sample_marco	Your MySQL username
Password	spiteman83	...and MySQL password.
Database Host	localhost	You should be able to get this info from your web host, if localhost does not work.
Table Prefix	wp_	If you want to run multiple WordPress installations in a single database, change this.

Submit

Figure 1.5. Inserting your database information

7. Run the installation.

After running a brief check to ensure it can talk to the database with the information you just provided, WordPress tells you that after a bit more descriptive information on your part, it's ready to go. Let's give it what it wants as in Figure 1.6 … and run the install.

WordPress

All right sparky! You've made it through this part of the installation. WordPress can now communicate with your database. If you are ready, time now to...

Run the install

Figure 1.6. Clicking the install button

8. Provide your basic site info.

Now for the really basic stuff. WordPress is ready to set itself up, but it needs a little information from you about the site you are about to create, as indicated in Figure 1.7. Answer a few questions here and then push the button to install WordPress. Go ahead. Click it. Feel the power.

Figure 1.7. Feeling the power of WordPress

9. And you're ready to roll!

You've just installed WordPress. Easy.

Installing WordPress Manually

If the web-based installer seems a bit tedious, don't sweat it—you're in fine company. Especially when you find yourself installing WordPress often, the whole process can go faster by skipping the web-based interface altogether and just directly editing the **wp-config.php** file. The first three steps are identical to the previous process and then we change it up a bit. Let's have a look:

1. Download the current version of WordPress.

2. Upload and extract WordPress.

3. Create your MySQL database.

4. Rename and edit **wp-config-sample.php**.

WordPress relies heavily on a file called **wp-config.php** to function, and by default provides you with a template to show you how it works: **wp-config-sample.php**. Start off by renaming this file from **wp-config-sample.php** to **wp-config.php**, so that WordPress can see it when it starts running. Open it up in a text editor—you can do this directly on your server if you are so inclined, or on your local machine if you're more comfortable that way (but remember to upload the file back to the server after you're done editing it). Inside the file, you'll just have to add your database name, database user, and user password in the appropriate fields. You'll also want to make sure that your authentication unique keys and salts are set up, which exist to increase the security of your installation. WordPress provides an easy tool to randomly generate these lines of code,[13] which you can copy and paste right into your **wp-config.php** file.

Let's preview at what the modified portion of the wp-config.com will look like when you finish editing it:

chapter_01/completed-wp-config-abridged.php

```
// ** MySQL settings - You can get this info from your web host
   ** //
/** The name of the database for WordPress */
define('DB_NAME', 'sample_esquandolas');

/** MySQL database username */
define('DB_USER', 'sample_marco');

/** MySQL database password */
define('DB_PASSWORD', 'spiteman83');

/** MySQL hostname */
define('DB_HOST', 'localhost');

/** Database Charset to use in creating database tables. */
define('DB_CHARSET', 'utf8');

/** The Database Collate type. Don't change this if in doubt. */
define('DB_COLLATE', '');

/**#@+
 * Authentication Unique Keys and Salts.
 *
 * Change these to different unique phrases!
 * You can generate these using the {@link https://api.➡
```

---

[13] https://api.wordpress.org/secret-key/1.1/salt/

```
    wordpress.org/secret-key/1.1/salt/ WordPress.org ➡
    secret-key service}
  * You can change these at any point in time to invalidate all➡
    existing cookies. This will force all users to have to log➡
    in again.
  *
  * @since 2.6.0
  */
define('AUTH_KEY',          'QnGRcSzcDG+e+Kv{y+@h7l&Nm>MeGNQzbJ!➡
                            7k!-eF*35VG{+E9 6++^M!F@|Gq~|');
define('SECURE_AUTH_KEY',   'EEgr)P13 7tjQ)Hs>h%A8US/BQ2Or.2X+]➡
                            @~641=S|C%VMq|Ko|zdvp/1W)k@`+&');
define('LOGGED_IN_KEY',     'Y3--2:9a!V+_76{&9d$:UB7i{54ksw*f&$➡
                            !i>y&TF3LlcdJgkrnO+UmA:HUx[>3=');
define('NONCE_KEY',         'A-*,KFM%alj6lD,Gri3-z~&-tD`N*t1;➡
                            +/*X#fPgtF!q6/2d4oj+-gn^k#Ko>@9&');
define('AUTH_SALT',         'V;bXi_7=M,?}9*t49+2DxKq`DD(v]==N# ➡
                            xwicF![UoI:F^S`x,F|,(vrvK#*6kG');
define('SECURE_AUTH_SALT',  '*qi`X3#On+rRI2yc~o@cw!OQSm[z+|Qb+➡
                            E#!z-BdjT9j2FC`2XeWH>S-3s8Fmszd');
define('LOGGED_IN_SALT',    '2UOc--owpM}Sq<@zHv`|G_a:;)2T_B[H+^➡
                            nfn<CJi3xMmb<NOAFt%=gEVO*R5]2Z');
define('NONCE_SALT',        'kqpm(x+2j#bS]p-].h|3b5Hw3t6mw2$F-2C➡
                            /kiJ;S!OQ^AZh=P)sn-BdK>ItuxgO');

/**#@-*/
```

5. Provide basic site information and install WordPress.

From here on out, it's easy sailing (if it wasn't already). Just point your browser to the installation location on your server and you'll be greeted by the "basic site information needed" screen we saw previously. Fill it out and click **Install WordPress**, and bada boom—you're done!

A Word about Installers

Technically, there's a third method you can use to install WordPress, although we don't recommend it. Many hosting companies provide one-click installers like Fantastico or Simple Scripts that you can use to install a variety of open-source software, including WordPress. On the surface, it sounds like a great idea—after all, as easy as the aforementioned installation process sounds, why not just click a button and have it all taken care of for you immediately, right?

Actually, there are a couple of reasons to be wary of installers. First of all, and probably the least harmful, is the fact that the installer may not install the most recent version of WordPress. WordPress releases new versions all the time, and it's important to keep up with them for a variety of reasons, not the least of which is security. After all, WordPress is an extremely popular piece of software, and that makes it a target for malicious hackers. WordPress constantly fixes security holes, so many

updates don't introduce new features, but rather are security patches designed to make sure your site is as bulletproof as it can be.

You might think that there's still no real issue to be concerned about with installers—despite the fact they may not install the current version of WordPress—because of how easy WordPress is to upgrade automatically. However, some of these installers actually tie themselves into your installation, preventing upgrades unless they occur through their system rather than WordPress's. This is distressing on several levels: we need to be certain that the current WordPress version is installed, and we definitely want to be confident that we're dealing with a clean, unchanged version of WordPress.

Lastly, while it seems like a great idea to automate as much as you can, sometimes it can all go wrong. Especially in situations where the hosting environment hasn't been accounted for by the author of an installer, matters can and sometimes do go bump, and you can end up with a WordPress site that's installed incorrectly. The point is that it's very easy to install WordPress—so do yourself a favor and install it the correct way.

Giving WordPress Its Own Directory

When WordPress is not the only software being run on a particular domain, many developers choose to give WordPress its own directory on the web server, instead of installing it in the root public HTML directory you'd like the system to propagate to. So you might physically install WordPress at http://www.esquandolas.com/wordpress, but actually look to have the website respond properly at just http://www.esquandolas.com, as indicated in Figure 1.8. This technique is often used when you need to redevelop an existing website on the same server that the current website is running on, but don't want to interrupt the existing website until you are ready to flip the switch and make it go live. It's also a handy way to keep the directory structure clean and organized on your web server, and avoids mixing in other files and directories being used for a purpose outside WordPress.

WordPress address (URL)   http://www.esquandolas.com/wordpress/

Site address (URL)   http://www.esquandolas.com/

E-mail address   marco@esquandolas.com

Figure 1.8. WordPress URL, Site URL, and admin email address in the General Settings page

 A Word About Multisite

When you enable multisite, WordPress must be installed in a root directory; it won't work correctly if you attempt to use the aforementioned technique. That said, if you are enabling multisite, you're likely to not be doing anything else in that server directory space, so it's barely an issue anyway. See Chapter 10 for more on multisite.

Giving WordPress its own directory is an easy process. Simply install WordPress like you would normally—but in its own directory. Then, when you want to port it to show up in a different location, log into your WordPress installation, go to **Settings** > **General**, and change the site URL to reflect where you'd like the site to propagate to. Now save your changes. Finally, copy the **index.php** and **.htaccess** files to the new directory where the new site should actually resolve to and open up the **index.php** file. Assuming you've installed WordPress into a subdirectory of the directory you'd like the website stored inside, and called it **wordpress** as per our example, you'll need to find this line in the copied **index.php** file:

```
require('./wp-blog-header.php');
```

And change it to this new line:

```
require('./wordpress/wp-blog-header.php');
```

After you save the file, you're all done, unless you've already set up your pretty permalinks (more on these in the section called "Permalinks" in Chapter 2). If that's the case, go back into your WordPress admin dashboard and navigate to **Settings** > **Permalinks**; save the existing permalink structure one more time. This will refresh your permalink structure in the **.htaccess** file and make the entire site route properly. For more detailed information on this process, check out the WordPress Codex page.[14]

Resources and Learning Tools

What most developers come to appreciate upon digging into the WordPress community is just that—there's a real, vibrant, intelligent, and helpful development community that is constantly building, improving, refining, translating, and otherwise adding to the conversation that is WordPress. Be it through documentation, forums, local meetups, or chat rooms, you'll find numerous mediums to give and receive help within the community. Let's now look at some of the more popular ways to become involved and interact with the community.

The WordPress Codex

Although it's the least interactive of any of the tools we'll mention here, the WordPress Codex[15] is by far the most powerful resource that the community has to offer. The Codex is WordPress's online documentation. It's a complete resource that is perpetually kept up to date by volunteer contributors within the community, and may well be the most useful tool available for learning how to use WordPress from the ground up. It's also handy for looking up specific functions and processes. While the Codex is technically a wiki, and as such contains information that is out of date from

---

[14] http://codex.wordpress.org/Giving_WordPress_Its_Own_Directory
[15] http://codex.wordpress.org/

time to time, the Codex will teach you much more about understanding how to complete tasks than simply memorize specific functions (although the more you know, the easier your life will ultimately be). If you struggle to understand a concept or need clarification on how to use a particular function, the Codex should always be your first stop. It's your very best friend.

Support Forums

Interactive places that offer help can be found in any number of support forums on the Web. In particular, the official WordPress Support Forum[16] is a great place to start. Powered by bbPress, the forum software we discussed earlier, the WordPress Support Forum is especially unique in that it automatically creates a forum for every plugin listed within the WordPress Plugin Directory, and includes functionality that allows for plugin developers to mark support questions as resolved. There are plenty of other WordPress forums to be found across the Web, including SitePoint's own WordPress forum.[17]

WordCamp and Local Meetups

If you are more of a reach-out-and-touch-somebody type of person, have a look to see if there might be a local group of WordPress developers and enthusiasts that connects on a regular basis.[18] Local meetups tend to draw people from all aspects of the WordPress community, including developers, designers, entrepreneurs, academics, hobbyists, marketers, and more. They've proven extremely beneficial for both novice and seasoned WordPressers alike. In larger communities, you may find several groups segmented for more specific purposes, but it really depends on what the general interests are of the people within your community.

Once a group becomes sizeable and there's enough interest shown, somebody either inside the group or within the general WordPress community may seek to organize a WordCamp. In any given locality, WordCamp is an event that often serves as the annual keystone for local meetup groups. Usually comprising two days, such events are often sponsored by Automattic, encouraging a large number of local experts to give presentations on WordPress-related topics, along with national and international experts who introduce new information, ideas, and influences into the local community. If you've never been to a WordCamp and are interested in WordPress and everything that goes along with it, it's an event that is well worth your time. Check out the schedule of upcoming WordCamps[19] and attend an event near you.

---

[16] http://wordpress.org/support/
[17] http://www.sitepoint.com/forums/wordpress-300/
[18] http://wordpress.meetup.com/
[19] http://central.wordcamp.org/

WordPress.tv

If you're unable to make it to a WordCamp, but want to see replays of presentations or are looking for video tutorials and related WordPress video-based content, WordPress.tv is for you.[20] Here you'll find information pertinent to both self-hosted WordPress and wordpress.com.

Chat Rooms

If you are an IRC (Internet Relay Chat) fan, there are several chat rooms that offer real-time assistance to your issues. If you've never used IRC before, you'll need an IRC client on your computer to connect to the service. Once you have your IRC client ready to roll, connect to the Freenode server at http://webchat.freenode.net/, and have a look at the following chat rooms that cover these topics:

#wordpress   This is the main WordPress support channel. If you have general questions, this is really the best place to hang out.

#wordpress-dev   This is the main channel covering discussions about WordPress core development. It is best to skip this one if you are looking for general WordPress assistance. Topics here regard core development only.

#buddypress-dev   This channel is for anything and everything related to BuddyPress.

#bbpress   The channel for anything and everything related to bbPress.

Google

Look, the truth is that WordPress is pretty darn popular, so to try to create an exhaustive list of quality WordPress learning tools and resources might literally up take half of this book—not to mention become out of date quickly because of new resources that continually crop up. As with anything else, an excellent tactic is to simply use the almighty Google and type in exactly what it is you're seeking to learn about. You'll find tutorials, videos, support forums, and blog posts galore that touch upon every aspect of WordPress.

People, we have a big, helpful community out there, so make sure you use it. Don't be afraid to become involved, and remember to give back to help out the next newbie. At the end of the day, we're all amateurs; some of us are just a lot more professional about it than others!

Ready to Press On

Well, that's a whole bunch of stuff we just covered, huh? We looked at a brief history of modern web development, from its origins through the development of mature content management systems, as well as how Matt Mullenweg and Mike Little brought WordPress into being. We also covered

---

[20] http://wordpress.tv/

the way the WordPress community works due to its core developers and contributors, as well as the general development community that creates and supports both free and premium plugins and themes.

We discovered the most common uses for WordPress, the general approaches to take to accomplish a particular type of project, and when you're better off looking in a different direction for a solution to a web application. Finally, you should now have at least one WordPress installation up and humming along nicely, and an army of resources where you can go to find help. So, with all that said and your shiny new WordPress site at the ready, let's jump on in and have a look around, shall we?

WordPress 101

WordPress is a powerful development platform that can scale to handle the simplest of websites, as well as more robust and complex custom web applications. Before we dig into the nitty-gritty of code manipulation, it's useful to return to the beginning and take a look at the functionality provided by default in every core WordPress installation.

An Overview of Core WordPress

For newbie website administrators, this chapter will serve as a primer on the basics of what you'll find within a modern CMS. And if you're already well-versed in alternative commercial or open-source content management systems, it will provide a thorough road map that illustrates how content management concepts apply in the WordPress universe. If either of these descriptions resonate with you, or if you just feel like reviewing what's available and possible, we invite you to sit back, relax, and come along with us on a tour of the core WordPress administrative back end. If this wasn't a book, we'd offer refreshments, but sadly you're out of luck.

Setting the Mood

Like many things in life, it can be helpful to set the stage for whatever it is you're doing before jumping into the main event. After all, if you're planning a romantic dinner for your significant other, it's more than just cooking a really nice meal … you'll want to set the table, light some candles, dim the lights, and put some Barry White on, right? In the same way, it's a good idea to have a look around the WordPress admin back end and configure some basic settings before you launch into adding content.

The Dashboard

The Dashboard is essentially the home page for the WordPress administrative dashboard, and it's what you'll first encounter every time you log into WordPress. It is designed to give you a visual overview of some of the key elements going on within the website by utilizing movable Dashboard widgets. As you can see in Figure 2.1, the Dashboard features several rectangular areas that each encapsulate a piece of information or functionality.

Figure 2.1. The WordPress Dashboard

Each of these sections are actually self-contained, movable Dashboard widgets that we can arrange by simply dragging them around into the order and configuration we choose. As soon as we move a particular Dashboard widget, the new configuration is automatically saved; it'll always be right where we left it unless we move it again.

 Take It or Leave It

It's useful to note that you'll either absolutely love or largely disregard the Dashboard. There's nothing on the Dashboard that you won't find elsewhere within the administrative back end, and usually with more fleshed-out functionality. Still, a lot of users quite like it, because it allows them an overview of lots of elements from one vantage.

Core WordPress comes with a bunch of pre-installed Dashboard widgets that you can move around and play with, but some plugins will introduce additional Dashboard widgets for your use. If you find yourself using the Dashboard quite a bit but would like to customize its appearance or remove several widgets that take up too much space, you can have a look at its screen options.

Screen Options

Many areas of the administrative back end feature screen options, evident in Figure 2.2. When screen options exist for a particular WordPress section, you'll find an appropriately labeled button in the upper right-hand corner of your screen that will reveal a menu specific to the area you're working on.

Figure 2.2. Screen options in the WordPress Dashboard

For the Dashboard, you'll notice that WordPress provide two types of feature controls: the ability to show and hide different Dashboard widgets, and vary the number of vertical columns to display your Dashboard widgets. As a user, this gives you a great deal of flexibility in customizing your Dashboard.

Keep It Relative

If you are a developer who plans on integrating a Dashboard widget into a plugin, you'll want to take the width of a Dashboard widget into account. Keep in mind that your widget could be running in a relatively wide, one-column environment, or crunched up in a much narrower four-column environment. Be sure to use relative widths for visual outputs in these instances, and recognize that you simply lack *any* control as to how the Dashboard widget will ultimately be viewed.

The Admin Menu

Running along the left-hand side of the back end, you'll find the main **Admin** menu used within WordPress. Over the years, the **Admin** menu has seen some of the most significant overhauls of any of the visual aspects within the administrative back end, originating as a top-running horizontal menu and remaining that way until WordPress 2.7, when the design was shifted to a vertical positioning. Along with several other administrative visual elements, WordPress 3.2 took it a step further and made the menu minimal and narrow; a design improvement that does a better job of staying out of your way, and gives you more workspace on smaller browsers.

Each main section within the core is a top-level menu item in the **Admin** menu. Moving your cursor over to the right of each top-level menu label will reveal a drop-down arrow that expands to a submenu beneath. In Figure 2.3, you'll notice that the **Updates** menu item displays a gray circle with a number one in it, indicating that we have one plugin or theme that has updates available

that we can automatically upgrade to. Additionally, the menu highlights the section you're working in, pointing to it with a subtle right-handed arrow. Finally, if you want to see less of the menu, you can always click the **Collapse menu** link at the bottom of the menu, which will decrease its width by about 80%. This leaves only the main icons visible, so you still have access to your navigational controls.

 ### An Ever-expanding Menu

Figure 2.3 shows the default **Admin** menu when you first install core WordPress, but once you begin adding plugins to your site, your menu will become more cluttered. When you do install plugins and look to use your new functionality, understand that its settings page can technically be located anywhere on this menu, as hooks exist to add to each section (we'll learn more about hooks later on in the section called "Action Hooks and Filter Hooks" in Chapter 5). However, you'll most commonly find plugin settings pages listed as subitems in either the **Settings** or **Tools** menus, or added as their own top-level menu.

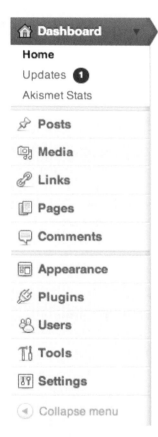

Figure 2.3. The main **Admin** menu in WordPress

General Settings

The next piece we should have a look at is the General Settings screen, seen in Figure 2.4 and located at **Settings** > **General**. General Settings are where you can set the most fundamental variables used throughout the installation.

Figure 2.4. The General Settings page

Site Title and **Tagline** are self-explanatory, and many themes use them by default in your website header and title tags. We've already touched upon site addresses in Chapter 1, with the WordPress address being the physical location where WordPress is installed, while the site address is the URL that the website should actually propagate and display to (if you are unclear on this, go back and have a look at the section called "Giving WordPress Its Own Directory" in Chapter 1). The rest of the options are also self-evident by their names: primary administrative email address, new user default role, time zone, date format, time format, and what day you want to start your calendar on if you choose to use the calendar widget that comes standard with core.

The only option that may need explanation is **Membership**, which is where you can indicate who can sign up to be a user on the website—whether through the automated user registration functions built into core, or more restricted access with a manual registration of all users. Let's keep moving, though; the tour gets better.

Themes

When you move into a new house, you only feel comfortable once there's furniture in your front room and some artwork on your walls. It doesn't have to be perfect—just as long as it's not blank and bare. The same holds true for your website, and luckily WordPress ships with a default theme that can be customized. Furthermore, while you can only have one theme activated at a time, you can add themes to your site to your heart's content. Pop over to **Appearance** > **Themes** and you'll see your **Manage Themes** screen, which will show you all the themes you've already loaded to your site. For each inactive theme, you'll have three available options: **Activate**, **Preview**, and **Delete**. When you have content populated in your site, the **Preview** option is especially nice, as you'll get a good idea of what a new theme will look like without having to actually make the change to your live site.

You can also add new themes from right inside your back end by clicking the **Install Themes** tab at the top of your screen, as seen in Figure 2.5. There's also the option to look for additional themes through the WordPress Theme Directory if you wish.

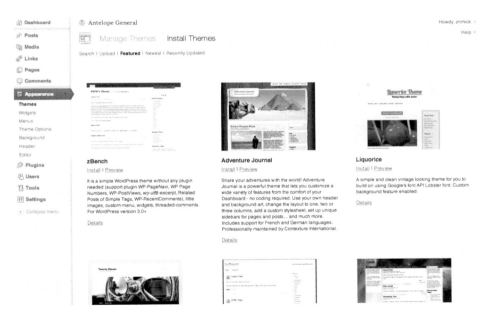

Figure 2.5. Some of the theme options in **Install Themes**

WordPress will let you search themes from the Theme Directory by keyword and visual attribute, or you can look through featured, recently updated, or brand new themes that have been made available. Each theme can be previewed and installed right away, giving you plenty of options to make your website look killer—even if you have no particular graphic design skills. You can also use the **Upload** link to install a theme in a **.zip** file you might have on your local machine.

Since we're talking about themes, there are a couple more points worth noting. As we'll see later in this book, many themes include theme-specific, user-configurable options. In these instances,

the theme can act like a plugin, and may add submenu items in the **Appearance** menu. For instance, we have WordPress 3.2's default theme—Twenty Eleven—active in the previous example, which has in turn added **Theme Options**, **Background**, and **Header** submenu items to our **Appearance** menu. If we change to another theme, these menu items will disappear and be replaced with different options unless the new theme has specifically configured them to be there. An additional tool that you should be aware (but wary) of is the theme editor, found at **Appearance** > **Editor**. This tool gives you direct access to view and (if you have relaxed enough permissions) make changes to the theme code directly while it is live. Be very, very careful with this tool: it's never best practice to make coding changes in a live environment, since even experts can accidentally miss a semicolon here or a bracket there, resulting in mayhem.

Finally, while you technically can change your theme easily and as often as you like, if you're trying to build a brand for your company or website in general, making frequent theme changes is generally a bad idea, unless you happen to be the most *avant-garde* of artists. People can be confused easily, and visual brand continuity means a lot. Remember that while dressing up your website can be tons of fun, it isn't like dressing yourself in the morning—save the frills for what you're wearing.

Privacy Settings

In what may be the easiest, most straightforward setting in WordPress, **Privacy Settings** (available by navigating to **Settings** > **Privacy**) determine whether or not you want to add `noindex`, `noarchive`, and `nofollow` tags to every page on your website. This effectively makes it invisible to search engines, and hence just about anyone who's unaware of the direct URL of the website. It's really handy when you are rebuilding an existing website in a public location, and want to ensure your timing is right when relaunching the new one, or if you are looking to run a public corporate intranet, but have no need for your pages to be indexed by engines. When privacy is set to block search engines, a message is displayed in the **Right Now** Dashboard widget, letting you know that search engine logging is blocked.

Automatically Updating

Finally, WordPress gives users the ability to upgrade conveniently and directly from within the WordPress administrative back end. Whenever a new release of WordPress is available, you'll receive a notification with a corresponding upgrade link at the top of every page in the back end. Click the link and you'll be taken to a formal update page, which will give you the option to upgrade WordPress, as well as any out-of-date plugins that you have in batch. The automated upgrade utility is excellent, and makes keeping up with feature updates and security patches a piece of cake.

 Back Up, Back Up, Back Up!

While it should genuinely go without saying (and before you actually click the **Upgrade** button you must read past a message that reminds you), please, pretty please, with sugar on top ... make sure you have a backup of your website. WordPress core itself has no integrated backup solution for a

number of reasons, most notably because of the varied environments that WordPress will run on; however, if you are doing anything of note with your website and have any long-term care for it at all, you really owe it to yourself to regularly back up your data. There are two common methods for backing up and restoring WordPress—either a WordPress backup plugin (and there are several premium plugins out there that do a great job), or some type of server-based backup option that covers both your website and your other web-based server data (such as email, DNS and the like). We won't dig much more into backup solutions here as it's beyond the scope of this book, but avoid making the mistake of overlooking its importance before it's too late.

Creating and Managing Text-based Content

Now that we've covered the background and setup stuff that we need with every WordPress install, we can finally get down to what this is really all about: working with, organizing, and managing content. Content can pragmatically be thought of as any piece of information we're going to be adding to our website, and commonly describes text, images, videos, and audio files. However, placed within the context of WordPress, most people tend to refer to text throughout a website as **content**, while images, videos, audio files, PDFs, and the like are categorized as media. By definition it's all content, but you'll find people referring to it in different ways. Don't worry, we'll cover all of it, beginning with the text-based stuff.

Pages

In WordPress, the most basic and intuitive form of text-based content is a page. Pages are meant to be used for static informational content; that is, content that's only changed infrequently. If you think about it in terms of the generic small business brochure website, example pages might include **About Us**, **Map and Directions**, or **Contact Us**. In each of these, the content may need occasional adjustments, but it shouldn't change all that much.

In order to view all the pages that you have loaded into your site, go to the **Pages** top-level menu in the **Admin** menu, and click on either the main **Pages** heading or the **All Pages** submenu item. This will give you a complete listing of all the pages that have been created, as well as their publishing status (whether they're in draft, published, or scheduled to be published—more on this in a bit), the author who created them, and the date they were created or published. Adding pages is as simple as clicking the **Add New** button at the top of the **Pages** management screen, or the submenu item of the same name in the **Pages** section of the **Admin** menu. Editing existing pages, on the other hand, can be done by simply locating the page you'd like to edit within the page listing, and clicking on the name of that page. You'll then be brought to a screen that looks like Figure 2.6.

Before we jump into the guts of page editing, it's useful to note that for both the primary types of text-based content in WordPress—pages and posts—the editing screens are similar. They are divided into two sections: the content editor, and supporting attributes that are displayed via meta boxes (see the section called "Meta Boxes"). We'll examine both sections within the context of pages so

that we don't need to spend as much time on them when we look at posts, which are a little more complicated conceptually.

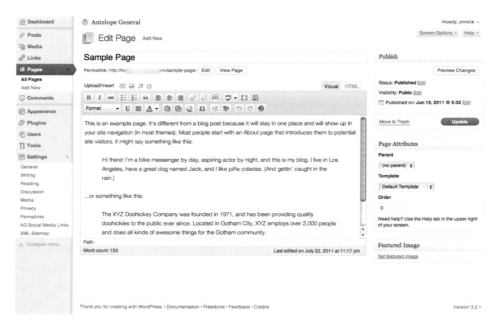

Figure 2.6. Editing a page

Upon initial installation, WordPress is good enough to provide a sample page to play with, so that you can get a feel for how things work; this is what the **Edit Page** screen looks like for that page. The main portion is fairly obvious; at the top is the main title for the page—in this instance, it's **Sample Page**. Below the title box is the permalink, which we'll cover this later on in the chapter, and in even greater detail in Chapter 12; for now it suffices to understand that if you have **Pretty permalinks** enabled, the page's slug will default to the sanitized version of the page title. Below this is the content editor: the place where you can actually enter and edit your page content.

The Content Editor

As we've described, pages (and posts, covered later) make identical use of the **content editor**, which you can think of as a kind of word processing program. After typing or pasting your page copy into the main content area, you can then format it as you intuitively would do in any commonly used word processor: through a formatting bar at the top of the content area. This toolbar has the buttons that provide your most important formatting functionality: highlight a word or phrase and click the bold, italic, or strikethrough buttons, place your cursor in your text where you want to create bulleted lists or block quotes, or align your content as you want it—it's all there. Hovering over each button will produce a tooltip, in case you need to discover its purpose. When you want to add a link, highlight the copy where it will be, and click the button that looks like a chain link. This will give you a dialog box with all the standard hyperlinking options that you're accustomed to, as well as additional features that let you search and link to existing content within your site. It's just as easy

to edit an existing link: place your cursor on the link you want to work with and click the same button. Deleting a link follows the same process, but instead of clicking the button that looks like a chain link, click the button that looks like a *broken* chain link. (See what we just did there? Tough stuff!)

Adding images, video, and audio is done by clicking the appropriate icon next to the **Upload/Insert** link above the content editor. This will bring up a dialog screen where you can either upload a file directly from your computer, or insert one you already have in your media library. We'll cover this in more detail in the section called "Working with Media and the Media Library".

Another essential feature built into the content editor is the ability to flip between visual and HTML versions of the page you're working with. To do so, click the appropriate tab in the upper right-hand corner of the editor to modify your view. Ultimately, keep in mind that everything you build in WordPress is going to be displayed in an HTML format; therefore, while a visual editor is helpful in knowing how your page will look, it's sometimes necessary to look at and make adjustments to the underlying HTML that will support that content. It's also an absolute necessity anytime you need to add a script of some sort to your copy. Companies that provide ready-to-use services for website owners—such as hosted streaming video players, mailing list services, and even hosted ecommerce solutions—routinely provide raw HTML or JavaScript code blocks that they require you to insert into your page copy where you want their service to appear on your web page. This means you need to have the ability to directly access the underlying HTML of your content copy through the content editor.

 Keep It Plain

If you are pasting in your copy from another source rather than typing it in, be aware of the following. Although you can paste directly from Microsoft Word to WordPress, or convert copy to plain text before pasting it, it's advisable to use a plain text editor such as Notepad or TextEdit instead. This ensures you are adding it in plain text (rather than rich text), thus avoiding any extraneous formatting or random characters that can cause display issues within WordPress.

Completing the tour of the content editor is the enhanced fullscreen editing feature commonly referred to as distraction-free writing. In the top toolbar, click on the menu item with the icon featuring four arrows that point towards the corners in an expanding fashion. You should see a similar view as in Figure 2.7.

Figure 2.7. Writing without distractions

Introduced with WordPress 3.2, distraction-free, fullscreen writing is a popular feature among copywriters who spend a lot of time writing directly into WordPress. Upon entering the fullscreen mode, you are initially shown the pared-down content editing options as displayed in Figure 2.7; but place your cursor in the content area and start typing, and all those minimal functionality queues fade away, leaving you with just your thoughts and words on a white screen. It's a Zen-like feature that can help the creative process by getting rid of overstimulating clutter, letting you focus on the content you are writing. Move your cursor again and your minimal navigation pops back up, complete with the option to leave fullscreen and go back to the normal editing screen.

Meta Boxes

The next major component in the page editing screen is all about the supporting attributes associated with any given page (or post). These supporting attributes are housed in **meta boxes**—boxes within the graphical user interface that compartmentalize information—and display on the right side of the page editing screen. While plugins or themes will offer you the ability to add custom meta boxes to the sidebar or beneath the content editor in different ways, the two that you should be aware of first up involve publishing information and primary page attributes.

At the top of the right-hand sidebar is the **Publish** meta box, which handles publishing information for the page. The main attributes that you can change and modify here are:

Status

Pages and posts can be saved in WordPress and marked with the status of **Published**, **Pending Review**, or **Draft**. Pages that have a status of **Draft** are just that: they are works in progress, and unable to be viewed in any manner at the front end of the website. Pages that are **Pending Review** are similar to those in **Draft**, with the exception that website editors with publishing privileges

can effectively moderate the content on these pages, making changes prior to publishing. **Published** pages are live on the site.

Visibility

Relevant once a page has actually been published, this attribute describes the rules allowing website visitors to view that particular page. **Private** pages are available on the front end of the website only to the creator of the page, while **Password Protected** pages require a password to be viewed, which can be set in this location upon selecting the option. **Public** pages are visible to all.

Published on

Defaulting to the current time, this attribute allows you to define the specific time a page should be published to the site. You can backdate the publishing date of a page if you wish, or you can schedule a page to be published at a date and time in the future. This attribute is more useful in batch scheduling the publishing of posts rather than pages, but there are cases where scheduling a page might be appropriate. For instance, a physician's office might have a page for each of the doctors working in the office. If a new doctor was hired and scheduled to begin work several weeks from that date, the person responsible for web content could add that doctor's profile page to the site immediately, but not publish it until the day the doctor started work.

Directly underneath the **Publish** meta box is the **Page Attributes** meta box, which features these particularly important attributes:

Parent

Pages have the ability to be built into hierarchical structures; this is extremely useful for organizing your site information and setting up your website permalinks properly (more on permalinks in the section called "Permalinks"). Pages are structured to have parent-child relationships, which enable a more specialized version (child information) of a more general version (parent information) of a particular page. For instance, if we were building a website that revolved around the topic of energy and fuel, we may have a page for liquid fuel. If we chose to break out individual pages that detailed different types of liquid fuel—say gasoline, diesel, and jet fuel—we would seek to create a parent-child relationship within individual pages. After creating a page for each of these topics, we'd then locate and select the Liquid Fuels page in the drop-down box on each of the three different fuel type pages (Jet Fuel, Gasoline, and Diesel); this indicates that each fuel type page are subsets (or children) of the originating page, Liquid Fuel).

Template

Every WordPress theme by definition comes with at least one page template, which is defined by the **index.php** file as we'll learn in Chapter 6; however, you can add as many page templates as you'd like to any given theme. Page templates can control how any WordPress page appears and, in some cases, operates.

To Be, or Not to Be Seen

Many aspects of WordPress won't be visible on the screen until you have a need for an option to be displayed. For instance, when you initially install WordPress, you'll be provided with one sample page. If you happen to go looking for the parent drop-down box where you only have one page loaded to WordPress, you won't find it; WordPress is smart enough to know that it's impossible to have a parent-child relationship if only one page exists. Similarly, in a category listing, a particular category will remain unseen unless there is actually a post in that category to display. This really is intuitive information, but when you're learning how to use the system initially, it can be a bit confusing. So, as you learn techniques and features of WordPress, always keep in mind that you may actually need to add content in order to see something work the way you expect it to.

Saving (Your Backside)

The final two elements of note on the page editing screen are the **Update** button and the **Move to Trash** button. The **Update** button is straightforward: it's your main save and update button for the page. If you do try to navigate away from a page before updating, WordPress will try its best to save your behind: a pop-up notice will ask if you really want to leave the page before saving your work. If you still decide to move on and end up losing something you really needed—remember, we did try to warn you.

Publish First

Technically, the **Update** button will only display if you've already published your post or page; otherwise, it will be replaced with the **Publish** button, allowing you to publish the page or post to the site. You'll have your **Save Draft** option as well.

The **Move to Trash** button does just that—moves the page to the trash. This brings up an important point: WordPress doesn't just delete stuff—its **Trash** function is similar to the one you might be familiar with on your PC or Mac. When you delete a page or a post from your site, WordPress doesn't remove it immediately; rather, it throws it into a holding queue that effectively removes it from view, but holds on to it for 30 days in case you change your mind and decide that you actually need it. To retrieve it, click on your trash bin in either the **Pages** or **Posts** area, restore it, and presto—it's back, all shiny and new! There's WordPress again, doing its best to cover your backside.

Quick Edit and Bulk Edit

A handy feature that both pages and posts share is **Quick Edit**. Sometimes you may need to change a page or post attribute in WordPress, but would prefer to avoid loading up the entire page editing screen to do so. This is often the case when you need to make changes to several pages or posts all at once. One way to handle this is through the **Quick Edit** screen, seen in Figure 2.8.

Figure 2.8. The Quick Edit Screen

When you go to either the page or post listings page in the back end, a small menu will be revealed when you move your cursor over any given page or post. This menu will give you four options: **Edit**, **Quick Edit**, **Trash**, or **View**. We've covered **Edit** and **Trash**, and **View** just shows you what the page or post looks like on your site. **Quick Edit** will open up a set of controls inline with your listings as seen in Figure 2.8. Furthermore, if you need to make the same basic changes to several pages or posts in your site, WordPress gives you a **Bulk Edit** feature to work with as well.

In the drop-down menu above the page/post listings, you'll find a further drop-down that lists **Bulk Actions**. Select the pages or posts you need to work with and then select **Edit** from the **Bulk Actions** drop-down. You'll be presented with the inline screen seen in Figure 2.9, allowing you to make wholesale changes to entries in your site very quickly.

Figure 2.9. Using the **Bulk Edit** option

Understanding Posts and Categories

Now let's learn about posts, the other primary text-based content type in WordPress. From an editing perspective, posts are similar to pages, as we've already seen. The main difference between posts and pages is that while pages are meant to be stand-alone pieces of information, **posts** are individual pieces of content of a dynamic nature that need to be grouped together and categorized in meaningful ways. The key word to note is *dynamic*, where content is (or can be) perpetually added

to a degree that would make its sheer volume unmanageable without a system. And of course, WordPress provides a system using categories. Before we look at the *how* of posts and categories, let's make sure we conceptually understand what they are and why they're structured the way they are.

Posts and categories can be best illustrated by looking at an example from the offline world. A classic example can be found in print newspapers. Let's create a fictitious newspaper that we'll call *The Mockingbird Gazette*. Like most newspapers, *The Mockingbird* has standard sections: Sports, Business News, Finance, Lifestyle, and of course the main News section. Within each of these sections, *Mockingbird* editors have formed subsections to better organize the articles within the newspaper, making it easier for readers. In the Lifestyle section, for instance, there might be subsections for Movies, Music, Books, Community Events, and Food and Drink. Let's say that the newspaper printed an article about a trendy microbrewery called The Wedge, which opened up in a cool, urban, reclamation-style location that sat adjacent to some train tracks. If you were recommending the article to a friend, you might hand them a copy of *The Mockingbird* and direct them to the Lifestyle section. If you wanted to be more specific, you could tell your friend that it was in the Food and Drink section of the Lifestyle section, making it easier for that person to go and find it.

In WordPress, posts and categories work in the same fashion. Drawing from our example, let's say we wanted to ditch the paper aspect of our newspaper altogether, publishing *The Mockingbird* online for environmental, economic, and accessibility reasons (sounds familiar, doesn't it?). We'll replace our newspaper sections with what we refer to in WordPress as categories, and write our articles in the form of posts. *The Mockingbird* online now has a WordPress website with categories that include **Featured News**, **Sports**, **Business News**, **Finance**, and **Lifestyle**. Furthermore, we'll divide our **Lifestyle** category into subcategories: **Movies**, **Music**, **Books**, **Events**, and **Food and Drink**. We can even organize our posts further, so that when a visitor looks for the article about The Wedge brewery we talked about earlier, it will be in both the **Lifestyle** category as well as the more refined **Lifestyle** > **Food and Drink** category. When our visitor has finished reading about the free peanuts on offer while drinking the top-class beer at The Wedge, and wants to know about the community events going on elsewhere around town, they can then click over to **Lifestyle** > **Community Events**. This method of organizing posts into categories and subcategories is just one of the ways that WordPress lets you organize information. Let's now look at another.

Understanding Tags

What's really cool about content management systems in general is that you're able to instantly extend functionality beyond what you'd ever have been able to do in the bricks-and-mortar world. Sticking with our example post on The Wedge microbrewery, we know where we can find the article within the category and subcategory system. We also know that if we were to search for "The Wedge" in our search box, we'll find it that way.

But what about the other stuff we learned about The Wedge? That it's a microbrewery in an urban reclamation-style location. It sits next to active train tracks. Let's say they also play free movies there, and it's dog-friendly. And please, let's not forget about the free peanuts, okay? All of these facts are big plusses, so it sure would be cool to find more places with similar characteristics, especially if you have a dog that you like to take with you when you chill out in town. Tags help make that a reality.

Tags are predefined keywords that the author or editor of a post can use to describe it; they're generally not broad enough to necessitate their own category. For instance, in all but the most niche markets, it would never make sense to list "dog-friendly" or "free peanuts" as a category to routinely post to; however, you still might mention this sort of information when it's relevant. For our example post on The Wedge, it would be appropriate to add tags such as "microbrewery," "urban reclamation," "train tracks," "free movies," "dog friendly," and, of course, "free peanuts."

Creating and Working with Posts

Now that we understand how posts are used, let's return to the WordPress administrative back end to see how we actually create and apply posts, categories, and tags. Creating a post is much like creating a page. In the main **Admin** menu, open the **Posts** menu and select **All Posts**; then click the **Add New** button above the listing of posts currently saved within the site. Alternatively, click the **Add New** submenu item button in the **Posts** Menu. This will bring you to a page that looks similar to the **Add New Page** screen. In fact, almost everything about adding a new post to WordPress is identical to adding a new page to WordPress, with the exception that individual posts do not have parent-child relationships with one another (categories do in the form of subcategories, as described in our example). You'll also notice several new meta boxes on the right-hand side of the **Add New Post** screen, as shown in Figure 2.10.

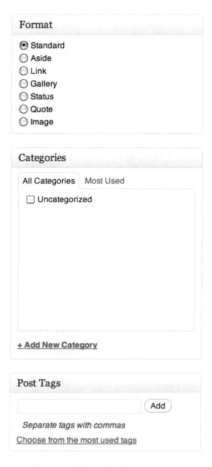

Figure 2.10. New meta boxes in the **Add New Post** screen

First up is the **Format** meta box, and it's being included here because it would be confusing not to do so. Simply put, this was introduced into core during the WordPress 3.1 release, and its purpose is to standardize how WordPress conveys the type of information contained within a specific post to a theme or external blogging tools. As of the time of this writing, it's not widely utilized, so its future is unclear in terms of ongoing usage. Furthermore, if the active theme lacks support for post metadata, this box won't display. For the most part, it's fairly safe to just use the standard format and move right along, but it's useful to keep this in mind when your usage expectations might shift. For more information, have a look at post formats on the WordPress Codex.[1]

Closer to the heart of the matter are the **Categories** and **Post Tags** meta boxes that follow **Formats**. These are fairly intuitive, with some cool logic integrated. Within the **Categories** box, you're presented with a list of available site categories to choose from; adding your post to a category is as simple as ticking the adjacent checkbox. Bear in mind that posts can be listed in multiple categories, which is handy if it's appropriate, but it's advisable to use some restraint with this feature. In

---

[1] http://codex.wordpress.org/Post_Formats

situations where you have a multitude of categories, it can be useful to click the **Most Used** tab and select from this listing instead. Finally, you can also add new categories on the fly, which is especially useful in the early stages of site development. In the event that you need to create a category, click on the **Add New Category** button and you'll be able to create it inline. Click the **Update** button, and you're good to go!

 ## Minimize Your Categories

It's a common mistake among newcomers to WordPress (and the creators of content management systems in general) to create far too many categories; they subsequently end up with only one or two posts per category in any given space. The category system quickly loses its effectiveness because it becomes unclear for your users where anything should be located. So, instead, focus on maintaining a small, reasonable number of categories that better classifies your data, and rely on tags for more specific categorization. The exact number of top-level categories for a website is entirely up to the website administrator, but from an information hierarchy design standpoint, four to eight main level categories is recommended. Always err on the side that fewer categories is better.

While the **Post Tags** meta box is equally straightforward in terms of use, it's important to guard against doubles or misspellings that ultimately dilute the effectiveness of the tag. For instance, if you use the tag "dog friendly" on one post, and then the tag "dog-friendly" on another post, you literally cut the effectiveness of your tags in half. After all, if a user clicks on the tag with a hyphen, only those posts tagged that way will be visible, with those sans hyphen remaining hidden. This problem is also common with plural versions of words ("dog" versus "dogs"), as well as words that are commonly misspelled.

WordPress tries to help by offering an autofill function, revealing available options as you begin to type tags into the post tag box. So when you type in the characters "do," you will automatically be presented with tags already listed in your WordPress site that start this way, such as "doctor's office," "Doppler radar," "Donald Trump," and "dog friendly." Another method is to simply click on the **Choose from the most used tags** button, and click the relevant tags. If you do need to add a new tag to your system for use on the post, you need merely click the **Add** button. Finish it all up by clicking the **Update** button, and you're all set.

Managing Categories and Tags

It's great that we can apply tags and categories to a post at the point of adding or editing it, but we also need some type of central management for both pieces of functionality. WordPress gives this to us in the form of the **Categories** and **Post Tags** management screens. Let's begin by navigating to the categories management screen in the **Admin** menu—as seen in Figure 2.11—by going to **Posts** > **Categories**.

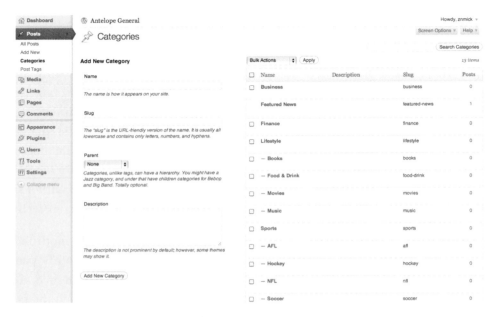

Figure 2.11. The **Categories** management screen

Once inside, you'll see both your current category structure on the right-hand side, complete with subdirectories (officially referred to with the same parent-child nomenclature we discussed earlier regarding pages), as well as the ability to create and organize new categories on the left-hand side of the screen. Adding new categories is simple, and all that's required is the name field. Adding a name will automatically generate the rest of the values within the category and place the new category in the location where you last created a category. Slugs are particularly important for search engine optimization when you have pretty permalinks enabled (which is covered in the section called "Permalinks"). If the category you are creating is meant to be a subcategory, be sure to select the appropriate category as the parent. Finally, it's safe to disregard the category description in most instances; this largely unused field is irrelevant for search engine optimization purposes. Editing existing categories is equally intuitive: just click on the category you're looking to modify, make the changes you need, and click **Update**.

The **Post Tags** management page is essentially identical to the **Categories** management page, except there is no **Parent** drop-down option to contend with. Easy peasy.

Working with the Links Content Type

Another content type found within WordPress are links, which you can access in the **Admin** menu by clicking on the **Links** submenu and any of its related submenu items. While they're less frequently utilized than other types of WordPress content, links can be useful if you're looking to display external website links in your footer or on sidebars. Links also share all the same organizational features of posts and pages. However, they comprise a type of functionality distinct from inserting internal or external links in your website copy, and many users simply don't use this content type at all. As links are a main **Admin** menu item, they're still worth mentioning here.

Permalinks

So far, we've made repeated references to permalinks and slugs. We'll cover permalinks and their practical application and configuration in more depth in Chapter 12, which deals with search engine optimization and marketing. But because we've now dug into our basic category types, we have enough background information to frame a basic explanation. Put simply, **permalinks** are permanent URLS associated with any given page, post, category, tag, or other piece of media that can have a slug attached to it. **Slugs** are sanitized text strings that are associated with a specific piece of content, category, or tag, and always form the last component of a URL. Slugs contain only letters, numbers, and specific characters such as hyphens and underscores. So if we have a page with a slug named "testimonials," the permalink for that page might be http://www.esquandolas.com/testimonials.

Permalinking structures are highly configurable within WordPress, and can be modified by navigating to **Settings > Permalinks**. In the **Permalinks Settings** screen, you're able to modify your site's permalinking structure to one of your own choosing. WordPress provides you with several commonly used options, but if none of them suit you, you can create your own here through the creative use of permalink structure tags. We'll cover this in more detail inChapter 12, but you can also obtain a complete listing of structure tags on the WordPress Codex page that discusses permalinks.[2]

In order for permalinks to work properly (or at all), you must have the correct server permissions set up and available. This will allow WordPress to write directly to the **.htaccess** file in the directory hosting the site URL, as defined in **Settings > General**. Without the correct permissions, you'll have to copy the file input that WordPress provides after setting the permalink structure settings. You'll then need to manually add the entry to the **.htaccess** file before your linking will display.

 ### Where's My .htaccess?

You'll notice that we are describing the **.htaccess** file, which needs to be modified. If your WordPress installation is running on a Windows server, you won't be able to do this, because Windows servers have no **.htaccess** files. Instead, you'll need to make modifications directly to IIS, the web server that manages and runs Windows-based web servers; however, this will literally be impossible unless you have root access to the server and are able to directly work with IIS.

The reason for this is because WordPress is a PHP-based program, and PHP itself is a scripting language native to Linux servers rather than Windows servers; the latter have their own server-side scripting counterpart, ASPX. While it's technically possible to run WordPress on a Windows server, that doesn't mean it's a good idea; frankly, if you're running on a Windows server, you're just doing it wrong. If you still must use a Windows server and want to use permalinks, feel free to pour over the help text in the WordPress Codex.

---

[2] http://codex.wordpress.org/Using_Permalinks

Alternative Ways to Post Text-based Content

If you'd prefer to not use WordPress's built-in web-based mechanisms to post new content, there are other options. Navigate to the **Writing Settings** page at **Settings > Writing**, and you'll find three methods integrated directly with core WordPress. It's possible to post via email by creating a dedicated email account and giving WordPress access to periodically check it. After selecting a default category for your posts, each time you send an email to that address, it will automatically post directly to your site in the specified category. Additionally, API hooks exist that can be activated in this area, allowing you to post to the site via the RSS-based Atom Publishing Protocol or XML-RPC.

Finally, a few miscellaneous items are located on the **Writings Settings** page, if and when you need to take advantage of them. Most notably, the ability to modify the default post category (as well as post format and link category) are here, as well as the dialog box to add extra pinging services, aside from the stellar Ping-O-Matic[3] tool managed by Automattic. Pinging services notify article directories, search engines, and other site indexing services that your site has been updated, so they're useful for search engine optimization purposes. However, Ping-O-Matic automatically pings all the most important services available in one fell swoop each time you update your site, eliminating your need to worry about notifying them individually.

Working with Media and the Media Library

Now that we've explored text-based content in detail, it's time to turn our attention toward the other forms of content that we'll work with in WordPress: media. **Media** is the collective term that refers to images, video, audio recordings, and other files that you might upload and use within your website. In order to use any given piece of media within WordPress, that media needs to live on a web server, so that it can be regularly accessed by the pages and posts trying to display it. WordPress sports a handy, easy-to-use system called the Media Library that makes managing media a breeze.

The Media Library

Accessed by going to **Media > Library** within the **Admin** menu, the Media Library provides a visual representation of all the images, videos, audio files, and other file types such as PDFs that you upload to your site. Whether you're working within a page or a post, if you right-click on the **Add New** button in the Media Library—or in the **Media** submenu of the **Admin** menu—new media files will appear here whenever you upload them to WordPress. The Media Library page bears a solid resemblance to the post or page listing pages, giving a quick overview of everything that's been added to the system.

---

[3] http://pingomatic.com/

Adding Images into a Page or Post

To insert an image into a page or post, place your text cursor in the content editor where you want the image placed. Click on one of the upload media icons above the content editor, as shown in Figure 2.12.

Figure 2.12. Icons for inserting media

WordPress will display a lightbox, which gives you the option of either uploading an image directly from your computer, or looking through the Media Library for an image that's already been loaded. Whether you upload a new image or use an existing one, you'll be brought to the **Add an Image** dialog box, as in Figure 2.13.

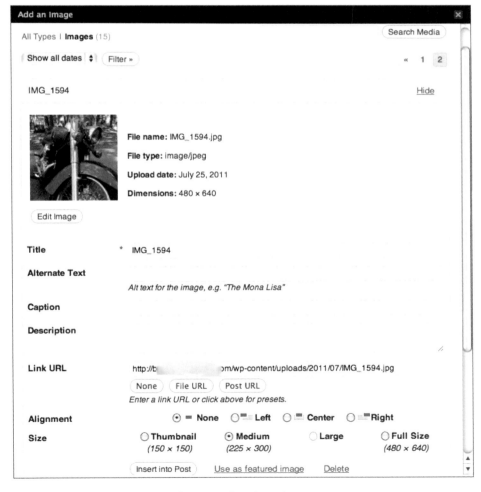

Figure 2.13. Inserting an image

This screen gives you a bevy of options and parameters you can set for your image, many of which are standard image parameters supplied by the `<img>` HTML tag. The only required parameter is the **Title**, which defaults to the filename of the image. Adding in relevant data for all these fields is a good idea for search engine optimization purposes, but are unnecessary from a functional perspective. Align the image and indicate whether it's a small, medium, or large size (an option configurable in the **Media Settings** page located at **Settings > Media**), and click the **Insert into Post** button. Finally, be sure to click the **Update** button to save the page/post and commit the changes to the database.

Modifying Images

Once you add an image, it's common to want to tweak how it appears in your page or post, or even delete it altogether. To make these modifications, click on the image in the content editor. This will highlight and darken the image, causing two icons to appear in its upper left-hand corner, as in Figure 2.14.

Figure 2.14. Editing or deleting an image

If you want to delete the image from your page, just click on the red circle with a slash through it; note that this will only remove it from the page, and not from the Media Library. If you just want to make some sizing or alignment changes, click the button on the left with the small photo in it. This will bring up the **Edit Image** dialog box, which by default lets you change the image's alignment; it also displays some fairly basic options like **Title**, **Alternate Text**, and **Caption**, which are useful mostly for search engine optimization. If you click the **Advanced Settings** tab, you'll be given more detailed image display properties to play with, as evident in Figure 2.15.

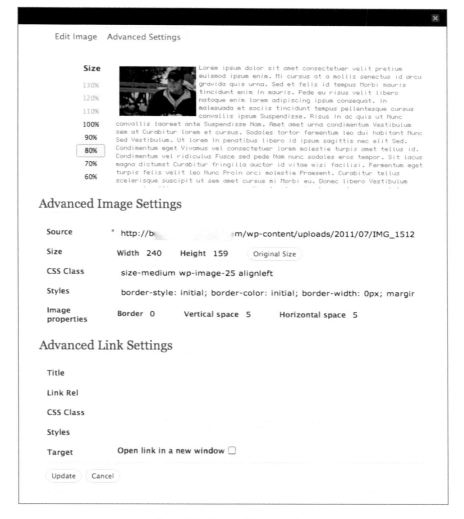

Figure 2.15. Advanced image settings

In this area, you'll be able to scale and preview the image at various percentage sizes, or add CSS properties to either the image or a link connected to the image in the content editor. One nice feature here is the **Image Properties** settings, which allow you to define inline styles on your image for border, vertical space, and horizontal space.

 What's the link URL?

Occasionally, some plugins and themes will ask you to provide the link URL for images, in order to use them for various functions within their own processes. The link URL is nothing more than the physical location of your image on the web server, and you can always find the unique link URL for any given image in the Media Library.

Image Manipulation within WordPress

It's worth noting that WordPress provides some basic source image manipulation and editing directly within the Media Library. Image manipulation differs from modifying how images appear in that no changes are made directly to the image file when you modify how it appears. Image manipulation, on the other hand, actually changes the image file. So if you scale an image with image manipulation, you are making the file physically larger or smaller, (and hence the file size), instead of just changing the dimensions of how that file is displayed.

In order to make changes to an image, select it in the Media Library, and click the **Edit Image** button, which will bring you to a screen like in Figure 2.16.

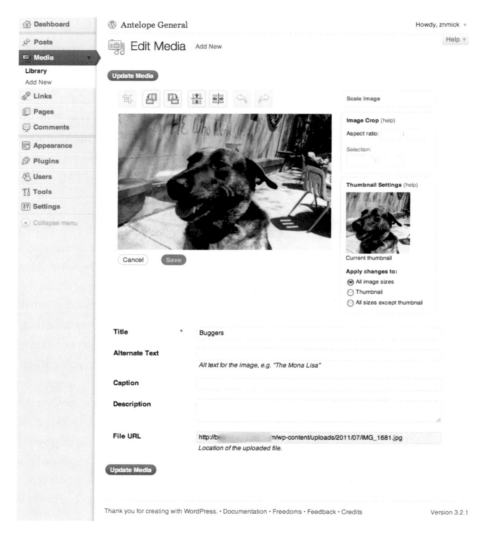

Figure 2.16. Editing media will affect the file itself, not just how it appears

WordPress shows you a working preview of your image, along with a row of tool buttons above it. The first is a crop tool for trimming the image down. The next two buttons rotate the image 90 degrees left or right, while the further two invert the image vertically or horizontally. Finally, there are your standard, handy undo and redo buttons should you make a mistake! To the right of the preview photo are additional photo manipulation tools that can either scale the image, or modify the thumbnail settings that are set up and managed by WordPress.

Managing Media Outside of WordPress

There are times when it makes sense to manage your media files outside the scope of WordPress, even if you plan to display it on the WordPress site itself; it's actually common practice for audio and video files. Such files differ from image files in that they require media players that interface with web or mobile browsers in order to function. Furthermore, different formats of both audio and video require their own types of players to work properly, and while you can upload audio or video files to the media library, WordPress has no integrated audio or video players installed with core. You'll need to find a solution to be able to play these types of files on your website.

To this end, social media services like YouTube[4] and Vimeo[5] are extremely popular. Such services are free, host the media files for you, and provide the benefit of tying into popular social media platforms that can help publicize and drive traffic back to your website. These types of hosting services provide you with a chunk of code, which you paste right into the HTML tab of your page/post's content editor, and you're on your way!

Another solution is to use a player that's configured as a plugin, and then create instances of that player that refer to the audio or video file on the appropriate pages. It's a very common way of handling audio and video, allowing you to upload files directly to WordPress and then reference them in the player. This is typically triggered through a **shortcode**—a piece of code used to create a macro, which is added where you'd like it to show up in the content. However, while you technically can host your audio and video files in WordPress, you might question whether you really want to. Audio and video files are often extremely large and tax your web server severely. Websites with moderate to heavy amounts of traffic can become bogged down and downright slow because of heavy usage, which can be an issue. Furthermore, if you have particularly large files on your website, your visitors can consume an inordinate amount of bandwidth by simply viewing and listening to to such files. Hosting plans are typically priced with bandwidth in mind, so this could lead to extremely high hosting bills, or even having your website shut down completely until more bandwidth is purchased and allocated. Either way, situations like this are commonly solved by utilizing third-party media file hosting providers like the Amazon S3 hosting service.[6] In this instance, you can still use all your WordPress video and audio player plugins, but instead of giving

---

[4] http://www.youtube.com/

[5] http://vimeo.com/

[6] http://aws.amazon.com/s3/

the WordPress-hosted link URL found in the media manager, you reference the file to an external URL provided by your media file hosting service.

A final solution popular amongst many small business owners is to work with a **SaaS** (software as a service) platform. This provides large media file hosting, as well as an array of video and audio players that you can embed anywhere in your website with a small code chunk. Such a solution cuts the guesswork out of the equation for many website administrators.

Media Settings

As we've already touched upon, WordPress provides some miscellaneous media settings that can be managed by visiting the **Media Settings** page at **Settings > Media**. Site-wide defaults for **Thumbnail**, **Medium**, and **Large** image dimensions can be set here, as well as global settings for the server path you want to store images in. Global settings for embedding third-party media are available here as well.

Everyone Wants a Say

When people throw the "Web 2.0" buzzword around, the heart of what they're talking about is creating and maintaining conversation. To that end, one of the most powerful aspects of WordPress is its built-in commenting capabilities. By default, WordPress enables website visitors to post comments on any of the posts in your website if they've had at least one previously approved comment. Users who are yet to have an approved comment will need their initial comment moderated and approved by an administrator before it's published. Once published, the comment becomes visible to other website visitors, who can then respond to it, as well as to the original post, or the individual comments that have been posted. In this way, WordPress creates discussion among the visitors that frequent a particular site.

Managing Comments

WordPress gives administrators several methods to manage comments on a website, but the most commonly used is the **Comments** section, seen in Figure 2.17. It is located by clicking on **Comments** in the **Admin** menu.

Figure 2.17. The Comments page

From the **Comments** area in the back end, administrators can view all comments from one location; a contextual menu is revealed for each comment when moused over. This menu allows administrators to approve or reject a comment on the fly, reply directly to a comment for display on the front end of the website, edit the comment, mark it as spam, or trash it. This panel is particularly useful in situations where all comments on a site are configured to be moderated by an administrator prior to publishing, a practice that completely eliminates comment spam.

Comment Spam

Comment spam consists of nuisance, unwanted comments that typically promote other services or websites. It's a rampant issue plaguing many content management systems including WordPress, and is most commonly entered into WordPress sites via automated scripts. These scripts locate WordPress sites and automatically comment on their posts; it's usually off-topic and never intends to genuinely engage your real website visitors in an honest, meaningful way. There are a variety of plugins that provide protection against content spam, notably the Akismet plugin[7] that comes bundled with core WordPress. In order to take advantage of Akismet, you'll need to create and retrieve an API Key by setting up an account at http://akismet.com/wordpress/. Once you have your API Key, it's as simple as adding it into your plugin settings to verify your identity.

Discussion Settings

The settings that govern how comments are managed can be found in the **Discussion Settings** page, located at **Settings > Discussion**. WordPress offers fairly comprehensive control over how comments are managed and we won't cover all the options here, but a few worth mentioning in particular include the following:

- **Allow people to post comments on new articles**: effectively turns the commenting system on and off for new articles

---

[7] http://akismet.com/

- **Comment author must fill out name and email**: provides website users with a measure of accountability

- **Users must be logged in to comment**: ensures that all commenters are registered users of your website

- **Email me whenever anyone posts a comment**: notifies the administrative email address whenever a new comment is posted

- **Email me whenever a comment is held for moderation**: notifies an administrator whenever a comment is held for moderation

- **Before a comment appears, an administrator must always approve a comment**: represents the default moderation settings that ships with core WordPress

- **Before a comment appears, comment author must have a previously approved comment**: the most restrictive commenting option available short of disabling altogether

Leaving both **Before a comment appears, an administrator must always approve a comment** and **Before a comment appears, comment author must have a previously approved comment** unchecked effectively leaves the site wide open to comment spam, and is severely discouraged. It's also useful to note that while **Discussion Settings** manages global settings for use throughout a whole website, commenting can be turned on and off in individual posts at any time by editing that post and selecting the appropriate option.

For a more thorough description of the **Discussion Settings** screen, see the Codex.[8]

Avatars

Avatars are the profile images that are displayed next to a user's name upon posting a comment on a site, and tend to add life and personality to any website. Avatars can be turned on or off globally within the **Discussion Settings** page, and can be personalized by registered users on that site. By default, avatars in WordPress are automatically powered by gravatar.com,[9] a free service that you can use to associate an image with any email address you like.

Additional Display Elements

So far in our functional overview of core WordPress, we've looked at the two most important building blocks of WordPress sites: the settings that describe how the site will look and act, and how we create, manage, and interact with the different types of content on any given website. While these components are the primary building blocks of any WordPress site, it's important to explore

---

[8] http://codex.wordpress.org/Settings_Discussion_Screen
[9] http://en.gravatar.com/

the smaller yet equally important components that serve as the glue to bring it all together: navigation, sidebars, and additional functionality that can be added through the creative use of plugins.

Managing Custom Menus

Regardless of the content's quality, websites that lack thought-out, intuitive navigation to help users move around easily are dead in the water before they even get started. To this end, WordPress enables administrators to replace the default menu with their own customized version, which they can easily create and manage in themes and plugins supporting the feature.

The **Menus** screen is available via **Appearance** > **Menus**, and is frighteningly easy to use. To start, you'll need to create a menu by clicking on the **Create Menu** button and giving it a name. In Figure 2.18, we've gone ahead and created three menus that we can use to intuitively navigate throughout our site.

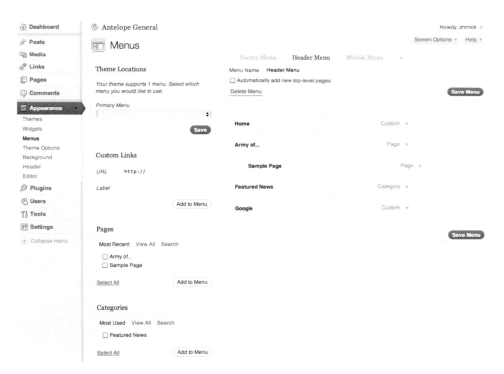

Figure 2.18. The Menus screen

Once a menu is created, adding pages or post categories is as simple as ticking the checkbox adjacent to the option, and then clicking the **Add to Menu** button to insert the pages in the menu organization area on the right. Once entries are in this area, you can move them into your desired order, or pull them slightly to the right so that they indent to create a submenu; you can see this in Figure 2.18 with **Sample Page** indented underneath **Army of ....** Once you've saved your menu, you can associate it with your theme and a specifically defined menu area by selecting the location where the menu should be displayed. This is done from the drop-down menu in the upper left-hand meta box titled

Theme Locations. Keep in mind that themes can support multiple menus, as can plugins, which is a common way to add mobile website functionality to a WordPress installation.

Sidebars and Widgets

Widgets are the figurative Swiss Army knife of the WordPress universe, and are best explained by first understanding how sidebars operate. In WordPress, whenever you see a sidebar on either side of a page, or when you notice content such as a Twitter feed or recent comments being displayed in a footer, chances are that the content is housed within some type of widgetized area. **Widgetized areas** are defined locations within WordPress page templates that allow users to easily insert and organize smaller blocks of functionality known as **widgets**.

You can work with widgets by navigating to **Appearance** > **Widgets** in the **Admin** menu, as seen in Figure 2.19, and they're dead simple to use.

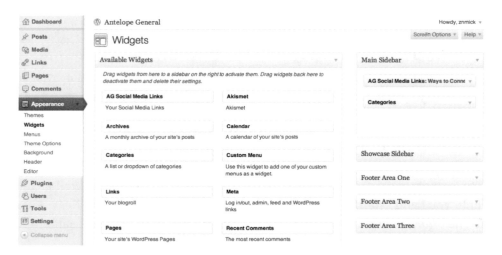

Figure 2.19. The Widgets main page

Core WordPress comes bundled with a variety of useful widgets, and plugins introduce new widgets all the time, allowing you to add the latest and greatest functionality to the widgetized areas in your theme at the drop of the hat. To do so, look for widget functionality that interests you in the **Available Widgets** area in the center of the screen. Now open the drop-in area on the widgetized sidebar where you'd like to add the widget by clicking on the drop-down arrow, and drag the available widget into that area. If there's more than one widget, you can order them however you like, or distribute them to other widgetized areas displaying elsewhere on the website.

Many widgets have options that allow them to perform an action differently from other instances of the same type of widget. For example, WordPress comes bundled with the Text widget, which lets you add in any plain text or raw HTML or JavaScript to do different tasks. In this way, you could easily use a Text widget to display simple textual information in a footer, all while using

another Text widget in the sidebar to house JavaScript code from a third-party mailing list service, which creates a newsletter sign-up form on your website.

Extending WordPress through Plugins

We've already referenced plugins many times throughout this book and we're devoting an entire chapter to them later on (see Chapter 5), but they do deserve a cursory mention in this space. **Plugins** are packaged pieces of functionality that can be easily added to any WordPress installation, and are an essential tool that extends the functionality of WordPress to meet different needs.

From an organizational standpoint in the back end, plugins are set up a lot like themes. Expand the **Plugins** submenu in the **Admin** menu and you'll find **Installed Plugins**, which provides a complete listing of currently installed plugins (both active and inactive); an **Add New** submenu item, which takes you to the plugin installation screen; and **Editor**, which lets you (gulp) directly edit the source code of both active and inactive plugins.

 Leave the Plugins Alone!

It's never considered best practice to edit active PHP programs. While you probably won't cause permanent damage to your website if you have a solid understanding of PHP and remember exactly what you did to cause a problem, it's best to make sure you really know what you're doing before you even conceive of using the plugin editor to make changes. Remember that there is no undo function inside the editor. Be afraid. Be very, very afraid.

For a complete, comprehensive look at the good, bad, and ugly of plugins, as well as how you can use them to help you bend WordPress to your will in the same way that Keanu Reeves bends reality to his will in *The Matrix*, have a look at Chapter 5 and get busy with your bad self.

Import and Export Tools

Speaking of plugins, a specific set of them are maintained by the WordPress development community to assist with importing and exporting page and post content into and out of WordPress. These plugins can be installed and utilized by visiting the **Tools** > **Import** or **Tools** > **Export** menu options in the **Admin** menu. These tools make it easier to migrate WordPress from server to server, as well as provide essential links to liquidate older free blogs running on services like Blogger, TypePad, and LiveJournal, if you want to migrate them to the self-hosted WordPress platform.

Users Roles and Permissions

The final component worth mentioning with core WordPress is the user management system that comes bundled with it. **User roles** are the types of user you can expect to find within WordPress; each user role has its own permissions that dictate different levels of accessibility.

Default User Roles

By default, core WordPress comes with five user roles, each with its unique set of permissions. Let's have a quick look at what they are and what they can do:

Administrator
> has access to all features and functionality across the WordPress site, and is the user role assigned to the first user created when a WordPress installation is created

Editor
> has significantly less authority than an Administrator, but is able to create, manage, and edit posts, whether or not they belong to other users; Editors also have the ability to approve posts submitted by users assigned to Contributor roles

Author
> has the authority to create, edit, and publish their own posts solely

Contributor
> has the authority to create and edit their own posts, but cannot publish them; Contributor articles must be moderated and published by Editors

Subscriber
> can read posts and add and read comments, but has no authority to create post content of any kind; after the initial Administrator is created during installation, WordPress creates all users as Subscribers by default unless otherwise configured

Administrator and Subscriber roles are more than sufficient for the vast majority of websites, and full-blown publishing sites will commonly find the default user roles built into WordPress quite adequate. Still, a website that seeks to operate as more of a corporate content management system —able to create new user roles and define customized permissions for each—can find the functionality they are looking for through plugins. At the time of writing, there are three plugins in particular that are useful in managing this process: Members, Role Scoper, and Capability Manager.

Members (http://wordpress.org/extend/plugins/members/)
> Members is an exceptional plugin that is frequently updated and extends users and roles; it also introduces some very useful content management functionality. You can make a site or its feed entirely private, as well as use shortcodes to determine who has access to specific content—well worth a look.

Role Scoper (http://wordpress.org/extend/plugins/role-scoper/)
> Role Scoper is a killer plugin that allows you to extend user roles in many ways. Aside from giving you the ability to define groups and assign them specific roles, it also provides the opportunity to assign roles and restrictions to specific posts, pages, or categories. Role Scoper is

also supported by Multisite (see Chapter 10), and allows you to give Subscribers content editing privileges.

Capability Manager (http://wordpress.org/extend/plugins/capsman/)

Capability Manager allows you to change the capabilities of any role as well as add new roles, copying and modifying the existing rules into the new ones. Capability Manager also features a backup/restore tool, which enables administrators to save current roles and capabilities before making any changes, and restore them in case problems arise from the role modifications.

Extending User Profiles

Sometimes it's useful to extend the information in a typical user profile past the bare bones options provided with core WordPress. There are two specific plugins useful in this purpose:

Cimy User Extra Fields (http://wordpress.org/extend/plugins/cimy-user-extra-fields/)

Cimy User Extra Fields allows you to create additional user fields to your heart's content, complete with form validation configurable by an administrator to verify that fields are all properly filled. It's also Multisite compliant.

Register Plus (http://wordpress.org/extend/plugins/register-plus/)

Register Plus is a comprehensive plugin that lets you add custom user fields, but also does all sorts of tasks for you including adding a custom logo, adding Captcha verification on your registration forms, letting users choose their own passwords when signing up, and much, much more.

Now You Know the Basics ...

We hope you have enjoyed the dime tour through core WordPress, but don't worry—there's still lots in store as we go deeper into the rabbit hole. It's impossible to really understand what we can achieve with WordPress without an appreciation for the fundamental processes WordPress supports.

So what did we cover? Well, first we got a feel for the basic functional and visual settings in a WordPress installation, and then took a look at pages, and how the content editor works. We took a tasty trip to The Wedge to learn about how WordPress handles posts, categories, and tags, which helped us better understand the organizational structure of websites and blogs in general.

After that, we talked a bit about images and best practices involved in using audio and video files on our website. Finally, we finished our trip through the WordPress core with a look at some of the less sexy but important functions inside the system, including navigation, widgets and widgetized areas, and user roles and permissions. It's been a whirlwind trip so far, but take a deep breath and hold on tight—we're about to get downright jiggy with the guts of WordPress. So pull out your PHP manuals and get ready to learn about WordPress's beating heart—The Loop!

Chapter **3**

The Loop and WordPress File System

While one of the main reasons for the massive popularity of WordPress is the approachable and simple-to-use GUI it boasts, ultimately it's nothing more than a piece of software, and as a developer you're going to have to get your hands dirty with some code. Not to fear, though; like everything else WordPress-related, there are systematic rules to follow that help you understand where different files live. Say hello to the standard WordPress file structure.

The Standard WordPress File Structure

Like most content management systems, WordPress has a standardized way of describing how it's put together as a cohesive piece of software by adhering to a standardized file structure. This is shown in Figure 3.1. This is the standard WordPress file structure shared by every single WordPress site running on the Web, regardless of what the site looks like or how it operates. It's powerful because it's fairly elegant, simple, and familiar to WordPress coders across the globe. Let's take a moment to get familiar with the structure.

Name	Date Modified	Size	Kind
36 items, 142.42 GB available			
index.php	May 26, 2008 11:33 AM	4 KB	PHP. ...cument
license.txt	Dec 6, 2008 11:47 PM	16 KB	Plain Text
readme.html	Nov 12, 2009 3:22 PM	8 KB	HTML ...ument
wp-admin	Nov 13, 2009 9:49 AM	--	Folder
wp-app.php	Aug 14, 2009 11:47 AM	41 KB	PHP. ...cument
wp-atom.php	Oct 14, 2008 10:22 PM	4 KB	PHP. ...cument
wp-blog-header.php	May 26, 2008 6:50 AM	4 KB	PHP. ...cument
wp-comments-post.php	May 19, 2009 7:00 AM	4 KB	PHP. ...cument
wp-commentsrss2.php	Oct 14, 2008 10:22 PM	4 KB	PHP. ...cument
wp-config-sample.php	Mar 1, 2009 1:55 AM	4 KB	PHP. ...cument
wp-config.php	Mar 1, 2009 1:55 AM	4 KB	PHP. ...cument
wp-content	Today, 5:14 PM	--	Folder
index.php	May 5, 2007 12:48 PM	4 KB	PHP. ...cument
plugins	Nov 13, 2009 9:49 AM	--	Folder
akismet	Nov 13, 2009 9:49 AM	--	Folder
hello.php	Jun 29, 2009 3:40 PM	4 KB	PHP. ...cument
index.php	Apr 16, 2009 10:57 AM	4 KB	PHP. ...cument
themes	Nov 13, 2009 9:49 AM	--	Folder
classic	Nov 13, 2009 9:49 AM	--	Folder
default	Nov 13, 2009 9:49 AM	--	Folder
index.php	Apr 16, 2009 10:57 AM	4 KB	PHP. ...cument
wp-cron.php	Feb 8, 2009 5:32 AM	4 KB	PHP. ...cument
wp-feed.php	Oct 14, 2008 10:22 PM	4 KB	PHP. ...cument
wp-includes	Nov 13, 2009 9:49 AM	--	Folder
wp-links-opml.php	May 6, 2009 10:43 AM	4 KB	PHP. ...cument
wp-load.php	May 21, 2009 7:32 AM	4 KB	PHP. ...cument
wp-login.php	Aug 11, 2009 9:03 PM	25 KB	PHP. ...cument
wp-mail.php	May 19, 2009 6:11 AM	8 KB	PHP. ...cument
wp-pass.php	Apr 21, 2009 12:50 PM	4 KB	PHP. ...cument
wp-rdf.php	Oct 14, 2008 10:22 PM	4 KB	PHP. ...cument
wp-register.php	May 26, 2008 6:50 AM	4 KB	PHP. ...cument
wp-rss.php	Oct 14, 2008 10:22 PM	4 KB	PHP. ...cument
wp-rss2.php	Oct 14, 2008 10:22 PM	4 KB	PHP. ...cument
wp-settings.php	Jun 28, 2009 3:44 PM	25 KB	PHP. ...cument
wp-trackback.php	Oct 20, 2009 7:11 AM	4 KB	PHP. ...cument
xmlrpc.php	Aug 20, 2009 10:06 PM	94 KB	PHP. ...cument

Figure 3.1. The standard WordPress file structure

The file structure itself can be cleanly divided into two types of files and folders: system files and user-manageable files. System files include everything in the **wp-admin** and **wp-includes** directories, as well as all the actual files in the root directory except for **wp-config.php**. User-manageable files include everything that's left: the **wp-config.php** file, the **wp-content** directory, and (on most servers) the **.htaccess** file. In case you're curious, here's a brief description of what everything is and does.

System files and folders

- These are all the .php files in the root directory, and serve as linchpins of WordPress, initiating the key functions that need to happen in order to make the system work. For example, **index.php** initiates the website page serving functionality, while **wp-register.php** contains all the logic necessary to initiate the user registration process, and **wp-cron.php** initiates the scheduled event functionality within WordPress.

- **wp-admin**: All the files and folders within **wp-admin** comprise all the various tools and interfaces necessary to make WordPress run.

- **wp-includes**: All the files and folders within **wp-includes** comprise the various pieces of code that actually execute WordPress and make all the magic happen.

User-manageable files and folders

- **wp-config.php**: We've already worked with this file quite a bit. **wp-config.php** begins its life in a newborn WordPress installation as **wp-config-sample.php** before being renamed, and controls all the primary settings and control keys for the installation. This includes defining the database location and credentials, setting the language being used in the site, and establishing unique keys that demonstrate authenticity and authority for the installation as a whole.

- **wp-content**: This directory is where just about everything you ever add or modify will live in your WordPress installation, including plugins, themes, and absolutely every image you upload to the site.

- **.htaccess**: While not visible in our screenshot, the **.htaccess** file is crucial in determining routing and general rules for how things operate. **.htaccess** is a file that can only be created on Linux and Unix-based servers, and doesn't ship with a typical WordPress installation; you have to actually make it for yourself, or WordPress will often create it on its own when you initially set your permalink settings (if the server you're running WordPress on allows sufficient permission to do so).

 Color Inside the Lines

Unless you really know what you're doing, it's never a good idea to change the core WordPress files outside **wp-config.php** or the **wp-content** directory. As we've already learned, WordPress has the ability to update itself at the click of a button, and physically this is accomplished by overwriting what are considered to be standard system files. If you make changes to any of these files regardless of where they are, you run the risk of having your file modifications overwritten at some point in time. For this reason, it's highly advisable to color inside the lines, and make sure that you make all your changes either in the **wp-config.php** file, or in the proper plugin and theme files in **wp-content**.

If where you hang your hat is where you call home, for the purposes of the WordPress universe, home may as well have the address of **wp-content**, as that's where we'll keep all our stuff. We've already had a cursory discussion of themes and plugins, but it's important to realize that whether we have only a single theme and three plugins or 20 themes and 200 plugins, they'll all be stored in either the **wp-content/plugins** or **wp-content/themes** directories. Additionally, when you begin to upload media to your website, the **wp-content/uploads** directory (or some form of it) will automatically be created, and will house all the media on your site.

So there you have it: a brief overview of where you can find just about anything inside a typical WordPress installation. While now we know where just about everything lives, it's high time we rolled up our sleeves and started digging into some PHP code—so hold on to your hats!

The Role of Queries and The Loop

Let's start out by digging into a theme in our WordPress installation and looking at the code we can find in the **index.php** file therein. Now whenever you load that WordPress page, WordPress queries the database for the posts that need to be shown. The posts that are returned depend, of course, on what's been asked for in the code of the page; for example, a request for the home page generally results in a query asking for the most recent posts. Even the templates for a single post or page query the database and make a list, albeit a list with only one item. WordPress loads up all these posts into a `posts` object.

Once we have that object, we can use a piece of code called **The Loop** to control how these posts are treated. The Loop simply runs through the posts that are stored in the object, and defines how each should behave. We can use a blend of WordPress's **template tags**—functions to display post data—and regular HTML markup to control the appearance of the posts.

If you're working with templates like the home page, a tag or category listing, a date-based archive, or a search page, the query to retrieve the posts you need is built right into WordPress; this means that your only task is to manipulate The Loop. When you want to produce your own custom set of posts, however, you'll need to create your own query for a custom loop to work with. In this chapter, we'll start by playing with the basic loops, and once we have the hang of that, we'll move on to creating custom queries.

 What *is* the default loop doing?

It's easy enough to find out what sorts of posts are being retrieved in a given page's loop. In WordPress, the `query_vars` object stores all the different parts of The Loop's query. See what's inside by echoing the query's `query_vars`:

```php
<?php
echo "<pre>";
print_r($wp_query->query_vars);
echo "</pre>";
?>
```

You'll soon find out a wealth of information about what's been asked for in each query.

The Loop: Exposed!

Because The Loop controls the appearance of a group of posts, you'll often find yourself working with it when you're editing template files. A quick trawl through the WordPress support forums will reveal that The Loop is, by far, one of the single most popular questions to ask about, and rightly so—it's one of the most important parts of the WordPress experience. That has to be one big and scary bit of code, right?

Actually, it's fairly lightweight. Stripped back to its basics, The Loop generally looks like this:

```php
<?php if (have_posts()):
?>
    ... anything that should appear before your group of posts
<?php while (have_posts()) : the_post();
?>
    ... instructions for each post
<?php endwhile;
?>
    ... anything after your group of posts
<?php else:
?>
    ... what to show if there were no posts
<?php endif;
?>
```

What's going on here? If you're cosy with PHP, you already know what an **if statement** is for—it's checking to see if we have posts. If so, a **while loop** kicks in—that's a piece of code that repeats based on a given condition. In our case, we repeat this loop once for each post. And if there are no posts, we'll do the instructions that follow `else`.

Of course, this is only as simple as it is because a lot of the hard work has been abstracted away into different functions: `have_posts()`, `the_post()`, and so on. For our purposes in this chapter, it's enough to know that they simply work, but if you're especially keen to find out, the Codex will explain it all.

The Loop and Template Tags

Of course, the above loop is stripped back to its most basic components, and if you were to go ahead and put it into your theme right now, you'd see very little indeed. In order to actually see anything interesting on your page, you'll need to include some template tags.

As we mentioned earlier, template tags are the functions responsible for showing stuff—generally it's information about your WordPress site, or about individual posts. There's a dizzying array of these for all kinds of purposes; roughly, you could divide them into simpler approaches, and more complex ones.

Some Easy Tags: the_

Simpler tags are those functions that can be used with little or no funny business with PHP. The easy tags are generally characterized by starting with the word `the`.

the_title()

This tag generates the post's title. You'll often use this within a heading element, in conjunction with `the_permalink()`, like so:

```
<h2>
    <a href="<?php the_permalink();
            ?>">
        <?php the_title(); ?>
    </a>
</h2>
```

the_permalink()

This is used to output the URL of the post, or the URL of where the post would always be found, the latter which is known as **permalinking**. In our previous code example, we've used it to wrap around the title. You'll also often find it in themes where a footer is used to provide post information. We used `the_permalink()` in the `<a>` element in our previous example.

the_author()

This is the tag that shows the author's name. In a user's WordPress administrator profile screen, it's possible to choose how you'd like your name to be displayed—login name, full name, first name, and so on. By default, the preference you choose is the one that's shown for this tag:

```
<p>
Posted by <?php the_author(); ?>
</p>
```

the_author_meta()

This is to show other kinds of information about the author, and accepts a parameter to define the information you'd like to show. For example, you can show a post author's contact details or website, or different variations on their name:

```
<p>
<?php the_author_meta('first_name'); ?>
   has been a member since
<?php the_author_meta('user_registered'); ?>.
</p>
```

`the_time()` and `the_modified_time()`

These tags show the timestamp for when the post was made, or edited, respectively. They accept four arguments: format, text to show before, text to show after, and whether to echo the date (`true` is the default) or simply return it for your own use (`false`).

The simplest way to call on either `the_time()` or `the_modified_time()` is to call it without arguments; WordPress will display the time that your post was made or updated with the format you specified in your blog's time settings. If you want to use it to call a date as well, simply pass it a format, using the PHP date symbols:[1]

```
<p>
Posted on <?php the_time('jS F Y'); ?>
at <?php the_time('g:i a'); ?>
</p>
```

`the_date()`

`the_date()` acts a little differently to `the_time()` in that it only appears once for each day; so for listing pages, like monthly archives, you can use it as a heading for groups of posts posted on the same day. As with `the_time()`, it accepts four parameters: the format, text to show before, text to show after, and whether to echo or return the text. The following example will put a date inside a level 2 heading:

```
<?php the_date( "jS F Y", "<h2>", "</h2>" ); ?>
```

`the_excerpt()`

This displays the text that was entered in a post's excerpt field. You'll find that `the_excerpt()` is put to good use in magazine-style themes where posts' descriptions are used. If a post lacks an excerpt, WordPress will show the first 55 words of a post, with all markup stripped. This tag takes no parameters, so our example is simply:

```
<?php the_excerpt(); ?>
```

`the_content()`

This tag shows the contents of a post. On the home page or a listing page, if your post contains the `more` **quicktag** (a quicktag is like an HTML formatting tag, but is used solely within Word-Press), `the_content()` only shows content up to this point, followed by a link inviting a visitor to read more. When you're on a single post's page, the entire post is shown.

`the_content()` accepts two parameters: a string that is shown for the **Read More** link, and a Boolean to define whether you want to omit the text before the `more` quicktag—false is the default.

---

[1] http://php.net/manual/en/function.date.php

In this example, we'll combine the_title() with the_content()'s string (that is, its "read more") parameter:

```php
<?php the_content("Continue reading "
    . the_title('', '', false)); ?>
```

the_meta()

If you're making use of WordPress's custom fields, the_meta() is a quick way to display all the fields' keys and values. These keys and values are output in an unordered list, and the function accepts no parameters.

the_category()

This shows a linked list of the categories that have been selected for this post. It accepts three parameters: a string to use as a separator, a choice of multiple or single to show parent categories or just child categories, and a post ID if you were using this outside The Loop. Commonly, you'll just pass the separator parameter. In the following example, we'll receive a list of items separated by a comma:

```php
<p>We filed it under: <?php
    the_category(', ');
    ?>
</p>
```

By default—that is, when called without a separator parameter—the list of categories is printed as an unordered list.

the_tags()

Like the_category(), you'd use this tag to show a list of the categories you've used for this post. Unlike the_category(), its parameters are for completely different purposes: text to show before the tags, a separator, and text to show after. By default, the output is the word **Tags:**, followed by each tag, separated by commas. In this example, we'll use list items for our tags, so that they match the default behavior of the_category():

```php
<?php the_tags('<ul><li>','</li><li>','</li></ul>'); ?>
```

 More Tags

We've touched on just a few of the functions that are commonly used while you're inside The Loop. You can find even more tags, and complete documentation on each, in the WordPress Function Reference.[2]

---

[2] http://codex.wordpress.org/Function_Reference

More Complex Functions: `get_`

For the most part, our arsenal of `the_` template tags will do the job; but sometimes the output that WordPress provides is less flexible than we'd like. Maybe we'd want to get at the information about each post, but we'd like to make a few tactical strikes with our PHP before it's printed.

Fortunately, WordPress provides a number of tags that retrieve, rather than simply print, post and page information (like our `the_` tags). These are generally prefixed with `get_`. These `get_` functions return strings or arrays that we can stash in a variable and manipulate. For every `the_` function, there's at least one `get_` function that can do a similar job. Let's look into how to use some of these.

`get_the_category()`

Imagine that for a post, you want to list each of its categories' names and descriptions as a definition list. Using `get_the_category()`, we can retrieve an object describing each category associated with the current post:

```php
<dl>
    <?php
    foreach((get_the_category()) as $category) {
      echo "<dt>" . $category->cat_name .
          "</dt>";
      echo "<dd>" . $category_description .
          "</dd>";
    }
    ?>
</dl>
```

`get_the_time()`

A common way to manipulate the time of a WordPress post is to use relative timestamps; that is, a statement like "Last posted 6 hours ago." In this example, we'll use `get_the_time()` and `get_the_modified_time()` in conjunction with `human_time_diff()`, a built-in WordPress function, to provide a friendly depiction of when content was edited. Of course, if the post has never been edited after the fact, we have no need to show this section, so we'll use an `if` statement to check whether the post's last edited timestamp is later than its published timestamp. Here goes:

```php
<?php
  $lastmodified = get_the_modified_time('U');
  $posted = get_the_time('U');

  if ($lastmodified > $posted) {
    echo "Edited " . human_time_diff(get_the_time('U'), ➥
        get_the_modified_time('U')) .
        " later";
  }
?>
```

get_post_custom()

We learned earlier that `the_meta()` fetches all the custom fields associated with a post. Custom fields are often used in plugins or for special post types, so it can be impractical to display them all indiscriminately. Instead, we can use `get_post_custom()` to retrieve just the fields we want. In this example, we've used this to retrieve any custom fields with a key of `song`, and then we'll print them into an unordered list. Naturally, if there's no `song` field for this post, we'll display nothing:

```php
<?php
  $custom_fields = get_post_custom();
  $song = $custom_fields['song'];

  if (isset($song)) {
    echo "<h3>Songs</h3>";
    echo "<ul>";

    foreach ( $song as $key => $value )
    echo "<li>" . $value . "</li>";
    echo "</ul>";
  }
?>
```

Conditional Tags: `is`

Conditional tags are those that answer questions about common conditions, such as whether we're viewing a single page, or whether a particular post matches certain criteria. It's a great way to introduce some simple logic to your loops.

`is` tags are used in conjunction with `if` statements in PHP. For example, you may decide that on your home page a sticky post should display a thumbnail, but a regular post should not. In your loop, you could simply pop your thumbnail code inside an `if` statement that checks to see if the post is sticky, and whether it has a thumbnail in the first place:

```php
<?php while (have_posts()) : the_post();
?>
<li>
  <h2><a href="<?php the_permalink() ?>">
      <?php the_title(); ?></a>
      <?php the_time("jS F"); ?>
  </h2>
  <?php if(is_sticky() && has_post_thumbnail()) {
          the_post_thumbnail();
        }
  ?>
  <p><?php the_excerpt(); ?></p>
```

```php
  <p><?php the_tags( "Tagged with: ", " / ", "" ); ?></p>
</li>
<?php endwhile; ?>
```

You can pass arguments to conditional tags, too, letting you perform actions at a very granular level. For example, `is_page()` will check if you're on a page, but if you pass it a page ID or a page title, you can perform those actions only on that page. Here's a snippet to try:

```php
<?php if(is_page('About Us')) { ?>
<div id="gallery">
  <h2>Gallery</h2>

    ⋮

</div>
<?php }?>
```

Conditional tags are described in detail in the Codex.[3]

Pagination

Your readers often want to navigate backwards and forwards through pages of posts—especially on blog- or news-style sites, so remember to include options for pagination in your themes. In WordPress, there are a few ways to achieve this. `posts_nav_link()` is a single template tag that creates a pair of links allowing the user to navigate to the next or previous posts; you can use it in archive templates or single post templates. If you want to split them up on an archive page, you can use `previous_posts_link()` and `next_posts_link()` to print a link to the previous and next set of results. To split these links on a single template, `previous_post_link()` and `next_post_link()` print a link to the previous and next single post.

`posts_nav_link()` accepts three parameters: text to sit between the links, the text for the previous link, and the text for the next link:

```php
<p><?php posts_nav_link(' &bull; ', 'Older posts', 'Newer posts');
    ?>.</p>
```

Used on listing pages, `previous_posts_link()` and `next_posts_link()` each accept two parameters: the link text, and the number of pages on which to show the links. The default for the second parameter is 0, meaning all pages:

```php
<p><?php next_posts_link('Go back in time...', 0); ?></p>
```

---

[3] http://codex.wordpress.org/Conditional_Tags

For single posts, `previous_post_link()` and `next_post_link()` act a little differently. They accept four parameters: a format for the link, the text of the link, whether we only want to show a post from the same category, and any categories from which we don't want to show posts. In most cases, you can go ahead and call this without passing any parameters, but if you do have a need to fiddle with the links, you can use the `%title` and `%link` tokens to fine-tune the output. In this example, we create a link to the previous and next post, and adjust the text output accordingly:

```php
<?php next_post_link('Older: <strong>%link</strong>'); ?>
<?php previous_post_link('Newer: <strong>%link</strong>'); ?>
```

 That's Backwards

WordPress considers the `next_post_link()` function to actually refer to the set of posts that came *previously* in time. `previous_post_link()` refers to the ones that came afterwards.

Find it a bit baffling? It helps if you think of this process as starting from your blog's home page, which contains the newest posts, and digging backwards. When you're working backwards, the *next* page is going to have older posts.

Let's Try a Simple loop

Now that we know what makes up a loop, let's try filling in some of the blanks. The following example is a loop that will show each entry's title, permalink, linked list of tags, and the excerpt. We'll wrap up all those posts in a tidy unordered list, and if there are no posts to show, we'll include a friendly message. Here goes:

chapter_03/loop-index.php *(excerpt)*

```php
<?php if (have_posts()) : ?>
  <h1>Latest Posts</h1>
  <ul class="mini-list">
    <?php while (have_posts()) : the_post(); ?>
      <li>
        <h2><a href="<?php the_permalink() ?>">
          <?php the_title(); ?></a>
          <?php the_time("jS F"); ?>
        </h2>
        <p><?php the_excerpt(); ?></p>
        <p><?php the_tags( "Tagged with: ", " / ", "" ); ?></p>
      </li>
    <?php endwhile; ?>
  </ul>
<?php else: ?>
<h1>No posts to show</h1>
```

```
<p>Sorry, we got nada. Nothing. Bupkis. Zippo.
Diddly-squat. Sorry to disappoint.</p>
<?php endif; ?>
```

Let's see how that loop looks if we use it in a home page template reminiscent of WordPress's Twenty Eleven style. Since it's on the home page, it's simply displaying the most recent posts in reverse chronological order. Figure 3.2 shows us what comes out of this loop.

Figure 3.2. Our compact loop, showing titles, tags, dates, and excerpts

Exciting? Hardly, but it serves to demonstrate how quickly and easily you can have a simple loop up and running in your templates. Soon we'll try some prettier examples.

Counters and The Loop

We often find it's useful to interrupt The Loop at a certain point, or to treat particular positions differently. For example, you might want to make the first post in your loop stand out more, or place an advertisement after the fifth post. You can accomplish this quite easily by introducing a counter to your loop. Every time The Loop prints out a post, we'll increment the counter. All you need is a bit of code to check the value of the counter, and act accordingly.

In the following example, we'll extend our simple mini loop from the previous section to show the first post's full content, and leave the others as excerpts:

chapter_03/loop-index.php *(excerpt)*

```php
<?php if (have_posts()) : $postcounter = 1; ?>
  <h1>Latest Posts</h1>
  <ul class="mini-list">
    <?php while (have_posts()) : the_post(); ?>
      <li>
        <h2><a href="<?php the_permalink() ?>">
            <?php the_title(); ?></a>
            <?php the_time("j M"); ?></h2>
        <p>
          <?php if ($postcounter == 1) {
                the_content();
              } else {
                 the_excerpt();
              } ?>
        </p>
        <p><?php the_tags( "Tagged with: ", " / ", "" ); ?> </p>
      </li>
<?php $postcounter++; ?>
```

You'll see that we start by creating a variable, postcounter, and at the beginning we assign it a value of 1. At the end of the while loop, we increment the value of postcounter by 1. And in the middle of the loop, we check the value of postcounter and decide whether to show the excerpt (the_excerpt()), or the post's content (the_content()).

Now, let's put that same counter to work in the pursuit of cold hard cash: we'll insert advertising blocks after every third post. After the end of the list items, we'll check to see whether the value of postcounter is divisible by three, and if so, we'll insert a subtle bit of advertising. The following example extends further on our previous one:

```
                                    chapter_03/loop-index.php (excerpt)
  ⋮

</li>
<?php
  if (($postcounter % 3) == 0) { ?>
    <li class="break">
      <a href="http://www.example.com">Buy lots of widgets please
      </a>
    </li>
<?php  }
$postcounter++; ?>
```

Let's see how that turned out, in Figure 3.3.

Figure 3.3. Our mini loop, now with ads—we'll be rich!

Of course, you might have better luck with raking in the cash if you use a more enticing ad from a reputable ad network, but no doubt you get the drift.

Rewinding The Loop

If you want to use more than one loop on a page, use the `rewind_posts()` function to reset The Loop's counters to the beginning. If you forget to do so, you might find that you're missing posts in your other loops, or experiencing funny behavior in pagination.

Beyond the Default: Custom Queries

It's all very well to be able to meddle with the default loops, but what about changing them completely, or even creating your own? Sometimes your project calls for a set of posts from a particular category or set of tags only. Maybe you'd like to show off your most recent photo attachments in a sidebar widget. You might want to change your author archives to show the posts in alphabetical order, instead of reverse chronological order. However you slice it, it's a certainty that one day you'll need to go beyond the safety of those default loops.

Like any CMS, WordPress's most important job is to retrieve and display posts. Accordingly, there are a few different methods for querying the database. Let's look at how these are done and when you might use each technique.

Manipulating the Default loop: `query_posts()`

We learned earlier that WordPress, being a helpful type of CMS, sets up its own queries on certain pages. What happens, though, when you want to alter that behavior ever so slightly? If your goal is simply to modify what should appear in the main WordPress loop, the `query_posts()` function[4] is for you. It's a function that overrides the current page's default loop, and it's useful whenever you want to make some quick tweaks to the type of posts that appear.

To use it, simply call on `query_posts()` before your loop begins, and set up the parameters you need from the available options. For example, we often find that we want to exclude certain categories from date-based archives or the home page. We can do this by simply adjusting the query to exclude those categories' IDs with a minus sign, like so:

```php
<?php query_posts('cat=-11,-8,-90');
if (have_posts()): while (have_posts()) : the_post(); ?>
... continue your loop as normal
```

To add more parameters, just pass on more of them, separated by ampersands:

```php
<?php query_posts('cat=-11,-8,-90&post_type=reviews&tag=action'); ?>
```

---

[4] http://codex.wordpress.org/Template_Tags/query_posts

What Parameters Can I Use?

All the available parameters are documented in the WordPress Codex's `WP_Query` documentation,[5] which is the class that underpins all the functions around fetching content.

Once you start adding more and more criteria, it becomes a little easier to read if you express these as a longhand-style array, and then pass the array into the `query_posts()` function:

```php
<?php $args = array(
        'cat' => '-11,-8,-90',
        'post_type' => 'reviews',
        'tag' => 'action',
        'posts_per_page' => 30,
        'order' => 'ASC',
        'order_by' => 'rand'
    );
    query_posts($args);
?>
```

When you've finished with your customized loop, it's important to clean up after yourself, and reset the query back to normal. `query_posts()` modifies a lot of global variables, many of which are also in use by plugins and themes; if you neglect to reset your query once you're done, it could have an adverse effect on plugins and the elements that assume the query has been left untouched. Overcoming it is simple—the `wp_reset_query()` function avoids all the drama:

```php
    ... The Loop
<?php else: ?>
    ... the no posts message
<?php endif;
 wp_reset_query(); ?>
```

Creating New Customized Loops: `get_posts`

The `query_posts()` function is great if you want to modify what happens on any given page's default loop. When you have a need to create completely customized loops, however, we have a different tool at our disposal: `get_posts()`.[6]

We often find ourselves using custom loops when we want to create complex pages. For example, the ever-popular magazine-style layout frequently makes use of a number of separate loops to achieve effects such as sliders and featured posts, or formats including topical sections. In this situation, modifying the existing loop isn't going to be enough.

---

[5] http://codex.wordpress.org/Class_Reference/WP_Query#Parameters
[6] http://codex.wordpress.org/Template_Tags/get_posts

For example, let's say that we're creating a page template that lists a particular series of posts. Each post in the series is tagged with **wordpress** and **tutorial**. We want to show the list of posts in ascending date order, so that a reader of the page knows which order to read them in.

To set up a loop that works for this scenario, we'll first need to make a new array with all the parameters we want to use to retrieve our posts. Then, we'll use `get_posts()` to create a new array of posts, `tutorials`, and use a `foreach` loop to iterate through them. By default, we're unable to use template tags like `the_content` in the usual way, so the addition of the `setup_postdata()` function takes each post and prepares it for easier use:

chapter_03/get_posts.php

```php
<?php $args = array(
    'numberposts' => 30,
    'tag' => 'wordpress+tutorial',
    'order' => 'ASC',
    'order_by' => 'date'
);

$tutorials = get_posts($args);
foreach($tutorials as $post) : setup_postdata($post); ?>
    <h2><a href="<?php the_permalink(); ?>">
      <?php the_title(); ?>
      </a>
    </h2>
    <?php the_excerpt(); ?>
<?php endforeach; ?>
```

 setup_postdata() Requires a post

In the above example, each item in the `tutorials` array is referred to as `post`. With the `setup_postdata()` function, you must always call on each post as `post`—no other variable will do.

 Post Query Parameters

When we're building our own queries, we have some incredibly powerful tools at our disposal. As always, there's no better place than the Codex[7] to learn about all the different parameters and how to combine them.

As we progress through this book, and cover different techniques and topics, we'll see how various parameters and methods help us get those jobs done.

---

[7] http://codex.wordpress.org/Class_Reference/WP_Query

Using the `WP_Query` Class Directly

The `WP_Query` class is what's responsible for returning the posts for a default loop, `get_posts()`, and `query_posts()`, alike; these functions call on the same class, just in different ways. Calling on it directly gets you a big object with a selection of posts, plus a good deal of information about the request itself.

If you're a creature of habit and consistency, a big benefit of this approach is that you can instantiate a new `WP_Query` object and treat it just like a regular WordPress loop, but dealing with `get_posts()` can be a little more tricky. Most of the techniques and functions are the same as the ones you'd use when you're manipulating a regular old loop, so it's very easy to pick up and use this method right away. With `get_posts()`, you'll find that there are a few caveats: pagination needs extra help, plugins work differently with a loop made from `get_posts()`, and so on.

Another benefit of the `WP_Query` approach is that you'll often find it in use with plugins, especially ones that modify the WordPress back end. If you're an aspiring plugin ninja, it's likely you'll deal with `WP_Query` often, so some consistency in how you retrieve content is handy to have.

It's still okay to use `get_posts()` to grab simpler lists of posts—in fact, it's been a popular method for so long that it will probably be around for a little while yet—but the ease of dealing with the `WP_Query` object directly makes it a great choice overall. You may find that you never need to worry about using `get_posts()` at all!

Let's look at how easy it is to deal with a `WP_Query` object. In this example, we're creating a similar loop to the one in the previous section, showing our WordPress tutorial series in chronological order—this time, using the `WP_Query` method. Before we begin, we'll put the existing query in a new variable for safekeeping:

chapter_03/WP_Query.php *(excerpt)*

```php
<?php
$original_query = $wp_query;
$wp_query = null;

$args = array(
    'numberposts' => 30,
    'tag' => 'wordpress+tutorial',
    'order' => 'ASC',
    'order_by' => 'date',
    'paged' => $paged
    );
$wp_query = new WP_Query($args);
?>
```

For Pagination, Only $wp_query Will Do

In this example, we'll be making our own query, but we'll be copying our original query to another variable and then naming that variable $wp_query. This is necessary for pagination methods and their associated tags. They simply fail to work when the query is stored in an object by any other name. Of course, you'll only need to concern yourself with this issue when you need pagination.

With us so far? Now that we've stashed the old query away and set up our new one, we can start using the new query in a loop:

chapter_03/WP_Query.php *(excerpt)*

```php
<?php if ($wp_query->have_posts()): ?>
<?php while ($wp_query->have_posts()) : $wp_query->the_post(); ?>
  <h2><a href="<?php the_permalink(); ?>">
      <?php the_title(); ?>
    </a>
  </h2>
  <?php the_excerpt(); ?>
<?php endwhile; else: ?>
    ... something to show if there were no posts
<?php endif; ?>
```

When you're finished playing with your WP_Query object, it's time to return everything to how you found it. We'll put the contents of $original_query back into $wp_query, and ensure everything's back to normal by using the wp_reset_postdata() function. This function uses the page's POST data to restore the post global variable to its original state:

```php
<?php
  $wp_query = $original_query;
  wp_reset_postdata();
?>
```

Roll Your Own Loop Magic

With a combination of custom queries, loops, and good old-fashioned HTML elbow grease, you'll be able to create some groovy features for your blog. Here are some examples of common techniques, and how queries and loops are used to achieve them. We've touched on a bit of theory in this chapter, but since The Loop is such an important part of the WordPress experience, you'll find that we delve into more interesting aspects of it throughout this book.

For now, let's just try out a few more examples.

Fetch Any Posts Matching a Custom Field

Imagine that you'd like to pull out a series of posts matching a given custom field. For example, if you've been keeping a note of the music you were listening to while you wrote each post, it might be amusing to pull out links to all the posts matching a given artist. WP_Query provides two custom field arguments, *meta_key* and *meta_value*, to construct a query:

chapter_03/custom-field.php *(excerpt)*

```php
<?php
$original_query = $wp_query;
$wp_query = null;

$args = array(
    'meta_key' => 'artist',
    'meta_value' => 'The Beatles',
    'order' => 'DESC',
    'order_by' => 'date',
    'post_count' => '10'
    );
$wp_query = new WP_Query($args);
?>
```

Now that we have our arguments and our query in place, we'll create a loop that shows a heading and list when there's matching posts. Since we have no need to show anything here if nothing exists, we'll just exit The Loop after our while loop:

chapter_03/custom-field.php *(excerpt)*

```php
<?php if (have_posts()): ?>
  <h3>This artist also inspired...</h3>
  <ul>
    <?php while (have_posts()) : the_post(); ?>
      <li><a href="<?php the_permalink(); ?>">
          <?php the_title(); ?>
          </a>
      </li>
    <?php endwhile; ?>
  </ul>
<?php endif; ?>
```

As we learned earlier, it's important to clean up your mess afterwards:

```php
<?php
// Reset post data
wp_reset_postdata();
```

```
// Restore some order
$wp_query = $original_query;
?>
```

Teasers of Future-dated Posts

If you're super-organized, you probably have a bunch of future-dated posts waiting to go up. Why not tease your readers with a taste of what's to come? In this example, we'll create a query that retrieves future posts, and shows their titles, excerpts, and an idea of how long readers need to wait till they can see it.

As before, we'll store away the original query in another object, and create a new WP_Query. In this case, we'll use the *post_status* argument to ask for posts that are set for publication in the future:

chapter_03/future-dated-posts.php *(excerpt)*

```php
<?php
$original_query = $wp_query;
$wp_query = null;
$args = array(
    'post_status' => 'future',
    'order' => 'ASC',
    'order_by' => 'date',
    'post_count' => '3'
    );
$wp_query = new WP_Query($args);
?>
```

Easy enough so far. Now we'll show a title, the excerpt, and a human-friendly explanation of how long our readers will have to bite their nails and wait to read it:

chapter_03/future-dated-posts.php *(excerpt)*

```php
<?php
if (have_posts()) : while (have_posts()) : the_post(); ?>

<h2><?php the_title(); ?></h2>
<p><?php the_excerpt(); ?></p>
<?php
$now = time('U');
$posted = get_the_time('U');
echo "Going live in " . human_time_diff($posted, $now) . " time";

?>
<?php endwhile;
else: ?>
    <p>No future posts are planned.</p>
<?php endif; ?>
```

Any More Queries?

There are many different facets to developing a keen understanding of WordPress, but the none of them will make sense until you understand The Loop and template tags, how they work together, and where everything lives. In this chapter, we covered the standard WordPress file structure and described how and where to use The Loop. We went through a few examples of simple versions of The Loop, and then dug into some more custom manipulations where we created our own queries and looked at the difference between `query_posts()`, `get_posts()`, and `WP_Query`. On the surface, The Loop isn't the sexiest topic in WordPress, but it's the vital building block required to make everything else hum. Now let's start putting our new-found knowledge about template tags and The Loop into action and delve into the world of custom post types.

Post Types

One of the factors that elevates WordPress from being a mere blogging tool into a butt-kicking CMS ready for world domination is its custom post types capability. Custom post types let you go beyond the concept of a blog post or page, and move into just about any type of content you like. Imagine creating a recipe or tutorial site, a staff directory, or a portfolio of work.

In this chapter, we'll learn about why we might want to create our own post types, how to put them together, and how to create templates for them.

Moving Beyond the Blog

While many of us get along fine with the built-in content types provided in WordPress, sometimes you just have to stretch the system a little—you want to be able to make up your own content types, with customized fields, categories, and more.

Before WordPress 2.9, if you wanted to create a custom content type, you'd have to try to combine pages or posts with categories, tags, custom fields, and some judicious use of theming. While it achieved the task at hand, it was hardly an ideal solution; a blog post is still a blog post, no matter how well your theme could dress it up to look like a product page. More adventurous souls would build plugins and strange hacks that created custom database tables and did other mysterious tricks behind the scenes, but it was an approach fraught with trouble.

Custom post types, by comparison, give us a straightforward way to extend WordPress's native content types beyond the default types. Setting them up is stupendously easy: just a few lines of

configuration and some effort with our templates is all it takes to have intuitive and functional content types.

What's in a name?

When we're talking about **post types**, what we really mean is content types. The fact that it's called a post type in WordPress might make it seem like it's still intended for blogging, but don't be dissuaded—there's so much more that can be done with these.

Creating Your First Custom Post Types

Let's imagine that we've found ourselves in charge of creating a website for a small web conference. Any good conference website needs to have at least two important pieces of information: who is speaking, and what they are talking about.

This sounds like a great opportunity to explore post types. We can use these to help us describe each of the speakers and the sessions. We'll also have information pages and a conference blog, though we'll use standard pages and blog entries for these. We'll start by planning out the types of information we'd like to express:

Speakers pages

These will be simple enough. They should describe a little bit about each person, including an image, their business, short and long versions of their bio, and a link to a website. We'll list all the speakers on a listing page.

Sessions pages

These will be more complex. They should describe the name of the talk, its location, its date and time, a description, and a way to upload a slide deck of the talk. They should also have their own tags, so that a user can check out all the sessions that may be of interest to them. We'll be listing sessions on a page, too.

Let's begin with the speakers. Create a new plugin folder called **sitepoint** in wp-content/plugins, and place a new plugin file inside it with the filename **sitepoint-custom-types.php**. You'll need to give your plugin a header, which WordPress will use when initializing your plugin for use:

```
chapter_04/sitepoint-custom-types.php (excerpt)
<?php
/*
Plugin Name: SitePoint Custom Conference Types
Plugin URI: http://sitepoint.com
Description: This is a plugin that provides the Custom Post Types
  chapter of the WordPress Anthology.
Author: Your Name Here
```

```
Version: 0.1
Author URI: http://sitepoint.com/
*/
?>
```

You can define your custom post types in a plugin folder, or in a theme folder's `functions.php` file. So which should you choose?

If your custom content is for wide use, it might be best to present it as a plugin. If you're working on a client's project where you're fairly sure they'll stick to using the theme you provided—whether that's Twenty Eleven or your own creative choice—perhaps you'll be safe keeping it within the `functions.php` file in that particular theme's folder (which can be found in **wp-content/themes**). The litmus test for where your code belongs is really whether that functionality can be best described as site functionality or display logic—but for a deeper discussion of this, have a look at the section called "Does My Functionality Belong in a Plugin or Theme?" in Chapter 6. When in doubt, it's usually best to add your functionality in a plugin. If you are concerned that your client may accidentally turn the plugin off, consider simply making the plugin a must-use plugin (you can learn more about must-use plugins in Chapter 5).

In this chapter, we'll work on a plugin—not least because it makes it really easy for you to drop our example files into your own install. If it sounds like we're jumping ahead a little, we are. In fact, plugin development is covered in detail in Chapter 5, specifically in the section called "The Anatomy of a Plugin" in Chapter 5. We'll only be touching on the most basic parts of plugin setup here, and if you've been reading cover to cover and are yet to read Chapter 5, these instructions should still make sense. Of course, if you're just dying to find out now, feel free to flip ahead—we'll still be here when you return.

Head into the WordPress admin area, go to the **Plugins** submenu, and click on **Installed Plugins**. There's our plugin, listed alongside any others in the **wp-content/plugins** folder, with all the information from our header attached to it. Cool, huh? Again, for now, avoid fretting too much about the details behind this—it's all going to be fully fleshed out in Chapter 5.

Our plugin, as yet, does absolutely nothing, so you'll need to activate it in order to see your code take shape. Go ahead and click **Activate**. Make sure you keep your **Admin** panel open in a separate tab in your browser, too, as we're going to be coming back to it a lot.

 Must-use Plugins Are Active

If you've set up your plugin as a must-use plugin, it's unnecessary to manually activate the plugin. Must-use plugins are automatically active whenever they are present in the **wp-content/mu-plugins** directory. For more information on this, flip forward to the section called "Must-use Plugins" in Chapter 5.

Now for some action!

The Basics of `register_post_type()`

The `register_post_type()` function takes care of telling WordPress about how we define each new piece of content. Like most things WordPress, it's described in great detail over at the Codex,[1] along with its dizzying array of configuration arguments (See what we did there—array? Okay, tough crowd …). In this chapter, we'll just refer to the ones we need.

We'll wrap all these up in our own function, `conference_post_types_register()`, and call on that function whenever the `init` action occurs:

```
                                          chapter_04/sitepoint-custom-types.php (excerpt)
function conference_post_types_register() {
    register_post_type( 'conference_speaker',
        array(
            'labels' => array( ❶
                'name' => __( 'Speakers' ),
                'singular_name' => __( 'Speaker' ),
                'add_new' => __( 'Add New Speaker' ),
                'add_new_item' => __( 'Add New Speaker' ),
                'edit' => __( 'Edit' ),
                'edit_item' => __( 'Edit Speaker' ),
                'new_item' => __( 'New Speaker' ),
                'view' => __( 'View Speaker' ),
                'view_item' => __( 'View Speaker' ),
                'search_items' => __( 'Search Speakers' ),
                'not_found' => __( 'No speakers' ),
                'not_found_in_trash' => __( 'No speakers in the Trash' ),
            ),
            'hierarchical' => false, ❷
            'public' => true, ❸
            'menu_position' => 25, ❹
            'menu_icon' => plugins_url( 'icons/user_comment.png' , __FILE__ ), ❺
            'has_archive' => 'speakers', ❻
            'rewrite' => array('slug' => 'speaker'), ❼
            'supports' => array( 'title', 'excerpt', 'editor', 'thumbnail'), ❽
            'description' => "A conference speaker page is a page of➡
                information about a person who'll appear at this event."

        )
    );
}

add_action( 'init', 'conference_post_types_register' );
```

---

[1] http://codex.wordpress.org/Function_Reference/register_post_type

❶ The `labels` array takes care of how the custom type is represented in the WordPress back end. We'll use the word "speaker" in variations appropriate to the context.

❷ `hierarchical` tells WordPress whether the post type can have parents and children, like pages. In this instance, we'll be saying no.

❸ `public` helps define whether we'd like this post type to be viewable on the front end, whether it can be returned in search results, and whether we'd like it to be editable in the back end. You might wonder why you'd want these to be hidden. In some cases, especially if you're automating content creation or want to treat some kinds of content like a private database, you may want to hide some of these items.

❹ `menu_position` is a number that represents the place this post type's menu will occupy in the **Admin** menu. 25 will place it below the **Comments** submenu.

❺ `menu_icon` looks after the all-important icon that represents this post type in the WordPress **Admin** menu. For this example, we've used one of the very excellent Silk icons.[2] These have a fairly close resemblance in size and style to the existing WordPress icons, and look about a million times better than anything we could draw up.

❻ `has_archive` defines whether the post type has an archive page of its own—that is, a listing page. We'd like to have a speaker listing page, so the value we pass it is `speakers`; this is both saying that we want an archive (`true`), and also serves as the slug we want to see for our archive's permalink.

❼ `rewrite` looks after what will be used in the permalink rewrite rules for an individual speaker; in this case, it will be `speaker`.

❽ `supports`, tucked away at the end here, might be one of the most important parts of all. It defines which of the core fields are supported and shown by this post type. The available fields are:

- `title`: text input field to create a post title
- `editor`: the main text editing box—the area that forms a blog entry's post content
- `excerpt`: a plain text region for writing a custom excerpt
- `comments` or `trackbacks`: the comments or trackbacks configuration areas, respectively
- `revisions`: allows revisions to be made to your post
- `author`: displays a pull-down menu for changing the item's author
- `thumbnail`: shows the **Featured Image** uploading box
- `custom-fields`: custom fields input area; you can leave this out, and still store custom fields—in fact, that's what we'll be doing
- `page-attributes`: the attributes box for pages, such as the parent post or page template

---

[2] http://www.famfamfam.com/lab/icons/silk/

We chose just four of the default `supports` fields: `title`, `editor`, `excerpt`, and `thumbnail`, representing the speaker's name, long bio, short bio, and image, respectively. We'll use custom fields to take care of the others later.

Action? What's that?

Hooks and actions are incredibly important concepts in WordPress hackery. Once more, these are covered in detail in Chapter 5, so head there for a fuller explanation of what these are and how they work. For now, just be pleased they're making your page work beautifully!

And More!

There are even more arguments you can pass with `register_post_type()`. Explore them all at the Codex.[3]

That's a lot of arguments, but can you believe that this is all you need to create a basic new post type? It's true! Save your work and have a look at your WordPress admin screen. You should find that your menu now contains a new item for **Speakers**, as seen in Figure 4.1.

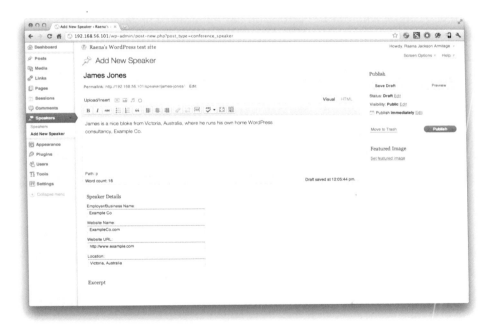

Figure 4.1. Creating a new speaker

Neat, hey? But we still need to add some new fields; that's what will come next.

---

[3] http://codex.wordpress.org/Function_Reference/register_post_type

Adding Custom Fields to the Edit Screen

Our conference speakers' pages need to include a note about who they work for (even if it's themselves), and their website's URL and title. Now, you could include these in the text of each page, if you wanted, but that's hardly the same as properly structured data.

This problem's been solved for a long time in the world of WordPress, of course; its **custom fields** feature allows you to create metadata about a post. Used properly, custom fields are a deadly weapon in the hands of an expert WordPress ninja—unfortunately, it also means that our users need to remember which field goes with what type of data. For example, you might want certain blog posts that represent quotations to have a source name and URL, so you'd have to remember to pick the right label, put the source in, and hope there's nothing you've forgotten. And if you use custom fields for several types of posts, they're all shown right there in the **Custom Posts** pull-down, which just seems superfluous.

For improved usability, wouldn't it be better just to fill in a clearly labeled set of fields? Sure it would—that's why we've hidden that interface element from our posting screen. We'll write our own **Edit Screen**, with our own form fields.

Let's create a function that reads the values of a number of custom fields, and prints form fields for each. Here's a fairly simplistic bit of PHP form creation:

chapter_04/sitepoint-custom-types.php *(excerpt)*

```php
function conference_speaker_fields (){
    global $post;
    $custom = get_post_custom($post->ID);
    $conference_speaker_business = $custom["conference_speaker_business"][0];
    $conference_speaker_website_name = $custom
      ["conference_speaker_website_name"][0];
    $conference_speaker_website_url = $custom["conference_speaker_website_url"]
      [0];
    $conference_speaker_location = $custom["conference_speaker_location"][0];
    ?>

    <p>
    <label>Employer/Business Name:</label><br />
    <input size="45" name="conference_speaker_business"
       value="<?php echo $conference_speaker_business; ?>" />
    </p>
    <p>
    <label>Website Name:</label><br />
    <input size="45" name="conference_speaker_website_name"
       value="<?php echo $conference_speaker_website_name; ?>" />
    </p>
    <p>
    <label>Website URL:</label><br />
```

```
    <input size="45" name="conference_speaker_website_url"
      value="<?php echo $conference_speaker_website_url; ?>" />
    </p>
    <p>
    <label>Location:</label><br />
    <input size="45" name="conference_speaker_location"
      value="<?php echo $conference_speaker_location; ?>" /></p>

    <?php
}
```

Notice that we've prefixed every post meta field with `conference_speaker_`? You never know when you might install a plugin that has fields that clash with your existing ones. Using a prefix like this makes it less likely to occur.

How do we place them on the edit screen? `add_meta_box()` is the function that will help us, and it accepts seven arguments. The four mandatory arguments are:

- `id`: the HTML `id` of the division that WordPress will insert
- `title`: the title we'll show for this edit screen section
- `callback`: the function that prints out the HTML for the edit screen section
- `page`: the built-in type or custom post type we want to modify

Optional arguments are:

- `context`: being the part of the edit screen we want to put it in; acceptable options are `normal`, `advanced`, or `side` (side placement is great for small fields)

- `priority`: determines the position (importance) of where the boxes should show; the available options are `high`, `core`, `default`, or `low`

- `callback_args`: any further arguments to pass on to our callback function

Let's take all that HTML we made before in `conference_speaker_fields()`, and put it in a new meta box called `conference_speaker_info`, with a title of **Speaker Details**. Naturally, we only want this to appear in the `conference_speaker` content type. Here's a function to create it:

_chapter_04/sitepoint-custom-types.php (excerpt)_

```
function add_conference_speaker_box(){
  add_meta_box(
      "conference_speaker_info",
      "Speaker Details",
      "conference_speaker_fields",
```

```
            "conference_speaker"
        );
}
```

Here, we've only used the four mandatory arguments.

 Why meta?

> Hey, have you noticed how functions about custom fields always seem to refer to meta this and meta that? It's because in the past they were called **post meta fields**. We now call them custom fields because this makes more sense, but the functions' names remain the same.

We'll also need a function to save them. update_post_meta() is the WordPress function that inserts values as custom fields. We'll take the value of each field from the POST variable, and save them in an appropriately named custom field for the current post:

chapter_04/sitepoint-custom-types.php (excerpt)

```
function save_conference_speaker_attributes(){
    global $post;
    update_post_meta($post->ID, "conference_speaker_business",➥
      $_POST["conference_speaker_business"]);
    update_post_meta($post->ID, "conference_speaker_website_url",➥
      $_POST["conference_speaker_website_url"]);
    update_post_meta($post->ID, "conference_speaker_website_name",➥
      $_POST["conference_speaker_website_name"]);
    update_post_meta($post->ID, "conference_speaker_location",➥
      $_POST["conference_speaker_location"]);
}
```

The admin_init action is triggered whenever an admin page is loaded; accordingly, it's the right place to call on our function that adds the conference speaker box:

chapter_04/sitepoint-custom-types.php (excerpt)

```
add_action( 'admin_init', 'add_conference_speaker_box' );
```

We also want to jump aboard when the save and publish actions happen, so that we can save what's in our customized fields:

chapter_04/sitepoint-custom-types.php (excerpt)

```
add_action('save_post',
'save_conference_speaker_attributes');
add_action('publish_post',
'save_conference_speaker_attributes');
```

Adding Conference Sessions

Let's expand on our plugin a little further, and create our conference sessions post type, with a
Sessions submenu in the **Admin** menu. We have already learned how to set up one of these, so the
following `register_post_type()` should be reasonably familiar to you:

sitepoint-custom-types.php (excerpt)

```php
register_post_type( 'conference_session',
    array(
        'labels' => array(
            'name' => __( 'Sessions' ),
            'singular_name' => __( 'Session' ),
            'add_new' => __( 'Add New Session' ),
            'add_new_item' => __( 'Add New Session' ),
            'edit' => __( 'Edit' ),
            'edit_item' => __( 'Edit Session' ),
            'new_item' => __( 'New Session' ),
            'view' => __( 'View Session' ),
            'view_item' => __( 'View Session' ),
            'search_items' => __( 'Search Session' ),
            'not_found' => __( 'No sessions' ),
            'not_found_in_trash' => __( 'No sessions in the Trash' ),
        ),
        'public' => true,
        'hierarchical' => false,
        'exclude_from_search' => false,
        'menu_position' => 20,
        'menu_icon' => plugins_url( 'icons/calendar_view_day.png' ,➥
            __FILE__ ),
        'query_var' => true,
        'can_export' => true,
        'has_archive' => 'sessions',
        'description' => "A conference session is an event: a➥
            workshop, talk, panel, or get-together.",
        'rewrite' => array('slug' => 'sessions'),
        'supports' => array( 'title', 'excerpt', 'editor', 'thumbnail' )
    )
);
```

Again, although it's relatively long, it's also fairly straightforward. Each piece of session content
represents an event in our conference, but in many other respects it resembles a regular sort of post:
it'll have an excerpt, a post body, and a title. We'll also need some details about where and when
the session will be held, so we'll add another meta box, like so:

```
                                        sitepoint-custom-types.php (excerpt)
function conference_session_admin(){
    add_meta_box("conference_session_meta", "Session Details",➥
                "conference_session_meta", "conference_session",➥
                "normal", "core");
}

function conference_session_meta (){
    global $post;
    $custom = get_post_custom($post->ID);
    $conference_session_room = $custom["conference_session_room"][0];
    $conference_session_date = $custom["conference_session_date"][0];
    ?>

    <p>
    <label>Room</label><br />
    <select name="conference_session_room">
      <option value="Grand Ballroom">Grand Ballroom</option>
      <option value="Plenary A">Plenary A</option>
      <option value="Plenary B">Plenary B</option>
      <option value="Theatre">Theatre</option>
    </select>
    </p>

    <p><label>Session date and time</label><br />
    <input size="45" id="conference_session_date"
       name="conference_session_date"
       value="<?php echo $conference_session_date; ?>" />
    </p>

    <?php
}
```

In this example, we've chosen to use a pull-down for each of the conference session venues, since they won't change. The date and time information is open—that makes it easy to insert flexible statements like "From 8 till late" or "6:30pm for a 7pm start." So far, so good, and still familiar territory.

Where our sessions will differ significantly from our earlier efforts will be in how we treat the topic of, well, topics.

Custom Taxonomies

If you've attended a conference lately, you'll know how tricky it is to decide which sessions to attend—and if it was a really good conference, you would have found yourself spoiled for choice! It's helpful to be able to plan your timetable by gaining a sense of which sessions will best suit your interests and skills. How can we make this easy for our site's visitors? One way is by creating a

custom taxonomy for our conference sessions. In the general sense, a taxonomy is a scheme of classification. In the WordPress sense, taxonomies are what we call sets of categories and tags. A vanilla install of WordPress already comes with three: post tags, categories, and link categories. Custom taxonomies work like these familiar tags and categories to add more meaning to custom post types.

 Don't Tax Your Brain Just Yet

Custom taxonomies are discussed in great detail in Chapter 7. Once again, you should look at that chapter for more information about how it all works. In this section, we'll just touch on the basics.

In our conference scenario, we'll be expecting our speakers to hold forth on a number of web-type topics—such as JavaScript, usability, or WordPress—so it makes sense for our conference session post types to allow for this. You can create a new taxonomy using the `register_taxonomy()` function,[4] which accepts three parameters: the name of the taxonomy, the type of content it's to be used with, and an array of additional arguments. In the below example, we'll set up a new taxonomy for session topics:

1. The first variable will be the name of our taxonomy: `conference_topics`.

2. The second argument defines which post types it should apply to; `conference_session`, in our case.

3. Our third argument is an array of more arguments:

   - `hierarchical` lets us choose if the taxonomy should allow for a hierarchy, like categories, or no hierarchy, like tags. In our case, we'll use a tag-like construction.

   - `labels` define the names of the taxonomy as seen in the admin area, much like the labels for new post types we learned about earlier.

   - `query_var` determines whether the post type is able to be queried—that is, if you can form a loop with it.

   - People are likely to enter their tags with a comma between each one; `update_count_callback()` calls on a function that ensures that WordPress treats these correctly.

   - The `rewrite` value determines what will be shown in the URL for a post of this type.

We'll wrap it all up in a function, `create_conference_taxonomy()`, like so:

---

[4] http://codex.wordpress.org/Function_Reference/register_taxonomy

chapter_04/sitepoint-custom-types.php *(excerpt)*

```php
function create_conference_taxonomy() {

    $topiclabels = array(
        'name' => 'Topic',
        'singular_name' => 'topic',
        'search_items' =>  'Search topics',
        'popular_items' => 'Popular topics',
        'all_items' => 'All topics',
        'parent_item' => null,
        'parent_item_colon' => null,
        'edit_item' => 'Edit topic',
        'update_item' => 'Update topic',
        'add_new_item' => 'Add new topic',
        'new_item_name' => 'New topic name',
        'separate_items_with_commas' => 'Separate topics with commas',
        'add_or_remove_items' => 'Add or remove topics',
        'choose_from_most_used' => 'Choose from common topics',
        'menu_name' => 'Conference topics',
    );
    register_taxonomy( 'conference_topics', 'conference_session',
        array(
        'hierarchical' => false,
            'labels' => $topiclabels,
            'query_var' => true,
            'update_count_callback' => '_update_post_term_count',
            'rewrite' => array('slug' => 'topics' )
        )
    );
}
```

 ## Avoid These Terms in Your Taxonomy Name

Some special terms are reserved for WordPress's use, and if you use them to name your taxonomy, it will result in a cheeky error. Uppercase letters are also a no-no. If you're being a polite developer, you probably have little need to worry; after all, you're already prefixing your custom taxonomies uniquely, like we talked about earlier, right? Even so, keep an eye out for the reserved names, which are listed on the Codex.[5]

Finally, you'll need to initialize this function—associate it with the `init` action as follows:

```php
add_action('init', 'create_conference_taxonomy', 0);
```

---

[5] http://codex.wordpress.org/Function_Reference/register_taxonomy#Reserved_Terms

Once you've put all this together, your new taxonomy will be in your administration area, and should look like Figure 4.2. Since topics are associated with questions, you'll find them in the **Sessions** menu.

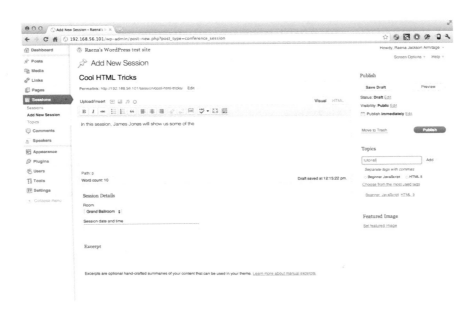

Figure 4.2. Our new taxonomy, ready for action

Providing Help

Remember the first time you jumped into WordPress? If you're anything like us, you would have found yourself lost among all those different screens in the WordPress administrative interface.

The good news is that on almost every WordPress admin screen, a friendly **Help** link is there to guide the way. Clicking it reveals a panel, which can be seen in Figure 4.3. The **Help** link often provides relevant links to the Codex or descriptions of each object. The even better news is that, as a WordPress developer, it's easy for you to add that same level of help to your own work. It's also a great opportunity to encourage users to visit any help pages you might have set up, or let them know how they can seek support.

Figure 4.3. The **Help** link reveals this handy panel

The `add_contextual_help` hook provides a simple, nonintrusive way to add or modify help panels, just like the ones that come with WordPress. It accepts two arguments: the name of the admin screen that you want to add help to, and some text to add.

Straightforward, right? But hey, wait a minute—how do you know the name of each of the different WordPress admin screens? The Codex provides a handy way to find out.[6] Where do you place this nifty little piece of code? Navigate to the theme folder that you're currently using. Right now, we're using Twenty Eleven, so our filepath will be **wp-content/themes/twentyeleven**. In here you'll find a **functions.php** file; this is where you'll input the following code:

```
function check_current_screen() {
  if(!is_admin()) return;
  global $current_screen;
  print_r($current_screen);
}
add_action('admin_notices', 'check_current_screen');
```

This function reveals a few bits of information about the screens you can call up in the admin area. Go and click on **Sessions**, and you will see that our `print_r()` function has output some useful information in the browser. The only piece of data we're interested in here is the `[id]`, which will be the name of the admin screen we're on. Placing this value in the `admin_notices` hook means that it'll be nice and obvious at the top of each page, just underneath the **Help** menu. It turns out

---

[6] http://codex.wordpress.org/Function_Reference/add_contextual_help#Finding_the_Screen_Name

that the page for editing conference sessions is called `edit-conference_session`, revealed in Figure 4.4, which is hardly surprising.

Figure 4.4. Our **Edit Session** page's name is revealed to be `edit-conference_session`

Once you have a page's name, you can hook into its contextual help menu. We'll bundle up our `add_contextual_help()` actions into a function we can call `conference_contextual_help()`, and then bring them all in using the `admin_init` hook. In this example, we've truncated the text in our help menus—normally, you'd want to be more explanatory—but you should have no trouble coming up with your own appropriately helpful content. Again, put this code into your **functions.php** file:

```php
function conference_contextual_help() {

    $editspeaker = "From this screen, you can view and update all➡
                    your conference's speakers...";
    $addspeaker = "Enter the details of a new speaker...";

    $editsession = "View and edit your conference's sessions...";
    $addsession = "Add a new session ...";

    $editsessiontopics = "Add and edit topics...";

    add_contextual_help('edit-conference_speaker', $editspeaker);
    add_contextual_help('conference_speaker', $addspeaker);

    add_contextual_help('edit-conference_sessions', $editsession);
    add_contextual_help('conference_sessions', $addsession);
```

```
    add_contextual_help('edit-conference_topics', $editsessiontopics);

}

add_action('admin_init', 'conference_contextual_help');
```

 Okay, Enough Help!

It can be very tempting, when writing contextual help, to try to pack in a full and frank explanation of everything that needs to happen. After all, that's what help menus are for, right?

Well, sometimes you can lose the reader's concentration with too much text—it becomes a bit overwhelming. If you look around in WordPress land, you'll see that it's all kept simple. Check out the help in WordPress's default screens, like **Media** or **Settings**, where you'll find a brief overview of the screen's functionality, and links to the WordPress Codex for anyone who wants to know more.

Remember, WordPress is about being easy and fun, not overwhelming and wordy. Try to take a similar approach to your inline documentation, too.

While you're poking around in **functions.php**, remember to remove—or at least disable—your `add_action( 'admin_notices', 'check_current_screen' );` function that we used earlier. It's handy for us to know, but your users can do without the unsightly mess on screen. Once you've done this, you should see that your help text appears in the right places whenever you press **Help** in any given submenu. Neat!

Displaying Your Custom Post Types

You've put together your custom post types, added a custom taxonomy to one of them, and even given the gift of help. All that's left now is to think about how your new post types will be displayed. And if you've already jumped ahead a bit and read Chapter 6, you already know just about everything you need in order to display your nifty new custom post types. It's true! If you love theming, this will be the easiest part of the chapter.

WordPress has a structured system to look for template information—it's called the Template Hierarchy.[7] To display a single item, WordPress will look in a particular theme folder for a template called **single-{post_type}**—like **single-conference_session** or **single-conference_speaker**. If a file of that name is not part of our theme, it will look next to **single.php**, and then to **index.php**. Similarly, if we're showing our custom taxonomy, WordPress has a hierarchy for that, too. It looks for:

- **taxonomy-{taxonomy_name}-{taxonomy-term}.php** first, then
- **taxonomy-{taxonomy_name}.php**, and finally to

---

[7] http://codex.wordpress.org/Template_Hierarchy

taxonomy_name.

The simplest path to cool custom post styles, then, is to create a template that falls into the template hierarchy of each of our customized features. In our theme folder, we'll need two PHP files for our post types: **single-conference_speaker.php**, and **single-conference_session.php**. For our purposes, it's unnecessary to worry about a separate template for each taxonomy term, so we'll just go with a template for all terms: **taxonomy-conference_topics.php**.

Showing off Our Conference Sessions and Speakers

In this example, we'll use a child theme for the the Twenty Eleven template. Let's save ourselves some extra work, and make a copy of Twenty Eleven's **single.php** template; then we'll rename it according to the rules of the Template Hierarchy—let's call it **single-conference_speaker.php**.

Looking inside the template, we'll see that there's a <nav> element containing forward and back links (remember `previous_post_link()` and `next_post_link()`?), a reference to a template part, and a reference to the comments template. These are all surplus to our requirements, so be merciless with the delete key! Get rid of this superfluous markup, and you should be left with an empty shell of a template containing an empty loop:

```
                                    chapter_04/single-conference_speaker.php (excerpt)

get_header(); ?>

        <div id="primary">
            <div id="content" role="main">

                <?php while ( have_posts() ) : the_post(); ?>


                <?php endwhile; // end of the loop. ?>

            </div><!-- #content -->
        </div><!-- #primary -->

<?php get_footer(); ?>
```

That certainly is a big, empty hole in the middle of that template. Let's fill it with template tags!

For our speakers, we'll list the speaker's name (the item's title), plus the company, website, and location (all post meta fields). After that, we'll show the entry's content. Here's some markup and template tags that will help us achieve that effect:

chapter_04/single-conference_speaker.php *(excerpt)*

```php
<?php while ( have_posts() ) : the_post(); ?>

    <article id="post-<?php the_ID(); ?>" <?php post_class(); ?>>
        <header class="entry-header">
            <h1 class="entry-title">
                Speaker Profile: <span><?php the_title(); ?></span>
            </h1>
            <p class="speaker-meta">
            Works at: <?php echo get_post_meta($post->ID,➡
                        'conference_speaker_business', true); ?>
            | Visit <a href="<?php echo get_post_meta($post->ID,➡
                        'conference_speaker_website_url', true); ?>">
                <?php echo get_post_meta($post->ID,➡
                    'conference_speaker_website_name', true); ?>
            </a>
            | Comes from: <?php echo get_post_meta($post->ID,➡
                        'conference_speaker_location', true); ?>
            </p>
        </header>

        <div class="entry-content">
            <?php the_content(); ?>
        </div><!-- .entry-content -->

    </article>


<?php endwhile; ?>
```

As you can see, it's just like theming a single post or page—but this time, we're making use of those custom meta fields. It will be similar for our sessions, but we'll also throw in an `if` statement that checks to see if the taxonomy exists. If it does, we'll use `get_the_term_list()` to build up a set of links:

chapter_04/single-conference_session.php *(excerpt)*

```php
<?php while ( have_posts() ) : the_post(); ?>

    <article id="post-<?php the_ID(); ?>" <?php post_class(); ?>>
        <header class="entry-header">
            <h1 class="entry-title"><?php the_title(); ?></h1>
            <div class="session-meta">
            <dl>
            <dt>Where</dt>
            <dd><?php echo get_post_meta($post->ID, 'conference_session_room',➡
                true); ?></dd>
            <dt>When</dt>
```

```
            <dd><?php echo get_post_meta($post->ID, 'conference_session_date',➡
               true); ?></dd>
            <?php
            if(taxonomy_exists('conference_topics')) {
                echo get_the_term_list( $post->ID, 'conference_topics',➡
                   '<dt>Topics</dt><dd>', ', ', '</dd>' );
                } ?>
            </dl>
            </div>
        </header>

        <div class="entry-content">
            <?php the_content(); ?>
        </div><!-- .entry-content -->

    </article>
<?php endwhile; ?>
```

There are very few differences between regular, built-in WordPress content types and your own custom ones. If you're a skilled themer, you'll have no problem showing off your custom types!

Custom Archives

Earlier in this chapter, we talked about how we could specify an archive page for each of our custom types—the pages that represent each archive will be found at **Speakers** and **Sessions**. Now that we're digging around in our theme, it's time to put these archives together. Looking back at our Template Hierarchy structure, we can see that WordPress will check for a file called **archive-{posttype}.php**, so we'll need two files, **archive-conference_session.php** and **archive-conference_speaker.php**.

Once again, we'll create an archive template by copying the one that comes with Twenty Eleven, stripping out the unnecessary parts, and enhancing the rest. We can also manipulate The Loop using our old friend query_posts(). In this example, we're collecting our conference_session items at 30 items per page, ordered by title:

chapter_04/archive-conference_session.php (excerpt)

```
$args = array(
        'posts_per_page' => 30,
        'order' => 'ASC',
        'orderby' => 'title',
        'post_type' => 'conference_session'
    );
  query_posts($args);
```

And if we have posts, we'll display our list. If we happen to have more than 30 events, we'll paginate. twentyeleven_content_nav() is a function defined by our parent theme that does the job here:

chapter_04/archive-conference_session.php *(excerpt)*

```php
if ( have_posts() ) : ?>

<header class="archive-header">
    <h1>
        Sessions
    </h1>
</header>
<p>You'll love our packed timetable! ...</p>

<?php twentyeleven_content_nav( 'nav-above' ); ?>

<?php /* Start the Loop */ ?>
<?php while ( have_posts() ) : the_post(); ?>

    <article class="session">
        <h2><a href="<?php the_permalink() ?>"><?php the_title();
            ?></a></h2>
        <div class="session-meta">
        <dl>
        <dt>Where</dt>
        <dd><?php echo get_post_meta($post->ID,➥
            'conference_session_room', true); ?></dd>
        <dt>When</dt>
        <dd><?php echo get_post_meta($post->ID,➥
            'conference_session_date', true); ?></dd>
        <?php if(taxonomy_exists('conference_topics')) {
            echo get_the_term_list( $post->ID, 'conference_topics',➥
            '<dt>Topics</dt><dd>', ', ', '</dd>' );
            } ?>
        </dl>
        </div>
        <?php the_excerpt(); ?>

    </article>

<?php endwhile; ?>

<?php twentyeleven_content_nav( 'nav-below' ); ?>
```

If there's nothing to display, it's probably because we're yet to post any sessions, so we'll show a message to that effect:

```php
<?php else : ?>

    <article id="post-0" class="post no-results not-found">
        <header class="entry-header">
            <h1 class="entry-title">Watch this space!</h1>
```

```
        </header><!-- .entry-header -->

        <div class="entry-content">
            <p>We've yet to post any sessions, but if you
                subscribe to our newsletter you'll be the first
                to find out!</p>
            <?php get_search_form(); ?>
        </div><!-- .entry-content -->
    </article><!-- #post-0 -->

<?php endif; ?>
```

Once you have your templates sorted, your custom post modifications are complete!

You're Custom-ready

As WordPress evolved, and as its popularity grew, users found themselves dealing with so much more than a mere blogging tool. Before we had this kind of support for custom content types, entire cottage industries grew up around hacking and bending WordPress to a webmaster's will. Nowadays, powerful CMS features are well within our reach, and in this chapter we've shown you just how easy it is to start creating your own powerful CMS features.

A huge slice of the world's most popular websites is WordPress-powered, and a large reason for that success is down to the fact that developers have let their imaginations grow beyond simple posts and pages. It's time for you to do the same!

Plugins

WordPress's core functionality is proven, tested, and thoroughly maintained by the core committers at Automattic, and throughout the rest of the WordPress community. However, while core WordPress provides you with the primary tools you need to manage a website—such as adding, modifying and deleting pages and posts, managing users, and other basic functions for a modern website—most sites need more functionality to be truly useful to the end user. To meet this need, WordPress offers plugins, a standard way to introduce additional functionality outside the scope of core WordPress to extend it for just about any purpose.

In truth, the ease with which users can add plugins to WordPress, along with the simple mechanisms available to developers for creating plugins, has contributed to making WordPress the most popular CMS on the Web today. If there's a task you want to perform on your website that isn't available specifically within core WordPress, there's probably a plugin for it.

The Basics

Plugins are incredibly powerful; they heighten the scope and functionality of any WordPress project, but they can also cause many of problems on any given site. For that reason, it's important to cover some basic information about plugins before we dive deep into the code.

The Upside to Plugins

Plugins are so easy to find and install. From right within the **Plugins** menu in the admin area, you can search for, browse, and install plugins that are listed—as seen in Figure 5.1—in the WordPress Plugin Directory.[1]

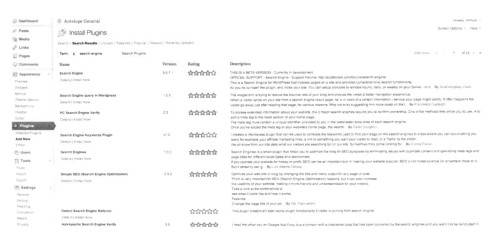

Figure 5.1. The WordPress Plugin Directory

Beware, though, that not all WordPress plugins are listed within the WordPress Plugin Directory, but as an end user seeking plugins, Google is a great option for you. Many premium, commonly used plugins like Gravity Forms or Shopp need to be purchased separately and installed into your WordPress installation through the **Upload** option.

Aside from their easy installation, there is a bunch of other useful aspects about plugins; for instance:

- You'll almost always be able to find a plugin for what you are looking to accomplish.

- It's common to be able to find several plugins that perform the same task in a different way, should you be unhappy with the way a particular plugin works.

- Plugins provide a certain level of future-proofing insurance for your site, because you're able to easily add the latest functionality when new technologies are quickly embraced by the public.

The Downside to Plugins

While the upsides are fairly obvious, there's a darker side to plugins that's often overlooked by end users, but all too apparent to the seasoned developer who's had to deal with the aftermath. While core WordPress is developed, maintained, and vetted by a team of trusted developers with core commit privileges, the plugin space is, in many ways, the equivalent of the Wild West.

---

[1] http://wordpress.org/extend/plugins/

On the most fundamental level, plugins typically comprise nothing more than a few PHP functions and possibly some supporting JavaScript or CSS. As we'll demonstrate in just a bit, writing a plugin and registering it with your WordPress installation is a simple process, but the quality of the code therein is only as solid and thought-out as the developer chooses to (or is able to) make it. Reality dictates that there are plugin developers all along the talent spectrum, ranging from beginners to experts, and, naturally, the products each developer produces directly corresponds to their level of proficiency. Furthermore, plugins are typically developed by either one developer or a small team of two to three working on the project. Things can get missed, and everybody has bad days.

In short, there are some poorly coded plugins out there.

While no method is 100% guaranteed, you can largely avoid poorly coded plugins by doing your homework on them before you install them. Start by looking at the overall star ranking of a plugin—these rankings are subjective, but a large enough sample user base will give you some reasonable expectations. You can also look at the discussion about the plugin right from the plugin's comments section: see if there have been complaints about the plugin (and if you are so inclined, try to make a judgment as to how relevant those complaints are). Another tried-and-tested way to check out plugins before installing is to simply google them and see what's been said about them. And, of course, even a highly rated plugin can be problematic if it hasn't been in production for some time, and was last compatible with an older WordPress version than you happen to be running.

Just what are some of the issues that come up with plugins? There is a litany, but here are a few common problems:

- A portion of plugins use deprecated action hooks that either are no longer in use, or are in the process of being phased out of core WordPress.

- Some plugins have poor naming conventions that conflict with other active plugins, thus creating unexpected results on the site.

- Occasionally, a plugin simply isn't coded correctly, so it just fails to work.

Another issue with many plugins—especially those in the WordPress Plugin Directory—is that since most of them are created by non-compensated developers in their spare time, you may not receive prompt technical support when the need arises; this fact has almost single-handedly driven the popularity of the premium WordPress plugin market, where tech support is more widespread.

Rules to Follow When Using Plugins

With all of that said, plugins are essential to bending WordPress to your will; it's just necessary to keep a few guidelines in mind when using them. As an end user, follow these two tips and you'll be fine:

Only use what you need

Every time you add a new plugin to WordPress, you are introducing a new set of PHP functions that are designed to perform tasks. By definition, adding PHP functions to a website adds programming that makes your WordPress installation a little more complex, and creates potential tripping points for problems to occur down the track. It's actually a lot like installing and running software programs on your computer: the more programs you have running at any one time, the slower your computer may run, especially if some of those programs are poorly put together. In this way, running superfluous plugins possibly increases your site's execution time, thus slowing it down. Given that search engines factor site speed as a part of their ranking algorithms, that's potentially a sensitive issue.

Deactivate or delete what's not being used

It's a corollary to the rule above, but when unused plugins are kept active, it's common to see conflicts crop up later on with other plugins (or themes), should you make a change to them. Your best practice is to—at the very least—keep unused plugins deactivated.

Must–use Plugins

Worth mentioning as well are **must-use plugins**, which comprise an underutilized but extremely useful technique for working with plugins. Must-use plugins are handy for developers who want to add plugins to a WordPress installation in a way that makes them more difficult for end users to deactivate. There's nothing particularly special about must-use plugins themselves—any plugin can be a must-use plugin. What's unique is how and where the plugins are installed. Instead of being downloaded from the WordPress Plugin Directory (or uploaded from your computer system) into the **wp-content/plugins** directory, they must be manually installed via FTP or your web host's control panel into the **wp-content/mu-plugins** directory. This directory does not exist by default—you'll need to create it—but when WordPress sees that it's there, it will automatically activate and load any plugin it finds therein.

Must-use plugins have several special properties in the way that they're handled by WordPress:

- You can't just drop a plugin subdirectory into **wp-content/mu-plugins**. Must-use plugins either need to be individual PHP files in the directory, or they need to have a PHP include file pointing to the subdirectory that the plugin is sitting in.

- If a plugin is loaded as a must-use plugin, there's no need to activate it—it's always on. This is useful to developers when they want to ensure that a client does not remove a particular plugin.

- WordPress won't notify you when a must-use plugin has an update. Instead, you'll need to manage updates manually … or not. This can be useful when you want to continue using an older version of a plugin for any reason.

■ Must-use plugins are loaded by PHP before all standard plugins, so API hooks added in a must-use plugin will apply to all other plugins.

Deactivation Can Be a Solution

When you're running a website on WordPress and you begin to experience problems, start by looking at your plugins and use this elimination technique. Deactivate all your plugins, and check to see whether your problem still exists on the website. If it does, you can be reasonably certain that the issue is either coming from within your content or within the WordPress core installation itself (it's rare, but it does happen).

It's common, however, for the issue to resolve itself after the deactivation of all your plugins. From here, reactivate your plugins one by one, starting with the most important plugins necessary for your site to function properly. Sooner or later, you'll locate the offending plugin, where you can then seek an alternate solution to managing that piece of functionality on your site.

Zip It

When you're troubleshooting WordPress by removing plugins, remember that must-use plugins won't show up in the main plugins listing. Unless you physically remove must-use plugins from the **wp-content/mu-plugins** directory, those plugins will be active and loading their functions into your WordPress environment. If you forget to remove them, you can foil your own divide-and-conquer trouble-shooting technique that we described above. A handy technique is to zip all your plugins up into a zip file or a tar file on your server for safekeeping, and then delete the runtime files. Once you're done troubleshooting, you can restore your zip or tar file, restoring your plugins to their original state.

Drop-in Plugins

Another special type of plugin is a drop-in plugin. **Drop-in plugins** replace entire portions of WordPress core functionality. They are specifically named files that you can create and customize, and must be located within the **wp-content/** directory. A complete listing of drop-in plugins can be found in Table 5.1, along with the context (single WordPress installation or WordPress Multisite installation) in which each is appropriate.

Table 5.1. Drop-in plugin availability chart

Drop-in Plugin Name	Description	Context
advanced-cache.php	Advanced caching plugin	Single
db.php	Custom database class	Single
db-error.php	Custom database error message	Single
install.php	Custom installation script	Single
maintenance.php	Custom maintenance message	Single
object-cache.php	External object cache	Single
sunrise.php	Advanced domain mapping	Multisite
blog-deleted.php	Custom blog deleted message	Multisite
blog-inactive.php	Custom blog inactive message	Multisite
blog-suspended.php	Custom blog suspended message	Multisite

Determining When to Create a New Plugin

Whether you're a developer or an end user, ask yourself whether it's necessary to develop (or contract out the development of) a plugin before you begin the work. There are literally dozens of ways to do many common programming tasks within WordPress, and with the prolific use of the platform, it's rare that you'd be creating a plugin that nobody else has attempted to do before you. Whether searching in the WordPress Plugin Directory or Google, you are apt to find several solutions that meet your needs. In the event that you're unable to find a suitable plugin solution, sometimes the creative use of several plugins can accomplish your goal equally as well.

While many of us in the development community cut our teeth on writing every single line of code ourselves, you'll often find that others who've tackled the same problems before us have created scripts with more fleshed out and better interfaces than we'd manage—at least, not without a significant investment of time and effort on our own. Use the open-source community; it's there to help you. If after an exhaustive search you still find that no existing plugin meets your needs, or you have an extremely specific piece of functionality that's unique to your application, by all means knock yourself out!

 Can I see your license?

If you choose to modify an existing plugin, you will need to pay attention to the software license associated with it. If you're modifying a plugin for the plugin directory, make sure it has a GPLv2 license, which allows any user to modify and reuse code so long as an attribution is given to its original author.

Debugging Your Plugin As You Go

None of us are perfect, and experienced plugin developers will testify that debugging your plugin as you develop it is just a fact of life. While there are several techniques you can use to debug your code, the most fundamental is to go into your **wp-config.php** file in your sandbox WordPress installation and ensure you've enabled WP_DEBUG, so that it appears in your code as follows:

```
define('WP_DEBUG', true);
```

This will automatically make WordPress spit out any PHP warnings or notices that you'll need to be aware of in order to correct, displaying them in real time as they happen. Furthermore, if you're going to be modifying any of WordPress's built-in JavaScript, make sure you enable SCRIPT_DEBUG as well, so that it appears in **wp-config.php** as follows:

```
define('SCRIPT_DEBUG', true);
```

In the same way as WP_DEBUG, SCRIPT_DEBUG will display JavaScript issues in real time as they occur.

Now that we've addressed the basics of what plugins are, how they're installed, what to be careful of when you use them, and when to actually create one yourself, let's get our hands dirty and pick them apart. Upwards and onwards!

The Anatomy of a Plugin

Conceptually, every plugin is broken up into two basic pieces:

- the wrapper, or packaging, which tells WordPress that it is, indeed, a valid plugin
- the scripting that makes the plugin actually perform a useful task

Let's investigate the wrapper component of a plugin first.

Standard Plugin Packaging

WordPress provides us with a standardized place to keep all the plugins within a particular WordPress installation: the **wp-content/plugins** directory. Because all plugins are stored in the same location, your plugin must have a unique name, lest it cause an error as WordPress attempts to initialize it upon running. This unique name should be built right into the main PHP file for the plugin that will live in the **wp-content/plugins** directory, or in the name of the directory that will house the primary plugin PHP file. While technically all a plugin needs to function is just one properly formatted PHP file, it's generally considered best practice to give each plugin its own directory, storing all files associated with the plugin within subdirectories therein. At the very top of our primary PHP file for our plugin, we'll add a standard identifying WordPress plugin header. We

introduced the concept of the plugin header briefly back in the section called "Creating Your First Custom Post Types" in Chapter 4, but it's worth going into more detail here:

chapter_05/standard-header.php

```php
<?php
/*
Plugin Name: The Name of Your Plugin Here
Plugin URI: Link to the Home page for the Plugin
Description: Brief descriptive text for the Plugin
Version: What Version is the Plugin
Author: Author Name
Author URI: Author Home page
*/
```

The only required line in this header is the `Plugin Name`, but the rest of the information is extremely important, and WordPress will use the information within this header when initializing your plugin for use. Aside from verifying that it is a valid WordPress plugin file, WordPress gathers the information about the plugin in this header for your users to view in the **Manage Plugins** screen, as shown in Figure 5.2.

Figure 5.2. The **Manage Plugins** screen

Making sure that you include correct, up-to-date information about who the plugin is written by and where users can go for updates ensures its usefulness over time. Additionally, you should make sure to include licensing information about the plugin. Most plugins are GPL-compatible, and indeed must be so if they are to be included within the WordPress Plugin Directory (more on that in the section called "The WordPress Plugin Directory"). Licensing information should directly follow your header information. Standard GPL licensing (with dummy text inserted for copyright year, plugin author name, and plugin author email) looks like this:

chapter_05/standard-gpl-license.php

```php
<?php
/*  Copyright YEAR  PLUGIN_AUTHOR_NAME(email : PLUGIN AUTHOR EMAIL)

    This program is free software; you can redistribute it and/or
    modify it under the terms of the GNU General Public License as
    published by the Free Software Foundation; either version 2
    of the License, or (at your option) any later version.
```

```
    This program is distributed in the hope that it will be useful,
    but WITHOUT ANY WARRANTY; without even the implied warranty of
    MERCHANTABILITY or FITNESS FOR A PARTICULAR PURPOSE.  See the
    GNU General Public License for more details.

    You should have received a copy of the GNU General Public
    License along with this program; if not, write to the Free Software
    Foundation, Inc., 51 Franklin St, Fifth Floor, Boston, MA
    02110-1301  USA
*/
```

While it is customary to insert the plugin license directly underneath the plugin header, it's also a nice idea to include it in a text file called **license.txt** within the plugin directory. An additional (and completely optional) step is to include a **readme.txt** file with your plugin, to provide any basic information or frequently asked questions to your plugin users that you might deem useful, but that's entirely up to you.

That's pretty much all we need to do in order to set up a plugin in the correct format so that WordPress can recognize it. Now's when the fun begins, and we can actually start doing something genuinely useful.

Action Hooks and Filter Hooks

We know that WordPress is a collection of PHP scripts that executes functions in a specific order, creating an end result that essentially comprises our website. One way to visualize the way core WordPress works is to think of it as a conveyor belt that moves through a specific process to get from point A to point B, producing a website as its end product. There's no black magic here, but rather an assembly line of PHP functions that moves information in different directions, depending on a set of predefined rules.

When we write plugins, what we are really doing is introducing new PHP functions that add to the predetermined rules WordPress has already given us. To make that happen, WordPress has been good enough to create a special set of PHP functions that give us the ability to connect with that conveyor belt in the specific place it is appropriate to do so. These functions are called **hooks**, and they are the essential tools we need to be able to take our great new ideas and latch them into WordPress in a way that makes them useful to our users. Two hooks exist: Action hooks and filter hooks.

Action hooks are used when specific events take place within WordPress's execution process. For instance, if you'd like to add some inline CSS code into the header of a page template, you could use the wp_head() action hook to do so, executing your function to create the appropriate lines of code when the wp_head() function is run in the standard assembly line of WordPress core functions. A properly formatted action hook call follows this format:

```php
<?php add_action( hook, function, priority, accepted_arguments ); ?>
```

Where the parameters are equivalent to:

- *hook* (string): the action hook to use (required)

- *function* (string): the name of your function to add (required)

- *priority* (arguments): the priority in which the function should be run (optional, and defaults to 10)

- *accepted_arguments* (arguments): the number of arguments the defined function can accept (optional, and defaults to 1)

Let's consider our simple CSS insertion example above, and see what that code might look like:

action-example.php

```php
<?php

function inline_css() { ?>
<style type="text/css"  >
  .mockingbird {padding-top:15px;}
  .mockingbird .famous {display:block;padding:1em;}
  .mockingbird .famous p.label_title {font-size:12px;font-weight:bold;
     display:block;margin-bottom:5px;}
  .mockingbird .famous label.no_bold {font-weight:normal;}
</style>

<?php }

add_action( 'wp_head', 'inline_css' );
?>
```

Easy stuff, right? We've just created a short function called `inline_css()` containing some CSS code that defines styles for a class called `mockingbird`, as well as a subclass that defines what a `famous mockingbird` might look like. Then, using our `add_action()` function, we employ the `wp_head()` action hook to add the code in this function to the header of our WordPress page; this is when events occur that are associated with the `wp_head` action hook.

There are many action hooks available to latch into our WordPress assembly line process where we want to, but here are some that are more commonly used:

- `wp_head`: triggered in the <head> section of the loaded theme

- `wp_footer`—triggered in the footer of the loaded theme

- init—triggered after WordPress has finished loading, but before any headers are sent; excellent place to intercept $_GET and $_POST HTML requests

- admin_init—same as init, but runs only on admin Dashboard pages

- admin_head—triggered in the <head> section of the admin Dashboard

- user_register—triggered whenever a new user is registered

- publish_post—triggered whenever a new post is published

- comment_post—triggered whenever a new comment is posted

Where action hooks are used to execute functions at a certain time during the WordPress assembly line process, **filter hooks**, are used when you want to modify information before saving it to a database or outputting it to a browser; they're typically used when modifying text in some way, shape, or form. The classic example of a filter would be in censoring out profane language that your users might try to add to pages or posts on your site. In this instance, you might apply a PHP function to a specific filtering hook such as the_content, so that you can remove words such as putz, dumdum head, or dimwit with a standard phrase like [mean name]. Let's take a peek at what an example of the PHP function and the associated filter might look like in this instance:

chapter_05/filter-example.php

```php
<?php
function play_nice($content) {
  $mean_words = array("putz","dumdum head","dimwit");
  $content=str_ireplace($mean_words,'[mean name]',$content);
  return $content;
}

add_filter ('the_content', 'play_nice');
?>
```

Here, we've written a little function that identifies and replaces words that we want to omit. Then, we've added our filter, instructing WordPress to run everything that goes through the_content (our filter hook) through our function, thus ensuring nobody can call anybody else a dimwit.

 You Say Po-TAY-to, I Say Po-TAH-to

Did you notice that the syntax of the filter hook in our example above looks a whole lot like the syntax for a properly formatted action hook? There's good reason: while filter hooks and action hooks serve very different purposes, the add_action() and add_filter() functions have identical syntaxes and take parameters in identical ways. In truth, you can really view the add_filter() function as a mechanism to keep concepts straight in your mind, and keep yourself

(and other programmers working on your code) sane when trying to figure out exactly what and how it works.

The Power of Paranoia: Data Validation

As much as we all like to be trusting, the truth is that every room has a shadow or two, and sometimes bad things lurk in the shadows. And if we have a user who tries to call another user a dumdum head on our public website for all to see, maybe they'll want to do worse! There's power in paranoia, kids, and for this reason you always need to be certain to validate and sanitize your data.

Much like brushing your teeth and (we trust) showering with soap every morning, data validation and sanitization should be treated as a habit every time you either output to a browser or save to your database. Essentially, what you want to do here is scrub every piece of data you can that is coming from a location *external* to your own code, as it may have illegal characters or genuine malicious intent.

WordPress gives us a standardized set of escaping functions we can use to scrub our data and ensure it's safe for our use. Consider Figure 5.3, which describes the WordPress escaping API.

Figure 5.3. WordPress escaping API

In this diagram, we see that there are three components to the function set, as described following:

1. `esc`: the prefix for the escaping function

2. `attr`: the context being escaped, with possible values including:
    - `attr`—HTML attribute scrubbing
    - `js`—JavaScript scrubbing
    - `html`: HTML character scrubbing such as <, >, ', and "
    - `sql`—MySQL query scrubbing
    - `url`—URL scrubbing
    - `url_raw`: URL scrubbing before saving to a database

3. `_e`: an optional translation suffix, with possible values including:
    - `__`: returns a translated value
    - `_e`: echoes a translated value

For example, in order to remove any HTML tags from a text string, you would use this format:

```php
<?php esc_html( $text ); ?>
```

Alternatively, if you were looking to escape any illegal characters from within an HTML attribute, you might code this:

```php
<input type="text" name="name" value="<?php echo esc_attr($text); ?>">
```

For more information on data validation, take a look at the WordPress Codex.[2]

Leave It Till Last

When you are validating and sanitizing your data, make sure you do it as late as you possibly can before outputting it or saving it to your database. Running your validation too early will leave your data susceptible to any errors or vulnerabilities introduced in code that's run after the validation has been complete, potentially causing issues. And nobody wants that.

Okay, we'll avoid acting like a parent here and beating this into the ground, but seriously: don't be an ingrate, remember to validate!

Dissecting a Plugin: Antelope General Social Media Links

For the purpose of illustrating how all the pieces of any given plugin work in practice, we'll use an example of a fictitious plugin created especially for you and this book: Antelope General Social Media Links (or AGSocialMedia, for short). AGSocialMedia is a simple plugin that will show us how to do some basic but useful tasks, such as:

- create a plugin settings screen inside WordPress that lets us update and manage links to our four favorite social media sites: Facebook, Twitter, YouTube, and LinkedIn

- add a **Settings** link in the plugin management screen that takes us directly to the aforementioned plugin settings page

- add a simple widget that lets us integrate our social media links wherever and however we want on our WordPress site

Of course, it's not *really* a fictitious plugin; in actuality, it works quite well and you can feel free to use it or extend it for yourself. After all, it's being presented to you by us under the GPL license, and you can find the code in this book's code archive.

---

[2] http://codex.wordpress.org/Data_Validation

Keeping Our Eye on the Prize

The purpose of this section is not to teach you how to code PHP—we'll assume you have a working knowledge of that. Rather, the purpose of this demonstration is to illustrate how your PHP code will interact with the various hooks and filters that connect your script to WordPress and make all the magic happen.

We'll begin our examination of AGSocialMedia by looking at the code for the entire plugin, and then pick it apart limb by limb:

chapter_05/AGSocialMedia/antelope-social-media-links.php

```php
<?php
/*
Plugin Name: Antelope General Social Media Links
Plugin URI: http://mickolinik.com/plugins/antelope-social-media-links
Description: Easily add links to your social media profiles
Version: 1.0
Author: Mick Olinik
Author URI: http://www.mickolinik.com
*/

/*  Copyright 2011  Mick Olinik  (email : mick@rockstarcoding.com)

    This program is free software; you can redistribute it and/or modify
    it under the terms of the GNU General Public License as published by
    the Free Software Foundation; either version 2 of the License, or
    (at your option) any later version.

    This program is distributed in the hope that it will be useful,
    but WITHOUT ANY WARRANTY; without even the implied warranty of
    MERCHANTABILITY or FITNESS FOR A PARTICULAR PURPOSE.  See the
    GNU General Public License for more details.

    You should have received a copy of the GNU General Public License
    along with this program; if not, write to the Free Software
    Foundation, Inc., 51 Franklin St, Fifth Floor, Boston, MA 02110-1301  USA
*/

//load textdomain for localization settings
load_plugin_textdomain('agsml', false, basename( dirname( __FILE__ ) ) .➥
  '/languages' );

add_action('admin_menu', 'agsml_create_menu');

function agsml_create_menu() {

  //create new top-level menu
  add_options_page('Antelope General Social Media Links',➥
```

```php
     'AG Social Media Links', 'manage_options', __FILE__, 'agsml_settings_page');
   add_filter( "plugin_action_links", "agsml_settings_link", 10, 2 );
   //call register settings function
   add_action( 'admin_init', 'agsml_register_settings' );
}


//add settings link to plugins list
function agsml_settings_link($links, $file) {
  static $this_plugin;
  if (!$this_plugin) $this_plugin = plugin_basename(__FILE__);
  if ($file == $this_plugin){
    $settings_link = '<a href="options-general.php?page=AGSocialMedia/➥
      antelope-social-media-links.php">'.__("Settings", "agsml_social_media").➥
      '</a>';
    array_unshift($links, $settings_link);
  }
  return $links;
  }

function agsml_register_settings() {
  //register our settings
  register_setting( 'antelope_social_group', 'agsml_facebook' );
  register_setting( 'antelope_social_group', 'agsml_twitter' );
  register_setting( 'antelope_social_group', 'agsml_youtube' );
  register_setting( 'antelope_social_group', 'agsml_linkedin' );
}

//create css for admin screen
function agsml_admin_css() { ?>
<style type="text/css"  >

.agsml_social_list {padding-top:15px;}
.agsml_social_list .setting {display:block;padding:1em;}
.agsml_social_list .setting p.label_title {font-size:12px;font-weight:bold;
  display:block;margin-bottom:5px;}
.agsml_social_list .setting label.no_bold {font-weight:normal;}
.agsml_social_list .setting label span.slim {width:200px;float:left;
  display:block;margin: 1px;padding: 3px;}
.agsml_social_list .setting p.desc {font-size:10px;font-style:italic;
  text-indent:10px; text-align:left;}
</style>

<?php }
add_action('admin_head', 'agsml_admin_css');

//html for settings form
function agsml_settings_page() { ?>

<div class="wrap agsml_social_list">
```

```
<h2>Antelope General Social Media Links</h2>

<form method="post" action="options.php">
  <?php settings_fields( 'antelope_social_group' ); ?>


      <div class="setting">

      <p class="label_title"><?php _e('Facebook Profile URL:', 'agsml') ?></p>
      <p><label class="no_bold" for="agsml_facebook">
         <span class="slim"><?php _e('Facebook URL', 'agsml')
         ?></span>
      <input name="agsml_facebook" type="text" id="agsml_facebook"
         value="<?php form_option('agsml_facebook'); ?>" /></label></p>
      <p class="desc"><?php _e('Enter the URL to your Facebook profile.')
         ?></p>

      <p class="label_title"><?php _e('Twitter Profile URL:', 'agsml') ?></p>
      <p><label class="no_bold" for="agsml_twitter">
         <span class="slim"><?php _e('Twitter URL', 'agsml')
         ?></span>
      <input name="agsml_twitter" type="text" id="agsml_twitter"
         value="<?php form_option('agsml_twitter'); ?>" /></label>
      </p>
      <p class="desc"><?php _e('Enter the URL to your Twitter profile.')
         ?></p>

      <p class="label_title"><?php _e('YouTube Profile URL:', 'agsml')
         ?></p>
      <p><label class="no_bold" for="agsml_youtube"><span class="slim">
         <?php _e('YouTube URL', 'agsml') ?></span>
      <input name="agsml_youtube" type="text" id="agsml_youtube"
         value="<?php form_option('agsml_youtube'); ?>" /></label></p>
      <p class="desc"><?php _e('Enter the URL to your YouTube profile.')
         ?></p>

      <p class="label_title"><?php _e('LinkedIn Profile URL:', 'agsml')
         ?></p>
      <p><label class="no_bold" for="agsml_linkedin"><span class="slim">
         <?php _e('LinkedIn URL', 'agsml') ?></span>
      <input name="agsml_linkedin" type="text" id="agsml_linkedin"
         value="<?php form_option('agsml_linkedin'); ?>" /></label></p>
      <p class="desc"><?php _e('Enter the URL to your LinkedIn profile.',➥
         'agsml') ?></p>

      <p class="setting">
      <input type="submit" class="button-primary" value="<?php _e➥
         ('Save Social Media Links', 'agsml') ?>" />
      </p>
```

```php
      </div>

   </form>

</div>

<?php }

function agsml_enqueue_styles() {

   // url to stylesheet
   $agsml_css_url= WP_PLUGIN_URL . '/' . plugin_basename(dirname(__FILE__)) .➡
     '/agsml-widget.css';

   //register and enqueue stylesheet
   wp_register_style('agsml_styles', $agsml_css_url);
   wp_enqueue_style( 'agsml_styles');

}

add_action( 'wp_print_styles', 'agsml_enqueue_styles' );

/* Register the widget */
function agsml_register_widget() {
   register_widget( 'Antelope_Widget' );
}

/* Begin Widget Class */
class Antelope_Widget extends WP_Widget {

/* Widget setup  */
function Antelope_Widget() {
   $widget_ops = array('classname' => 'agsml_widget', 'description' => ➡
     __( 'Your Social Media Links', 'agsml') );
   // The actual widget code goes here
   parent::WP_Widget( false, $name = 'AG Social Media Links', $widget_ops );
}

/* Display the widget  */
function widget( $args, $instance ) {

   //get widget arguments
   extract($args);
   //get widget title from instance variable
   $title = apply_filters('widget_title', $instance['title']);

   //insert before widget markup
   echo $before_widget;

   //if theres a title, echo it.
```

```php
  if( $title )
  echo $before_title . $title . $after_title;

  //start list
  $social_list .= '<ul>';

  // define list
  if (get_option('agsml_facebook' )){
    $social_list .= '<li class="facebook"><a href="'. ➥
      get_option('agsml_facebook').'">' . __('Friend us on Facebook', 'agsml') .➥
      '</a></li>';
  }
  if (get_option('agsml_twitter' )){
    $social_list .= '<li class="twitter"><a href="'.➥
      get_option('agsml_twitter').'">' . __('Follow us on Twitter', 'agsml') .➥
      '</a></li>';
  }
  if (get_option('agsml_linkedin' )){
    $social_list .= '<li class="linkedin"><a href="'. ➥
      get_option('agsml_linkedin').'">' . __('Link us on LinkedIn', 'agsml') .➥
      '</a></li>';
  }
  if (get_option('agsml_youtube' )){
    $social_list .= '<li class="youtube"><a href="'.➥
      get_option('agsml_youtube').'">' . __('Watch us on Youtube', 'agsml') .➥
      '</a></li>';
  }
  // end list
  $share_content .= '</ul>';

  //display assembled list
  echo $social_list;

  //insert before widget markup
  echo $after_widget;

}

/* Update the widget settings, just the title in this case  */
function update( $new_instance, $old_instance ) {
  $instance = $old_instance;
  $instance['title'] = strip_tags($new_instance['title']);
  return $instance;
}

//form to display in widget settings.  Allows user to set
//title of widget.
function form( $instance ) {
  $title = esc_attr($instance['title']);
    ?>
```

```php
        <p>
          <label for="<?php echo $this->get_field_id('title'); ?>">
          <?php _e('Title:'); ?></label>
          <input class="widefat" id="<?php echo $this->get_field_id('title');
            ?>" name="<?php echo $this->get_field_name('title'); ?>"
            type="text" value="<?php echo $title; ?>" />
        </p>
        <?php
  }
}


/* Load the widget */
add_action( 'widgets_init', 'agsml_register_widget' );
?>
```

This is the meat of the plugin. The **AGSocialMedia** folder also includes several other directories and files, including an external CSS file to provide essential styles for the widget output, an **/images** directory for the social media icons we'll use in our plugin, and a **/languages** directory with a **.pot** file for localization purposes. We'll touch on some of these files in other areas of the book; for now, let's just focus on the actual plugin file doing all the work.

Header and License

Let's take a look at that first chunk of code:

chapter_05/AGSocialMedia/agsml_header_license.php

```php
<?php
/*
Plugin Name: Antelope General Social Media Links
Plugin URI: http://mickolinik.com/plugins/antelope-social-media-links
Description: Easily add links to your social media profiles
Version: 1.0
Author: Mick Olinik
Author URI: http://www.mickolinik.com
*/


/*  Copyright 2011  Mick Olinik  (email : mick@rockstarcoding.com)

    This program is free software; you can redistribute it and/or modify
    it under the terms of the GNU General Public License as published by
    the Free Software Foundation; either version 2 of the License, or
    (at your option) any later version.

    This program is distributed in the hope that it will be useful,
    but WITHOUT ANY WARRANTY; without even the implied warranty of
    MERCHANTABILITY or FITNESS FOR A PARTICULAR PURPOSE.  See the
```

```
    GNU General Public License for more details.

    You should have received a copy of the GNU General Public License
    along with this program; if not, write to the Free Software
    Foundation, Inc., 51 Franklin St, Fifth Floor, Boston, MA  02110-1301   USA
*/
```

Nothing too exciting's going on here, but there's stuff we need to take care of anyway. We have our standard WordPress header detailing exactly what the name of the plugin is, what it's for, the version, who wrote it, and so on. We're also telling people what the terms of use are—will your end users need to promise you their firstborn child to use this thing, or are the terms of use easy like the summer breeze? Let the good people know whether it's GPL or commercial.

 Version Control

> WordPress queues plugin data in the plugin repository based on the information you provide within the header of your plugin. If you list your plugin in the Plugin Directory and forget to update the version number, WordPress installations running your plugin won't be prompted that there's an update available. Nobody wants to see your efforts wasted like that.

Localization Settings

Next comes the code for our localization settings:

chapter_05/AGSocialMedia/agsml_localization.php

```
//load textdomain for localization settings
load_plugin_textdomain('agsml', false, basename( dirname( __FILE__ ) ) .➥
  '/languages' );
```

Before we really do anything in our plugin, we should check to see whether we have a language translation file that matches the language that has been set in **wp-config.php**. WordPress is brought to you in English by default, and most plugins are as well, but if we have localized our plugin (and we have), we enable our users the ability to extend the plugin themselves by translating it into a language of their choice. Consider the function `load_plugin_textdomain()`, which takes the three parameters described below:

```
load_plugin_textdomain( $domain, $abs_rel_path, $plugin_rel_path )
```

- *$domain*—a unique identifier assigned to your custom translatable strings

- *$abs_rel_path*—an optional, deprecated function as of WordPress 2.7. Default it to false or just omit it; it's nothing to worry about

■ *$plugin_rel_path*—the relative path to your translation key file. If you fail to define this path, it will default to the root directory that the file is in. While this is by definition an optional parameter, it's best practice to keep your language translation files separate from your logic files, so you'll usually want to specify a value here.

A more detailed explanation of localization can be found in Chapter 11, but for our purposes here, we're looking in the **/languages** directory of our plugin to see if there's a language translation file that matches the language we're running WordPress in (if we're not running it in English already). If we find a match, `load_plugin_textdomain()` will grab all the translated text strings and swap them out for their counterparts; these counterparts are defined within the plugin's code as it executes and outputs to the screen.

Creating the Menu Item for the Settings Page

Now matters become interesting. Let's look at this next code block and break it down into pieces:

chapter_05/AGSocialMedia/agsml_createadmin.php

```
add_action('admin_menu', 'agsml_create_menu');

function agsml_create_menu() {

  //create new top-level menu
  add_options_page('Antelope General Social Media Links',➡
    'AG Social Media Links', 'manage_options', __FILE__, 'agsml_settings_page');
  add_filter( "plugin_action_links", "agsml_settings_link", 10, 2 );
  //call register settings function
  add_action( 'admin_init', 'agsml_register_settings' );
}



//add settings link to plugins list
function agsml_settings_link($links, $file) {
  static $this_plugin;
  if (!$this_plugin) $this_plugin = plugin_basename(__FILE__);
  if ($file == $this_plugin){
    $settings_link = '<a href="options-general.php?page=AGSocialMedia/➡
      antelope-social-media-links.php">'.__("Settings", "agsml_social_media").➡
      '</a>';
    array_unshift($links, $settings_link);
  }
  return $links;
}

function agsml_register_settings() {
  //register our settings
  register_setting( 'antelope_social_group', 'agsml_facebook' );
  register_setting( 'antelope_social_group', 'agsml_twitter' );
```

```
  register_setting( 'antelope_social_group', 'agsml_youtube' );
  register_setting( 'antelope_social_group', 'agsml_linkedin' );
}
```

In full, what we're doing here is laying the groundwork for working with our plugin inside the WordPress admin area. Let's start by looking at the top code block:

```
                                   chapter_05/AGSocialMedia/agsml_createadmin1.php

add_action('admin_menu', 'agsml_create_menu');

function agsml_create_menu() {

  //create new top-level menu
  add_options_page('Antelope General Social Media Links',➥
    'AG Social Media Links', 'manage_options', __FILE__, 'agsml_settings_page');
  add_filter( "plugin_action_links", "agsml_settings_link", 10, 2 );
  //call register settings function
  add_action( 'admin_init', 'agsml_register_settings' );
}
```

We start by first using an action hook, requesting that the **Admin** menu run the `agsml_create_menu()` function. And what does that function do? It utilizes the `add_options_page()` function to add the Antelope General Social Media Links plugin and label it AG Social Media Links. The other parameter of interest in the `add_options_page()` function is `agsml_settings_page`, which defines the callback function to be used that displays the contents of the page within the link. We'll cover this function further on in our explanation.

It's a Wrap

WordPress provides easy wrapper functions that allow developers to add sublevel menu items to the primary top-level administrative menu items such as **Dashboard**, **Posts**, **Media**, **Appearance**, **Settings**, and so on. For more information as to how to add them, have a look at the WordPress Codex.[3]

The next line is an example of a filter hook, whereby we are calling `plugin_action_links()` and running it through the `agsml_settings_link()` function that we'll explore in a moment. This filter serves to insert the function that creates the link to our plugin settings page directly within the **Manage Plugins** listing page, which is utilized by many of the nicer plugins.

Finally, we use another action hook to initialize the `agsml_register_settings()` function, which we'll use to save our data directly to the **wp_options** table in our WordPress database. More on this shortly.

---

[3] http://codex.wordpress.org/Administration_Menus#Using_Wrapper_Functions

Let's look at our next function:

```php
//add settings link to plugins list
function agsml_settings_link($links, $file) {
  static $this_plugin;
  if (!$this_plugin) $this_plugin = plugin_basename(__FILE__);
  if ($file == $this_plugin){
    $settings_link = '<a href="options-general.php?page=AGSocialMedia/➡
      antelope-social-media-links.php">'.__("Settings",➡
      "simple-social-sharing").'</a>';
    array_unshift($links, $settings_link);
  }
  return $links;
}
```

This little code block just defines the PHP code we'll use to actually create the link and label that we'll insert into our plugin settings page. This will be placed directly within the **Manage Plugins** listing page, as described previously in the filter hook in the `agsml_create_menu()` function. This is really just PHP code, and there's not much here that involves WordPress.

Next up comes our `agsml_register_settings()` function:

```php
function agsml_register_settings() {
  //register our settings
  register_setting( 'antelope_social_group', 'agsml_facebook' );
  register_setting( 'antelope_social_group', 'agsml_twitter' );
  register_setting( 'antelope_social_group', 'agsml_youtube' );
  register_setting( 'antelope_social_group', 'agsml_linkedin' );
}
```

Here we go, back to WordPress functions. This is a useful spot to discuss database considerations when dealing with WordPress plugins.

When you are working with WordPress plugins, you'll almost always need to save your data to the database at some point. There are generally two ways to do this:

- Save your data to the **wp_options** table within your WordPress database.
- Create a new table within your WordPress database and save your data there.

Space doesn't allow us to cover the creation of new tables for plugin data storage in the context of this chapter; however, bear in mind that when you go in this direction, there'll be several considerations you'll need to keep in mind including initially setting the table up, ensuring that there are no naming conflicts, and developing a mechanism to safely remove the table upon uninstall. With

that said, unless your plugin is extremely specialized and complex, and requires you to save an extensive quantity of data, you'll typically use the first method and store your data in the **wp_options** table.

The `register_setting()` function is useful for defining the data you want to save for your plugin, and takes the following parameters:

```
register_setting( $option_group, $option_name, $sanitize_callback )
```

- `$option_group` (string): a settings group name, typically used to identify your plugin (required)

- `$option_name` (string): the name of an option to sanitize and save (required)

- `$sanitize_callback` (string): a callback function that sanitizes the option's value (optional)

In our case, our intent is quite simple. We only really have four values we want to save with this plugin, so we register each of these with its own unique name and tag it back to a unique group name: `antelope_social_group`. Once we've done this, we have our framework in place and we're off to the races ... what's next?

Styling the Admin Screen

Check out the CSS file in the **AGSocialMedia** folder:

```
                                    chapter_05/AGSocialMedia/agsml-widget.css
/* Antelope General Social Media Links */
.agsml_widget {
  overflow: hidden;
  padding: 0;
}

.agsml_widget ul {
  list-style-type:none;
  margin:0;
  padding:5px 0;
}

.agsml_widget ul li a{
  padding: 5px 10px 5px 20px;
  line-height:18px;
  margin:0;
}

.agsml_widget ul li {
  padding-bottom:5px;
}
```

```
.agsml_widget ul li.twitter a {
  background:url(images/mini_twitter.png) no-repeat left;
  margin:0;
}

.agsml_widget ul li.facebook a {
  background:url(images/mini_facebook.png) no-repeat left;
  margin:0;
}

.agsml_widget ul li.linkedin a {
  background:url(images/mini_linkedin.png) no-repeat left;
  margin:0;
}

.agsml_widget ul li.youtube a {
  background:url(images/mini_youtube.png) no-repeat left;
  margin:0;
}
```

Again, not a whole lot to see here aside from demonstrating the addition of internal CSS styles within a plugin. We're just creating a function, inlaying some CSS for the purpose of styling our **Admin** page to make it look pretty, and then adding the function in to run with the *admin_head* action hook. At this point in the game, we've seen this stuff before; let's keep moving.

Formatting for the Settings Page

Following this comes a chunk of form-building HTML:

chapter_05/AGSocialMedia/agsml_settingspage.php

```php
//html for settings form
function agsml_settings_page() { ?>

<div class="wrap agsml_social_list">
  <h2>Antelope General Social Media Links</h2>

  <form method="post" action="options.php">
    <?php settings_fields( 'antelope_social_group' ); ?>


    <div class="setting">

      <p class="label_title"><?php _e('Facebook Profile URL:', 'agsml') ?></p>
      <p><label class="no_bold" for="agsml_facebook"><span class="slim">
        <?php _e('Facebook URL', 'agsml') ?></span>
      <input name="agsml_facebook" type="text" id="agsml_facebook"
        value="<?php form_option('agsml_facebook'); ?>" /></label></p>
```

```
    <p class="desc"><?php _e('Enter the URL to your Facebook profile.') ?></p>

    <p class="label_title"><?php _e('Twitter Profile URL:', 'agsml') ?></p>
    <p><label class="no_bold" for="agsml_twitter"><span class="slim">
        <?php _e('Twitter URL', 'agsml') ?></span>
    <input name="agsml_twitter" type="text" id="agsml_twitter"
        value="<?php form_option('agsml_twitter'); ?>" /></label></p>
    <p class="desc"><?php _e('Enter the URL to your Twitter profile.') ?></p>

    <p class="label_title"><?php _e('YouTube Profile URL:', 'agsml') ?></p>
    <p><label class="no_bold" for="agsml_youtube"><span class="slim">
        <?php _e('YouTube URL', 'agsml') ?></span>
    <input name="agsml_youtube" type="text" id="agsml_youtube"
         value="<?php form_option('agsml_youtube'); ?>" /></label></p>
    <p class="desc"><?php _e('Enter the URL to your YouTube profile.') ?></p>

    <p class="label_title"><?php _e('LinkedIn Profile URL:', 'agsml') ?></p>
    <p><label class="no_bold" for="agsml_linkedin"><span class="slim">
        <?php _e('LinkedIn URL', 'agsml') ?></span>
    <input name="agsml_linkedin" type="text" id="agsml_linkedin"
        value="<?php form_option('agsml_linkedin'); ?>" /></label></p>
    <p class="desc"><?php _e('Enter the URL to your LinkedIn profile.',➡
                    'agsml') ?>
    </p>

    <p class="setting">
    <input type="submit" class="button-primary"
        value="<?php _e('Save Social Media Links', 'agsml') ?>" />
    </p>

  </div>

  </form>

</div>

<?php }
```

There are three main points in this code block worth noting. First, we see our definition of our `agsml_settings_page()` function, which we last referenced as the callback function in our `add_options_page()` function further back in the code. In other words, it's this function that defines the instructions for displaying all the code for our actual **Settings** page in the **Admin** menu.

Secondly, since this is the administrative settings page output, it follows that we have text strings here being displayed to our users. Because we are thoughtful developers and want to make sure that folks all over the world are able to use our plugin in their own native language, we need to prepare our text strings for localization. This means that instead of just typing in an output string like this:

```
<p class="label_title">LinkedIn Profile URL:</p>
```

We've added our _e() wrapper tags around each of our strings to produce results that look more like this:

```
<p class="label_title"><?php _e('LinkedIn Profile URL:', 'agsml') ?></p>
```

You'll notice here that we've defined both the string to be translated (in this instance, 'LinkedIn Profile URL:') as well as the unique domain namespace we've created for our localization at the top of our code (agsml). Again, for more on localization, have a look at Chapter 11.

Finally, notice that we've taken care to sanitize the data here before committing anything to our database. Here, we've used form_option() to output our social media values. form_option() runs these values through esc_attr() to sanitize them, ensuring that they are safe for our use.

Getting Output Styles Ready

This next piece of code is an example of the proper and safe way to insert an external CSS sheet into your plugin:

```
                                            chapter_05/AGSocialMedia/agsml_enqueuestyles.php
function agsml_enqueue_styles() {

  // url to stylesheet
  $agsml_css_url= WP_PLUGIN_URL . '/' . plugin_basename(dirname(__FILE__)) .➥
    '/agsml-widget.css';

  //register and enqueue stylesheet
  wp_register_style('agsml_styles', $agsml_css_url);
  wp_enqueue_style( 'agsml_styles');

}

add_action( 'wp_print_styles', 'agsml_enqueue_styles' );
```

We create a function called agsml_enqueue_styles(), and then define the URL to the CSS for our widget to be displayed on the front end of our website, but the next two functions are really worth taking note of. Rather than just injecting the link to the CSS sheet directly into the <head> section of your WordPress site, enqueueing a WordPress CSS file allows you to specify dependencies that tell WordPress your CSS depends on another CSS file, and should be loaded afterwards. While the wp_register_style() function essentially serves as a helper function to prepare your data for wp_enqueue_style(), wp_enqueue_style() is where all the magic happens. Our example is a very simplified form of wp_enqueue_style(), and so in the situation of AGSocialMedia we're really including it for proper form, and to prepare to extend the plugin later on if we so choose.

Don't Force Your Design on Users

It's common to see plugin authors try to help people out by providing styles within the context of their plugins, essentially forcing user plugins to look a certain way. While the thought is usually well-intentioned, it can be a real pain in the behind for WordPress site developers trying to use your plugin on their own sites, especially when their visual style differs markedly to what you've supplied. Instead of creating a bevy of styles for your users choose from when using your plugin, make the choice to go minimal. Particularly if you are planning on releasing your plugin into the WordPress Plugin Directory, ask yourself this important question: "What's the least amount of CSS I can supply for this functionality to display properly?" When you come up with an answer, add only that styling, and try to err on the side of less is more. If you were to put a Do and a Don't list together for this, think of it this way: *Do* provide easy-to-use classes that designers can grab to style your plugin to suit their own needs. *Don't* try to force your own perception of how your plugin should appear onto your end users.

Widgets 101

Before we further continue tearing apart our Antelope General Social Media Links plugin, let's take a moment to talk about widgets and how they work.

Useful for dragging different pieces of functionality around to sidebars, footers, and other widgetized areas on a WordPress site, **widgets** extend the functionality of a plugin by allowing users to place it in an appropriate place on their websites. They're not appropriate to add to all plugins, but in the case of our AGSocialMedia plugin, they are, as the entire purpose of the plugin is to display icons and links to our four most used social media sites: Facebook, Twitter, LinkedIn, and YouTube.

Thanks to the widget API that WordPress gives us, creating and using widgets isn't as difficult as it could be. There are three basic steps to creating and using a widget in your plugin, broken down as follows:

1. registering your widget using the `register_widget()` function

2. defining the widget via the WordPress-provided widget class, which we'll touch on more in a moment

3. loading the widget via the `widgets_init` action hook

To further understand how widgets work, let's look briefly at the basic structure of the widget class in WordPress:

chapter_05/AGSocialMedia/widgetclass.php

```php
<?php
class Antelope_Widget extends WP_Widget {
  function Antelope_Widget() {
```

```
      // actual widget code that contains the function logic
    }

    function widget($args, $instance) {
      // display the widget on website
    }

    function update($new_instance, $old_instance) {
      // save widget options
    }

    function form($instance) {
      // form to display widget settings in WordPress admin
    }

  }
  ?>
```

As you can see, the widget class contains four basic components:

- declaration of the widget name that extends the `WP_Widget` object and the subsequent initialization of the function of the same name (in this case, `Antelope_Widget`)

- logic that actually outputs the widget coding to the website as desired

- functionality that allows you to create and save instances of the widget

- a form that allows users to make changes to the widget if the developer has made them available in the **Widgets** management screen

 Widgets Extend Classes

If you are fairly new to programming and have never dealt with objects and instances before, widgets might throw you a bit. Here's a layman's version of what you need to understand. When you are registering a widget, you're essentially creating an **object**, which can be thought of for our purposes as a template framework for how that particular widget should function and appear. Any given working example of that widget would then be referred to as an **instance** of the widget. Therefore, when we talk about widgets, we are really discussing two different aspects: initializing the template for how it will work (the object), and creating and outputting individual instances that you actually see and use. This may seem as clear as mud. It'll get easier.

Let's build upon these definitions and take up our AGSocialMedia plugin code where we left off: setting up the widget to output our links.

Registering Our Antelope General Widget

Check out our first piece of widget-related code:

chapter_05/AGSocialMedia/agsml_registerwidget.php

```php
/* Register the widget */
function agsml_register_widget() {
  register_widget( 'Antelope_Widget' );
}
```

The first piece here is super-easy, and it's our first step in creating and using a widget for our Antelope General Social Media Links plugin. We're just going to register our widget so that WordPress knows we have a new one coming, and it's called `Antelope_Widget`. Easy peasy.

Define What the Widget Should Do

Now we jump into step two of creating our widget, which is really step one of its own four-step process: defining the widget class functionality:

chapter_05/AGSocialMedia/agsml_widgetlogic.php

```php
/* Begin Widget Class */
class Antelope_Widget extends WP_Widget {

  //* Widget setup  */
  function Antelope_Widget() {
    $widget_ops = array('classname' => 'agsml_widget', 'description' =>➡
      __( 'Your Social Media Links', 'agsml') );

  // The actual widget code goes here
    parent::WP_Widget( false, $name = 'AG Social Media Links', $widget_ops );
  }
```

In the code, you can see that we begin by extending the `WP_Widget` object with the `Antelope_Widget` class, thus extending it and creating a namespace for ourselves to work with. After that, we create a basic localized array (note the double underscore wrapper that encompasses the string `'Your Social Media Links'` and which denotes the unique domain namespace we've created earlier in `'agsml'`) and toss it all into a variable. Then we utilize the widget API to create a new object for our actual widget, which we'll be able to find in the **Appearance** > **Widgets** menu area within WordPress. Notice that we have a label for our widget here (`'AG Social Media Links'`), and we're also passing our array in as well, so we have our object's data handy for use.

Display Logic

The second piece of the widget class involves actually outputting the instance of a given widget to the browser:

```php
/* Display the widget  */
function widget( $args, $instance ) {

  //get widget arguments
  extract($args);
  //get widget title from instance variable
  $title = apply_filters('widget_title', $instance['title']);

  //insert before widget markup
  echo $before_widget;

  //if theres a title, echo it.
  if( $title )
  echo $before_title . $title . $after_title;

  //start list
  $social_list .= '<ul>';

  // define list
  if (get_option('agsml_facebook' )){
    $social_list .= '<li class="facebook"><a href="'.➥
      get_option('agsml_facebook').'">' . __('Friend us on Facebook', 'agsml') .➥
      '</a></li>';
  }
  if (get_option('agsml_twitter' )){
    $social_list .= '<li class="twitter"><a href="'.➥
      get_option('agsml_twitter').'">' . __('Follow us on Twitter', 'agsml') .➥
      '</a></li>';
  }
  if (get_option('agsml_linkedin' )){
    $social_list .= '<li class="linkedin"><a href="'.➥
      get_option('agsml_linkedin').'">' . __('Link us on LinkedIn', 'agsml') .➥
      '</a></li>';
  }
  if (get_option('agsml_youtube' )){
    $social_list .= '<li class="youtube"><a href="'.➥
      get_option('agsml_youtube').'">' . __('Watch us on Youtube', 'agsml') .➥
      '</a></li>';
  }
  // end list
  $share_content .= '</ul>';

  //display assembled list
  echo $social_list;

  //insert before widget markup
```

```
    echo $after_widget;

}
```

Because we've passed the object's data to the instance of the widget as just described, the first step is to extract the $args so that we can use them. The AGSocialMedia widget has the capacity to create a custom title on an instance-by-instance basis as we'll see in a moment, so one of the first items here is the extraction and sanitization of the title string from our array, after which we drop it into the $title variable.

You may notice that there are several variables sprinkled throughout this code block that we aren't defining: $before_title, $after_title, $before_widget, and $after_widget. These tags are provided to you by the widget API, and are available to theme designers to manipulate in different ways, so that they can add code to make their websites look pretty. Make sure the tags stay as positioned, so those designers avoid running into any unforeseen and unexpected surprises.

Aside from that, the rest of this code is fairly self-explanatory. Because we're outputting to the browser here, we once again have strings that are being localized in the same format as before; it doesn't bear any more explanation, but when you are writing your own plugins, you will want to remember this important detail. Spread the WordPress love by localizing—have you noticed this as a recurring theme yet? We should make bumper stickers: "Be Wise and Localize!"

Updating the Instance of the Widget

The third piece of the widget class is the nearest we have to a standardized component, and it's very simple to see what's happening:

chapter_05/AGSocialMedia/agsml_widgetupdate.php

```
/* Update the widget settings, just the title in this case  */
function update( $new_instance, $old_instance ) {
  $instance = $old_instance;
  $instance['title'] = strip_tags($new_instance['title']);
  return $instance;
}
```

All we are doing here is sanitizing the only input we have for our widget—in this case the customized title—and saving it as a new instance, replacing the old instance if it existed.

Creating the Form to Change the Title

The final component of the widget class provides the logic for the form, which is necessary to update the title of the instance of the widget:

chapter_05/AGSocialMedia/agsml_widgetform.php

```php
//form to display in widget settings.  Allows user to set title of widget.
function form( $instance ) {
  $title = esc_attr($instance['title']);
?>
<p>
  <label for="<?php echo $this->get_field_id('title'); ?>"><?php _e('Title:');
    ?></label>
  <input class="widefat" id="<?php echo $this->get_field_id('title'); ?>"
    name="<?php echo $this->get_field_name('title'); ?>" type="text"
    value="<?php echo $title; ?>" />
</p>
<?php
}
}
```

Here we find a very simple form with just one label (that includes our now all-too-familiar localized string) and its corresponding input field, which autopopulates with the existing title, if one has been previously set.

Load Our Widget into WordPress

The final touches on our Antelope General Social Media Links plugin are finally within our grasp:

chapter_05/AGSocialMedia/agsml_loadwidget.php

```php
/* Load the widget */
add_action( 'widgets_init', 'agsml_register_widget' );
?>
```

Now all we need to do is use `widgets_init` to load up our `agsml_register_widget()` function. After this function fires, we're home, and while most antelopes run out of control, our antelope is running with all the controlled precision we could possibly hope for!

Taking Plugins Further

While we've pieced together an entire plugin bit by bit, we've only begun to touch on what you can do with plugins. In truth, the only limit to what you can accomplish with a plugin is your imagination, as there are thousands of hooks to work with, and even more standardized tools that you can use to continue to push the envelope with WordPress. While it made no sense to include them within the context of the Antelope General Social Media Links plugin example, there are two pieces of functionality commonly implemented within plugins that we should cover: meta boxes and shortcodes. We won't go into nearly as much depth on either piece of functionality, but we'll look at them so that you'll at least be able to use them. Let's start with a basic discussion of meta boxes.

Meta Boxes

In many plugins, you'll want to give your end users the ability to add information in a standardized way right on the page or post editing screen. One way to accomplish this is to utilize meta boxes, which we looked at back in the section called "Meta Boxes" in Chapter 2. If you recall, meta boxes are customized dialog boxes you can insert on administrative editing screens, seen in Figure 5.4.

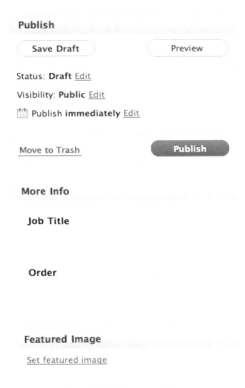

Figure 5.4. Custom meta boxes

Meta boxes are added using a standard function that takes seven parameters, as shown below:

```
add_meta_box($id, $title, $callback, $page, $context, $priority, $callback_args)
```

Each of the parameters is defined as follows:

- $id (string): CSS id attribute for the meta box (required)

- $title (string): the title displayed within the header of the meta box (required)

- $callback (string): the name of the function that displays the meta box information (required)

- $page (string): the type of page that you want the meta box displayed on; for example, post, page, link, or custom_post_type, where custom_post_type is the custom post type slug (required)

- $context (string): the specific area within the edit screen of where you want the meta box displayed, such as normal, advanced, or side (optional)

- $priority (string): the priority within the context where the meta box should be displayed, such as high, core, default, or low (optional)

- $callback_args (array): arguments to pass into your callback function (optional)

The add_meta_box() function is typically used in conjunction with the admin_init action hook, which you can use to create your custom meta box within page types associated with your plugin. While most of the parameters that add_meta_box() takes are self-explanatory, there's a couple of really cool ones that make this a particularly flexible function. Notably, the $page parameter queues up the type of page that your meta box can be displayed on; because it ties into custom post types, it gives you an additional level of control when morphing WordPress into the specialized CMS you envision for your website, as described in Chapter 4. The $context parameter is equally useful, giving you control over exactly where that meta box will show up on the page type editing screen. This is sexy stuff that lets you carve out WordPress to make it look and function however you see fit.

Shortcodes

Another extremely useful concept to dig into is shortcodes. Shortcodes are essentially sanitized placeholders for PHP functions that are either initialized by core WordPress, from within a plugin, or even from within the **functions.php** file of your theme. They can accept parameters that make them perform tasks, and are very useful when you want to insert fairly complicated code into a page or post without actually inserting that code. Instead, you can think of a shortcode as a placeholder that WordPress will identify when outputting your website, replacing it with the appropriate code associated with the shortcode. They are formatted with opening and closing brackets that look like this: [my_super_awesome_shortcode].

Shortcodes are easy to create, and for the most part you can embed any functionality you want into them. WordPress gives us the following standard function to use when we want to create one:

```
add_shortcode( 'shortcode-name', 'shortcode-function-name' )
```

Here, the parameters are straightforward, with the name of the shortcode (the text we insert in our brackets) being defined within the first string parameter, and the associated function that calls the PHP function we'll be executing where the shortcode is inserted in our page. Let's take a look at a very simple example of a shortcode in action:

```php
<?php

function thank_you() {
  return 'You can feel good about Hood.';
}

add_shortcode( 'mrminer', 'thank_you' );
?>
```

Here, we have defined an extremely simple shortcode named *mrminer*, which makes reference to a function called `thank_you()`. While you can be extremely creative and intricate with the functionality you'd like to introduce in your shortcode, we've kept it very simple here to illustrate the process. In our example, we can add the shortcode `[mrminer]` to any post or page, and it'll print out "You can feel good about Hood." in that space.

Return, Don't Echo

A common mistake that many plugin developers make when they are beginning to work with shortcodes is to try to `echo` the results of a shortcode, rather than `return` the response. Don't sweat it, though … now that you've read this tip, you'll avoid this pitfall!

The WordPress Plugin Directory

All right, so let's say you've created a plugin and you want to give back to the community by sharing your creation with the world. One of the easiest and most effective ways of doing that is to submit it to the WordPress Plugin Directory on WordPress.org. There are several really cool things that result from listing your plugin in the directory, most notably that it instantly becomes accessible to anybody who's running a WordPress installation. With just a few clicks and the right search, your plugin can come up in the plugin search and be added to anyone's WordPress site in just a few minutes. Additionally, when you update your plugin inside the directory, your users will be immediately notified and prompted to upgrade from right within their WordPress admin back end … and that just *feels* so cool the first time you ever see it happen with one of your plugins. Finally, WordPress.org also gives you access to statistics, so you'll be able to see exactly how many people have downloaded your plugin and the ratings they've given it, as well as view and respond to comments.

You'll need to adhere to several blanket terms and conditions if you want your plugin to be listed in the directory, namely:

- Your plugin should have a license that is GPL-compatible.
- Your plugin can't do anything illegal, or be morally offensive in any way.
- You'll need to host the plugin using the WordPress.org subversion repository.

- You'll need a valid **readme.txt** file for your plugin.
- Your plugin can't embed an external link to the author's site without giving the user an option to easily remove it.

If you choose to submit your plugin to the WordPress Plugin Directory, it's an easy process, even though it's not immediate. You'll need to be a WordPress.org registered user, and then you submit your plugin at http://www.WordPress.org/extend/plugins/add/. Upon adding your plugin, it will need to be reviewed and approved by the staff managing WordPress; it's a process that can take some time, as it is manual.

Upon having your plugin approved, you will be given access to the WordPress.org Subversion repository, where you'll commit the uncompressed plugin to the SVN repository, along with a valid **readme.txt** file that describes the information needed for listing a plugin in the directory. A sample **readme.txt** file can be found at http://wordpress.org/extend/plugins/about/readme.txt, and a **readme** validator that will help you determine whether you've added the required elements for a listing is available at http://www.WordPress.org/extend/plugins/about/validator/.

Some Food for Thought

Few things are worse in the WordPress community than a poorly supported plugin, especially if it starts off with a head of steam and gains a following. Such plugins are one of the reasons why WordPress earned a bad name in the past, so we encourage you to give some thought to how comfortable you are in providing a reasonable level of support to others using your plugin. When you submit a plugin to the WordPress Plugin Directory, you really are making a loose, implied agreement to provide a basic level of support to others who may use your plugin; otherwise, releasing it into the directory makes little sense outside of satisfying your ego. Submitting your plugin to the directory is a *choice* that you as the developer can make—it's not a requirement.

Plug In All the Way

Plugins are powerful pieces of functionality, and are essential in extending the functionality of any WordPress website. Poorly coded or out-of-date plugins are one of the most common reasons why WordPress websites occasionally have problems, so the easiest place to begin troubleshooting is to turn off all your plugins.

If you are a developer, you can make WordPress do backflips with the creative use of plugins (all right, maybe not backflips, but you could probably make it order pizza for you). Mastering action hooks and filter hooks are essential to making your plugins hum, but you'll need a solid foundation in PHP to make anything really go. Just remember, if you can dream it, you can do it with plugins in WordPress!

Themes

Well-designed content management systems seek to create a separation between design, content, and functionality, and WordPress is no exception. So far in this book, we've covered the fundamental building blocks of WordPress that primarily manage functionality: The Loop, post types, and plugins. **Themes**, on the other hand, comprise the structural CSS, HTML, and JavaScript code that handle the overall design, layout, and visual user experience of a website. In other words, themes are all about making your website look really good, and less about the programming that does all the heavy lifting in the background. There are plenty of considerations that muddy these waters, though, as we'll learn later in the chapter, but for the time being, let's focus on the basics of what goes into a theme.

Basic Components of a Theme

At their core, themes are really nothing more than the HTML code to create a structure that describes where different components will live on a website, and the CSS code that describes what those components will look like. For the purposes of this chapter, we'll assume you have a solid understanding of both HTML and CSS, and that you understand the fundamental components necessary to construct a successful web page. It's vital that you understand how all those pieces work together within a WordPress theme.

Just like with plugins, WordPress provides us with a standardized place to store our themes within a particular WordPress installation: the **wp-content/themes** directory. Although only one theme can be activated at any given time, WordPress does let you store as many themes as you like to activate and deactivate at your leisure. Keeping with the same pattern we saw with plugins, themes must

have unique names and be stored in their own unique directories within the **wp-content/themes** directory. So far, so good.

Required Elements of a Theme

Now that we know where to save the files within our theme, we need to start building those files. While we'll probably end up creating several more files, we technically only require two files to set up a valid theme:

- **styles.css**
- **index.php**

The **styles.css** file is the more crucial of the two, and is the first file that WordPress will look for when it gathers information about your theme prior to activation. Similar to the way in which it recognizes plugins, WordPress searches for a standardized header at the very top of the **styles.css** file to gather pertinent information about your theme. Since we won't be creating our own full-blown theme here within this chapter, let's take a look at how the team over at WordPress.org has done it with their latest and greatest theme, Twenty Eleven:

chapter_06/twenty-eleven-styles-header.php

```
/*
Theme Name: Twenty Eleven
Theme URI: http://wordpress.org/extend/themes/twentyeleven
Author: the WordPress team
Author URI: http://wordpress.org/
Description: The 2011 theme for WordPress is sophisticated, lightweight, and
  adaptable. Make it yours with a custom menu, header image, and background --
  then go further with available theme options for light or dark color scheme,
  custom link colors, and three layout choices. Twenty Eleven comes equipped
  with a Showcase page template that transforms your front page into a showcase
  to show off your best content, widget support galore (sidebar, three footer
  areas, and a Showcase page widget area), and a custom "Ephemera" widget to
  display your Aside, Link, Quote, or Status posts. Included are styles for
  print and for the admin editor, support for featured images (as custom header
  images on posts and pages and as large images on featured "sticky" posts), and
  special styles for six different post formats.
Version: 1.0
License: GNU General Public License
License URI: license.txt
Tags: dark, light, white, black, gray, one-column, two-columns, left-sidebar,
  right-sidebar, fixed-width, flexible-width, custom-background, custom-colors,
  custom-header, custom-menu, editor-style, featured-image-header,
  featured-images, full-width-template, microformats, post-formats,
  rtl-language-support, sticky-post, theme-options, translation-ready
*/
```

As you can see, this is fairly standard fare. What's important to remember is that no two themes loaded in the same WordPress installation can have the same name; so if you are building a theme by copying an existing theme and making modifications from there, make sure you change the header information here to your own unique values.

The remainder of the **styles.css** file is just standard CSS. You can use it to create all the cool styles you'll utilize to make your theme look awesome.

The **index.php** file, on the other hand, is the initial page that a browser will fire upon visiting your site, and serves as the key file to describe the layout of the main page (and potentially the entire site, as we'll discuss in a moment). We can place whatever HTML we want our theme to display inside this file, but since our goal here is to output our WordPress content via our theme, we'll take a more structured approach. Let's take a look at a stripped down **index.php** file we might commonly see in a theme:

chapter_06/basic-index.php

```php
<?php

// Insert the header.php file to begin the page output
get_header();

// Add in page logic via the Loop
if (have_posts()) :
   while (have_posts()) :
      the_post();
      the_content();
   endwhile;
endif;

// Insert the sidebar.php file to include widgetized sidebars
get_sidebar();

// Insert the footer.php file to complete the page output
get_footer();

?>
```

Right away, you'll notice that this **index.php** file is broken up into four sections:

- header area
- the location to add The Loop, which will define our page logic
- sidebar area
- footer area

Just by looking at the comments in the code, we can deduce that get_header() grabs and inserts the **header.php** file, while get_sidebar() and get_footer() perform the same function with

sidebar.php and **footer.php**, respectively. Fairly easy, right? There's no need to define the specific names of those files; WordPress assumes that you'll follow its nomenclature (a recurring theme, as we'll see here in a moment). We've already covered The Loop in detail in Chapter 3, so we should already be able to see where the content is going to be added. However, this does introduce three more files that we'll need to add to our theme:

- **header.php**
- **sidebar.php**
- **footer.php**

These files aren't vital, but you'll find almost every theme makes use of them. And just to keep you on your toes, they won't necessarily include what you think they might if you try to interpret them literally. For instance, the **header.php** file will contain all the display code required to create the code of a given page right up to where the content code is added into the outputted source code. This includes the `<DOCTYPE>` information for your outputted page, all the typical components you'd need in any `<head>` code such as meta information and links to your stylesheets, and the opening `<body>` tag to begin your display code. With all that said, there are two tasks you must include when creating your **header.php** file that will break WordPress without their presence:

- Reference the **styles.css** file you've set up to initialize your theme.
- Add the `wp_head()` function in the `<head>` code to initialize WordPress and ensure that all core functions work properly.

Similarly, the **footer.php** file can cover all the outputted source code from the bottom of the content block to the end of the file, although, in our example, we've inserted our **sidebar.php** file in this space, which serves to include logic for our widgetized areas. Typically, the footer contains the `</body>` and `</html>` tags, and must contain `wp_footer()` to allow core WordPress functions to manage footer settings as required; without it, unexpected results will occur when WordPress uses your theme.

 Tying It All Together

> If you were paying close attention in Chapter 5, you'll recall that two of our most common action hooks were the `wp_head` and `wp_footer` action hooks. The functions that we've just discussed above—`wp_head()` and `wp_footer()`—are the functions that actually trigger each of these action hooks, respectively. Nothing like tying it together with a nice little bow, right?

Let's stop for a moment and draw an analogy to illustrate this point further, using a hamburger (or a veggie burger if you prefer) as an example. Now, the way that we prefer our burgers may well be different from the way you prefer yours. While a lot of people prefer to put their pickles, mustard, and ketchup underneath the meat, with the cheese, lettuce, and tomato on top, we choose to have nothing underneath our burger, instead having all toppings between the meat and the top bun. Other people may choose to skip the mustard and ketchup, favoring mayonnaise as their only

condiment. Whatever your preference, what we all have in common on our burger is the fact that there's a top bun, a bottom bun, and the meat in the middle—what you add to the burger is really up to you.

In the same way, themes are really all about visual flavors and preferences. We all have stuff on the top (a header), stuff on the bottom (a footer), and meat in the middle (the content being added by The Loop). Other than that, as designers we like to be creative and make our themes uniquely our own, much like we do when we prepare our burgers. Consider Figure 6.1.

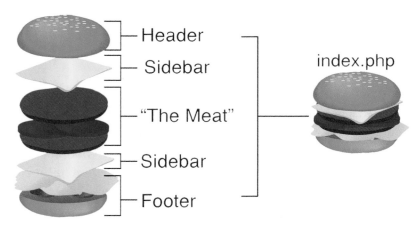

Figure 6.1. **index.php** structure dressed up like a hamburger

What the burger-maker has done here is change the very nature of the meal. It's no longer a hamburger, but a double cheeseburger, and we'll need to manage some options that deal with the cheese. Bringing the analogy back to the **index.php** file within our theme, we'll call these places where we need to manage options sidebars, and we can move them around however we like. In our initial example, we'd already added one sidebar between The Loop and the footer, but now we have to manage two sidebars that may have different options. The easiest way to do this is to create a left and a right sidebar, which we can do by passing the correct standard parameter to the `get_sidebar()` function, as is done in the revised example:

chapter_06/dual-sidebar-index.php

```
<?php

// Insert the header.php file to begin the page output
get_header();

// Add in page logic via The Loop
if (have_posts()) :
  while (have_posts()) :
    the_post();
    the_content();
  endwhile;
```

```
endif;

// Insert both widgetized sidebars
get_sidebar('left');
get_sidebar('right');

// Insert the footer.php file to complete the page output
get_footer();

?>
```

We're cooking with gas now, except … wait. We've added two sidebars to our theme, but we only have one **sidebar.php** file. What gives?

Easy—get_sidebar() takes one optional parameter, a name that corresponds directly to a standard nomenclature with **sidebar.php**. So when you use get_sidebar('left'), get_sidebar('right'), or even get_sidebar('footer'), WordPress will seek out **sidebar_left.php**, **sidebar_right.php**, or **sidebar_footer.php**, respectively. Nomenclature, in fact, plays a very big role in determining how WordPress parses out template files within your theme, as we are about to find out.

Nomenclature Hierarchy and Page Templates

We now have a handle on the fundamental components you can use to assemble your web pages within your WordPress theme. This is great, but what about extending those styles and changing your theme depending on where you are in your website? After all, it's quite common to make your home page appear different from your internal pages, and you just might want to have a distinct look for a 404 page that pops up when a user tries to visit a place on your site that doesn't actually exist. Regardless, WordPress has you covered in two ways:

- the template nomenclature hierarchy
- page templates

Let's tackle the nomenclature hierarchy first.

By default, WordPress requires that you only create one template file within your theme: **index.php**. If you create no other template files aside from **index.php**, WordPress will simply default to this visual styling for everything it needs to display on your website. However, WordPress provides us with a specific nomenclature system that provides a handy way for theme designers to automatically display templates for a particular type of page output, or even for a page, post, or category. All you need to do is make a copy of your **index.php** file, rename it to match up with the type of content you'll display, and then make your template modifications within that file. Consider the WordPress Template Hierarchy in Figure 6.2.

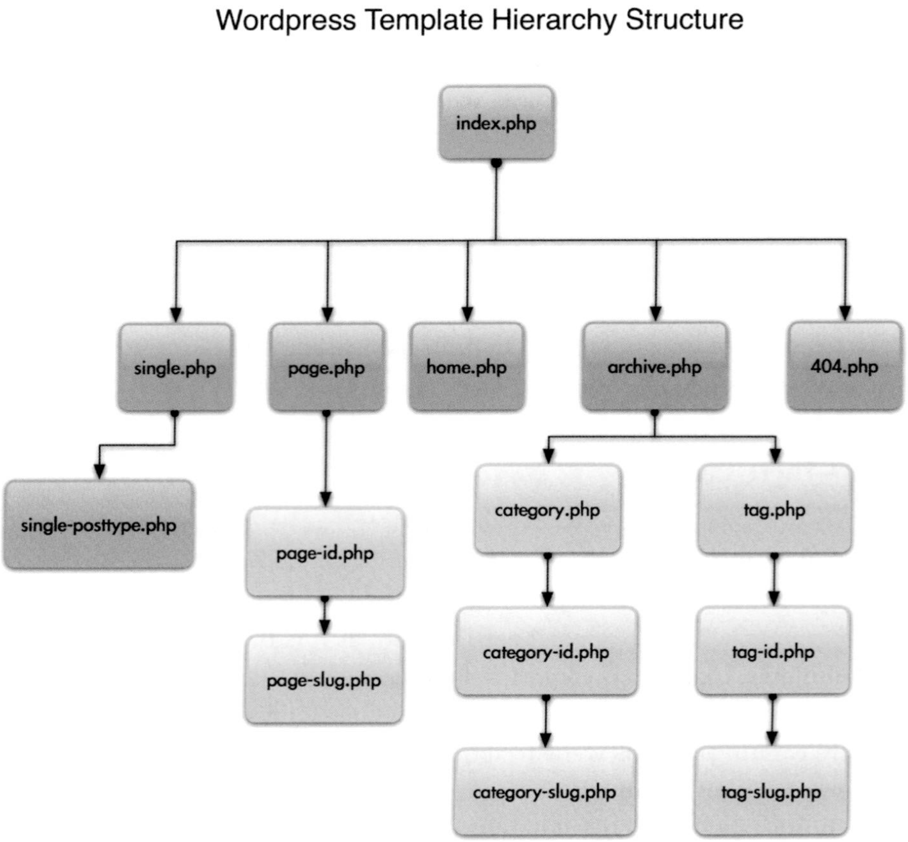

Wordpress Template Hierarchy Structure

Figure 6.2. A simplified version of the WordPress template hierarchy structure

This simplified hierarchy structure describes the process; it helps to think of it like a funnel, with a URL working top-down through the hierarchy. At the top of the structure, there are templates used to describe the most specific forms of content types we could have. If a template file exists for a specific slug or post ID, that template is used. If no slug or ID template file exists, WordPress would look for the next template file in the linear hierarchy and use the first available, defaulting to **index.php** if no file is found until that point.

For example, let's say that you would like to create a page template to manage the appearance of all your pages, but you'd like to give your About Us page its own look and feel. You could accomplish this by creating a template named **page.php** to handle all the pages within your theme, but then create a second file named **page-about.php** with the specialized display logic (assuming that "about" is the slug for that particular page).

The most common templates modified by theme designers, aside from **index.php**, are colored in blue in Figure 6.2. Here's what each of them modify:

■ **single.php** manages all display formatting for individual posts

- **page.php** manages all display formatting for individual pages

- **home.php** manages all display formatting for the home page (called from the is_home() function, rather than the is_front_page() function, which is managed by the **front-page.php** display template)

- **archive.php** manages all display formatting for post-listing pages (those that typically display post excerpts)

- **404.php** manages all display formatting for any pages not found (this can be useful for improving your visitors' experience by giving them helpful navigation tips, since you can safely deduce that they're experiencing what they didn't expect on your site)

 But Wait—There's More

Figure 6.2 lists only some of the most common page template types used by theme designers. For a more complete listing, have a look at the diagram provided by WordPress.[1]

The **archive.php** template is its own special case as well, as it is the root controlling template file for a variety of templates, including categories, tags, and several others such as taxonomies, which aren't pictured here. Other than this, the **archive.php** template works just like the others. For example, let's say that you're running a sports website about the Olympics, and you have a particular interest in swimming events. Working from the bottom up, you could create a specialized display template for posts about Olympic swimming by creating a file called **category-swimming.php**. However, you may also want to post about sports unrelated to swimming that have no need for a distinct appearance, so you could create a second template called **category.php** that serves this catch-all category. Finally, since you'll be doing this over the course of several Olympic Games, you may want to display older, less relevant posts differently; you could then use another display template for archived posts. Shockingly, this would be named **archive.php**!

Page Templates

The other way to create distinct layouts in WordPress is to use **page templates**. It's no surprise to find that you can only use page templates with individual pages, but they're useful for giving your end user an easy way to change the appearance of a page within the page editing screen.

Creating a new page template is easy as pie. Just copy an existing template you have within your theme and give it a unique name. There's no requirement to follow a nomenclature for filenames of page templates as it is with the template hierarchy; in fact, you'll want to make sure that you avoid naming your page templates one of the template names, as it will cause it to behave in a way you don't want. Instead, you register your page templates with WordPress in what should now be

---

[1] http://codex.WordPress.org/Template_Hierarchy

a very familiar way: having a standardized comment format at the top of your template file, as described here:

```
chapter_06/page-template-registration.php

<?php
/*
Template Name: Antelope General Special Sales Page Template
*/
?>
```

As the required `Template Name:` label suggests, the name of your custom page template is defined here, and once saved, you'll find it immediately in the page templates drop-down on your page editing screen. Nothing to it, as Figure 6.3 shows.

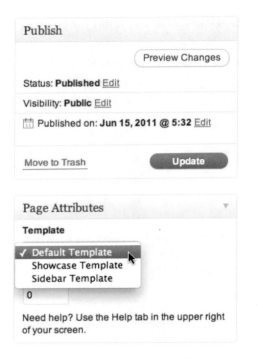

Figure 6.3. Page Templates dialog box

Adding Functionality to Your Theme

So far, we've talked in detail about how themes work and are structured, which is all well and good, but sooner or later you'll want to make your theme sing and dance, and that means adding some theme-specific functionality. For this reason, an important file that you'll find in most themes is the **functions.php** file. A file that WordPress automatically searches for when it loads a theme, **functions.php** is essentially treated as a theme-specific plugin. There are plenty of appropriate uses for it (and inappropriate uses, as we'll discuss in a bit); what's important to remember is that

functions.php is where you'll want to place custom PHP functions that make sense to use within the context of your theme, and your theme alone. Let's take a look at some of the more common uses of functions.php.

 Keep It Functional

Functions defined and written into **functions.php** are automatically loaded whenever the theme is in use; therefore, it's useful to keep in mind that long, unwieldy **functions.php** files can actually slow your website down.

Adding Custom Menus

While you can literally add any functions you'd like to the **functions.php** file, one of the most common functions theme designers use involve setting up custom menus for extended navigation on the site. WordPress gives us an exceptionally easy method for creating as many menus as we'd like, which is useful for producing top header menus, footer menus, contextual menus, and any other type you can dream up. In order to create our menus, we'll need to register them within our **functions.php** file using the register_nav_menus() function, which takes an array of menu slugs and descriptive names as its argument. Let's have a look at it in use:

chapter_06/functions-php-menus.php

```php
<?php

if ( function_exists( 'register_nav_menus' ) ) {
    register_nav_menus(
        array(
            'header_menu' => 'Header Menu',
            'footer_menu' => 'Footer Menu',
            'mobile_menu' => 'Mobile Menu'
        )
    );
}
```

As is fairly plain to see, we've registered the availability of three new menu files in this example—a header menu, a footer menu, and a mobile menu. With this code saved to our **functions.php**, we'll now have these menu options available to us when we navigate to the **Menus** screen in the Dashboard at **Appearance > Menus**; here we can make modifications to our heart's content. However, we still need to place them in our theme, and to do this we need only use the wp_nav_menu() function in the desired location within our theme, which looks like this in action:

```php
<?php wp_nav_menu('header_menu'); ?>
```

Working Backwards

The custom WordPress menu system was introduced in WordPress 3.0. If you want to make sure that your theme is compatible with WordPress versions older than 3.0, use the conditional `if (` `function_exists ( 'register_nav_menus()' )` code as described in our recent example.

Choose Your Format

While the standard usage of `wp_nav_menu()` is fairly basic, you can do all sorts of formatting tricks with it. Have a look in the WordPress Codex[2] for the range of parameters you can pass to the function to extend your custom menus.

Creating Widgetized Areas

Aside from adding customized menus, **functions.php** is often utilized to extend WordPress's functionality, creating additional widget-ready areas for use within your theme. Consider the following code:

chapter_06/register-widgetized-area.php

```php
<?php

// Register Antelope Featured Widgetized Area so it exists and we can use it
if ( function_exists('register_sidebar') )
register_sidebar(array(
  'name' => 'Antelope Featured Widgetized Area',
  'before_widget' => '',
  'after_widget' => '',
  'before_title' => '<h2>',
  'after_title' => '</h2>',
));

?>
```

Nothing to this, really. Here, we're just letting WordPress know that we have a new widgetized area called Antelope Featured Widgetized Area that we'll want to use. WordPress will respond by creating a namespace for you to work with; so now when you go to the **Appearance > Widgets** area within the admin area, you'll see a new sidebar named **Antelope Featured Widgetized Area**. Go ahead and fill it up with whatever widget functionality you'd like, and then we'll move on to the next (and final) step so that we can actually reap the benefits of our efforts.

Since we've just registered a new widgetized area, let's follow through and add it to our theme in a useful location for our purposes. Widgetized areas can be added anywhere in a theme, but they're

---

[2] http://codex.wordpress.org/Function_Reference/register_nav_menus

commonly added within **sidebar.php** templates (or derivatives thereof). Just locate the place in your code where you want to add your new widgetized area, and drop in the following PHP code:

```
                                                    chapter_06/display-widgetized-area.php

<?php

// Output Antelope Featured Widgetized Area in our theme
if ( !function_exists('dynamic_sidebar') || !dynamic_sidebar➡
  ("Antelope Featured Widgetized Area") ) : ?>

<!-- Default formatting code here  -->

<?php endif; ?>
```

We promised we'd avoid delving too deeply into PHP here, but this shouldn't be too scary. Here we are just being responsible and making sure that our theme has no issues; for example, if the theme is unable to find either the `dynamic_sidebar` function (highly unlikely, as it's a core function) or the widgetized area we just registered in our **functions.php** file (more likely, since everybody is prone to human error). In the event that the theme runs into an issue here, it'll just display the output code we've specified—in this case, a descriptive comment. However, so long as we have coded our widgetized area correctly and added widgets to it, we should see a useful addition here.

Adding Support for Visual Modifications

The other types of functions most commonly added to **functions.php** involve giving your users the ability to make visual changes to the theme from directly within the admin Dashboard.

Adding Support for Custom Headers

It's typical that users with a particular theme on their website will want to change the header to one of their own creations, and WordPress gives us a really easy, standardized method of doing so. In order to make this happen, WordPress provides us with a set of code additions that we'll need to build our **functions.php** file:

```
                                                    chapter_06/functions-php-custom-header.php

<?php

// Four constants that must be defined in order for the custom image
// header to work properly
define('HEADER_TEXTCOLOR', 'ffffff');
define('HEADER_IMAGE', get_bloginfo('styesheet_directory') .➡
  '/images/default_header.jpg');
define('HEADER_IMAGE_WIDTH', 900);
define('HEADER_IMAGE_HEIGHT', 150);
```

```
// Include the header within the theme
function header_style() {
    ?><style type="text/css">
        #header {
            background: url(<?php header_image(); ?>);
        }
    </style><?php
}

// Include the header within the admin interface
function admin_header_style() {
    ?><style type="text/css">
        #headimg {
            width: <?php echo HEADER_IMAGE_WIDTH; ?>px;
            height: <?php echo HEADER_IMAGE_HEIGHT; ?>px;
            background: no-repeat;
        }
    </style><?php
}

// Enabling the custom image header
add_custom_image_header('header_style', 'admin_header_style');
```

You'll notice that there are four basic blocks of code: the first defines four constants; the second adds the header to the front end of the theme; the third adds the header to the administrative portion of the theme; and the last actually enables it all within WordPress. From an editing perspective, it's important to pay attention as a theme developer to the first code block where we define our constants. Make sure to input the header dimensions accurately, as well as describe the location of the header image, and the color of any text that is added to the header. Without these constants, the custom header will simply fail to work.

Following the constants definition, the remaining three code blocks comprise pretty much our standard WordPress magic. First, we'll create a function that will load with the *wp_head* action hook that adds the header image and its attributes into your theme. The next code block loads the header to the admin Dashboard, followed by our activation function in add_custom_image_header(), which specifically calls the two functions we've just defined.

Adding Support for a Custom Background

In what may be the granddaddy of easy functionality to add to any theme, WordPress has a simple method that gives your users the ability to add a custom background to their themes. In your **functions.php** file, add the following line of code:

```
<?php add_custom_background(); ?>
```

Doing this will automatically add a set of functionality to your theme that will allow the website administrator to see the existing background image of the theme, upload a background to replace the old one, and tweak several of the commonly modified attributes of the background. Take a look at Figure 6.4.

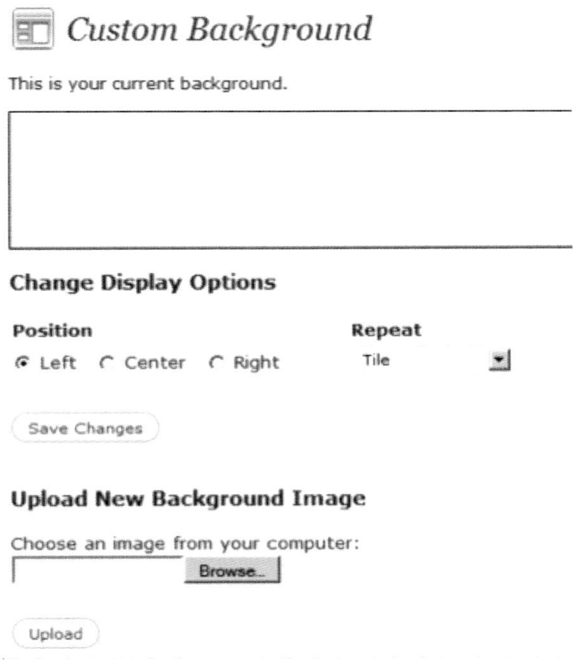

Custom Background

This is your current background.

Change Display Options

Position
⊙ Left   ○ Center   ○ Right

Repeat
Tile

Save Changes

Upload New Background Image

Choose an image from your computer:

Browse...

Upload

Figure 6.4. Adding a custom background

If you were expecting a more complicated process, don't knock it. Every once in a while you're given a gift, and this is one of them!

Does My Functionality Belong in a Plugin or Theme?

While you can technically add functionality wherever you like in your theme, the question of where it's appropriate to do so can be a bit murky when considering both the flexibility of WordPress and the divergent intentions of different web developers. Before we examine these nuances, though, let's first define exactly what we mean by *functionality*.

Defining Functionality

The term **functionality** is a common buzzword that is thrown around fairly loosely these days by developers, designers, and clients alike, but exactly what are we talking about when we reference it? For the most part, just about anybody involved would agree that it's a general term describing a specific feature set that has been introduced into a system. Within WordPress, almost all types of functionality can be broken down into four primary categories:

- core WordPress functionality

- functionality that enhances existing feature sets within core WordPress

- functionality that introduces entirely new feature sets unavailable within core WordPress (including third-party application integration; for example, Twitter)

- functionality that aids a specific theme in handling variables from a design and layout perspective

Whether you're looking to add a real-time feed of Tweets to your sidebar or a jQuery image gallery on your home page, or just to set up your site to be ranked better in search engines, the categories listed should cover just about anything you want to throw at WordPress. If we assert that all functionality in WordPress falls within one of these four categories, and consider that WordPress provides a logical location to house operations, we can project whether a specific piece of functionality belongs within a plugin or within a theme.

Core WordPress functionality is included within WordPress, and should never be directly edited at any time (if you do, bad stuff can happen; think "removing random pieces of your engine just to see what happens"). Functionality that either enhances existing WordPress core features or introduces brand new features typically belongs as plugins, so that they can be added and removed as necessary. Likewise, functionality that aids a theme belongs within that theme, but it's useful to note that it's scripting that helps display specific pieces of content rather than add or extend functions. In this way, the intent of the scripting is different; it's more about display logic than it is about site functionality, and it's probably the most important distinction to make in determining where to place your site's custom functionality.

The Difference between Display Logic and Site Functionality

Almost all functionality in WordPress is written in one of two languages: PHP or JavaScript. After all, whether you're creating a custom jQuery script to add a behavior to a slide show or modifying The Loop to add the three most recent posts in the **Featured** category to the front page, you are really working on the site's functionality. Right?

Sort of.

The truth is that while you are, indeed, working with functional pieces of scripting on your site, you should be able to squarely place any scripting into one of two categories. The script either adds to or enhances the actual features of your WordPress site (**site functionality**), or assists you in displaying that information to your audience (**display logic**). We all have a reasonable idea of what site functionality is, but display logic has everything to do with how we actually display useful data within the context of the theme. Common examples of display logic include:

- registering sidebars and widgetized areas
- registering new WordPress menus

- inserting custom conditional logic into The Loop
- using post thumbnail scripting references such as TimThumb[3]

Incorporating prefabricated site functionality via the plugin system by customizing a theme's display logic is the most common form of WordPress development performed by the typical WordPress developer, as most of us spend our time finding slicker and more effective ways of integrating existing tools across the Web to create client solutions. Often, the difference between good and poor coding practices is in recognizing the difference between actual site functionality and display logic, and coding each in the appropriate location.

A Case Study: ABC Real Estate

So if this is all as clear as mud, let's take a look at a practical example. Suppose that we have a new client—ABC Real Estate—who'd like us to develop a new website built upon WordPress with the following functionality requests:

- some form of event management system, as it will be running regular seminars

- that each property be displayed in a constant, intuitive way with space for multiple photos (to vary per house listing)

- six featured properties in a specific format to be selected for the home page

- site integration of Facebook comments so that visitors can easily share potential homes with their friends

Each of these requests seems more than reasonable and intuitive for a real estate website, but let's sort out exactly where we'd add each piece of functionality listed.

Some Form of Event Management System

This one is relatively simple. Because WordPress lacks an event management system in its core, we'll need to add one via the plugin system. Could we write our own and add it directly to the theme itself? Technically, we could, but it would make little sense, as there are already so many event management systems available to try in a heartbeat. Furthermore, if we were absolutely bent on writing our own system, it would be easiest to contain all the files necessary in their own place to keep it tidy. Sounds like a plugin.

Each Property Displayed in a Constant, Intuitive Way

This one is a touch more complex, and a bit of a trick question. Since we're talking about how elements are displayed, you might think we're immediately in the realm of display logic. However, WordPress 3.0 introduced the notion of post types, which allows for developers to create a certain

---

[3] http://code.google.com/p/timthumb/

display format for a specific type of post. You can collect a discrete set of data within the WordPress admin for each record within the post type, and then output that record to a post template inside the theme, allowing the post to be output to the screen in a unique way. Because of the particular way that post types operate, you are essentially forced to create both display logic as well as site functionality when you work with them. We'll go over this in a bit more detail further on in this chapter.

Six Featured Properties in a Specific Format for the Home Page

This is display logic. We're adding nothing new here at all, but rather picking specific pieces of stored content from the database. This is always done directly within the theme.

Site Integration of Facebook Comments

Third-party application integration—in this case, Facebook. Piece of cake; we'll add one of the myriad Facebook commenting plugins available for WordPress and integrate it appropriately.

My Way of Adding Site Functionality Works for Me!

And to that we say: we completely understand where you're coming from, but allow us to make a few compelling points that just might change your mind.

First of all, if you are developing site functionality yourself, you're likely to find it more useful to do so within the context of a plugin for purposes of portability, rather than directly within the theme. After all, even after a job has been completed and the site launched, a large percentage of developers retain the intellectual property rights of programs that they develop and utilize within sites they work on; sooner or later there is a need to reuse the same code (or a version of it) for another project. Plugins make this site functionality portable and easy to install, saving quite a bit of time in the long run.

Because WordPress plugins are structured to maintain all their files in separate directories away from other plugins and core WordPress features, they inherently provide order to the functions written throughout the site. For instance, if you are having an issue with the meta description on the home page and you know you are using an SEO plugin that handles that function (easily looked up by referencing the active plugin listing in the WordPress admin), you'll know exactly where to begin investigating the source of the issue, even if you weren't the original developer. In this way, plugins can actually provide a loose form of documentation in and of themselves, giving developers reasonable clues as to where certain functions might live, even in the poorest-documented of sites.

Troubleshooting is another fabulous reason to maintain site functionality within plugins rather than embed it directly into the theme. Adding new features to a WordPress site can occasionally cause conflicts and break a website, causing any number of display or performance issues that need to be corrected. When such issues go bump in the night, most seasoned developers begin examining existing plugins to see where scripting plugins may be happening. Using WordPress's plugin system

to activate and deactivate plugins provides a handy way to eliminate active scripts running on the site, and then bring them back one by one to determine which are the offending scripts. Without the ability to turn plugins on and off, a developer can be stuck trying to sort out exactly which scripts are conflicting with one another and causing a buggy result to the end user.

Finally, don't underestimate the importance of flexibility in your website functionality. The more of the site's core functionality that is directly built into the theme, the more difficult it becomes to make design changes to that theme, or even swap it out entirely. It may sound clichéd, but the Web is constantly shifting, and, ultimately, so will your site's needs. Hard-coding site functionality into a theme can lead to time-consuming edits, changes, and overhauls in the long term (and often the short term) as you realize that what you thought was crucial yesterday—basing your entire site development on it—is entirely obsolete next week. Honestly, it has happened to the best of us.

Breaking the Rules

"All right," we hear you say. "That's fine, but I have a good reason to deviate …" Every subjective argument like this has solid reasoning to go your own way, and it's useful to point out a few here.

Reason #1: Post Types

In our case study, we discussed putting together a customized post type to handle the display format for a property listing. Pragmatically, this involves putting two pieces of code together: an array initializing the data for the post type, and the post template to handle the display within the context of the theme. While the second component here is clearly an issue of display logic, the array initializations are a bit more fuzzy. This function is commonly defined within the theme's **functions.php** file, but it's important to note that it could be defined with a functions file initialized within the plugin system. In many ways, this makes a touch more sense as it keeps a clean separation between site functionality and design components, and would ensure that the site's functionality was retained if you were to swap themes out down the track. As of this writing, initializing the array within the theme's **functions.php** file is clearly the most common practice, but it's certainly a gray area.

Reason #2: Specialized Page Templates

Occasionally, it becomes important to create a page on a WordPress site that performs a particular function. Perhaps you're framing an item from another site, or pulling in some type of custom functionality that isn't really conducive to working within the constructs of the standard WordPress page template and content editor. When this is the case, a usual practice is to register a new page template with the standard WordPress syntax in the template file, and then include the functionality directly within that page. In this instance, the functionality is not portable to other sites at all, but often it is done in a situation where that is unnecessary.

Reason #3: Protecting the Client from Themselves

As much as we'd all like to believe that WordPress is a bulletproof system that clients are unable to break, we know that's inaccurate. Occasionally there is a good reason to hardcode. For example, let's say you have a client who has to edit the sidebar on their website, but continually adds to or edits the wrong item. In this instance, it can be useful to hardcode simple elements into the sidebar that you're reasonably sure the clients themselves will never need to update, guarding against the possibility of accidentally deleting it. Examples of what might be hardcoded include an email opt-in box or social media connection buttons.

Reason #4: Specialized Products for a Specific Industry

There are many theme developers out there who build targeted WordPress themes tailored to certain industries. These themes lack a certain amount of flexibility, but the upshot is that for the target market they serve, the additional flexibility is unnecessary. Examples of this include real estate-specific themes, product review themes, or question-and-answer aggregation themes.

Reason #5: Time and Budget Considerations

Point blank, it's sometimes faster to code directly into a theme than to make it modular and use a plugin. When time is a factor or your client has a tight budget, a legitimate reason exists to cut corners and code site functionality directly into the theme. It's important to note that this is certainly not a best practice, but it's a reason to do what you need to do to get the job done.

Looking Good

Ultimately, themes are all about making your site look pretty, and it's easy to do if you keep in mind a few points:

- Themes revolve around moving template tags into different positions within your page templates. For the most part, every template will have a header and a footer, inserting page logic in the middle via our trusted friend and ally, The Loop.

- There are some linear rules for determining how to name your template files, so that they automatically style the types of content you want them to.

- You can use page templates to allow users greater control in the page editing screen over how certain pages appear.

We also learned how to add functionality such as widgetized areas in a theme's **functions.php** file, and discussed the difference between site functionality and display logic. We've made the case that the best practice for adding functionality is to code display logic directly into the theme, while creating site functionality within the plugin system.

Taxonomies

So far within this book, we've touched upon the primary components that comprise the main content and operational functions of WordPress: the core WordPress installation; The Loop that handles WordPress's main content display logic; post types, which provide for extended flexibility in displaying different types of content; plugins, which add entirely new functionality at the drop of a hat; and themes, which determine how the site will look. While each of these elements are essential in creating the ability to add, manipulate, and display information differently, it is the ability to organize our content into intuitive, searchable groupings that ultimately makes WordPress a useful tool. To this end, WordPress employs **taxonomies**, which are defined as methods of grouping similar individual instances of content together in meaningful ways.

Before we dig deep into taxonomies as they are applied in WordPress, let's have a look at an example of how taxonomies are used in the real world. When you walk into any library, you know that there are thousands of publications to choose from. Most of those publications are books, but some are magazines, periodicals, compact discs, DVDs, or—if the library is really old-school—microfiche. While we know that these forms of media are usually kept in different places, imagine how confusing it would be if that was the only form of organization our library gave us! After all, could you imagine throwing an outdoor party and being forced to rifle through thousands of books trying to find the right one on barbecuing sausages? Instead, we have whole sections devoted to specific topics, including one on cooking, and then within it a subsection on barbecuing, and within that a subsection on barbecuing sausages. All the organization and suborganization that you find in any library is an excellent example of taxonomy at work in the real, physical world … and with the help of a real-life librarian or the Dewey Decimal System (google it, kids) you even have a built-in search function.

Now that we've covered a good example of what a taxonomy might look like in real life, let's dig into taxonomies as they are applied in WordPress.

Categories, Tags, and Custom Taxonomies

In WordPress, taxonomies are used to add a relational dimension to how you group elements together. Categories and tags are both used to group posts together, and indeed define the taxonomy for any given post once assigned. Core WordPress includes three taxonomies by default: categories, tags, and link categories. Each time you create a new category, tag, or link category, you are creating a term of that taxonomy. For instance, a category called **Neighborhoods** would be a term of the category taxonomy, while a tag named **Fiji** would be a term of the tag taxonomy.

While we've already talked about categories and tags at length in Chapter 2, what's important to recognize is that categories are hierarchical in nature. Individual categories can have subcategories, and then those subcategories can have their own subcategories, and so forth. Tags, on the other hand, are not hierarchical but merely labels that you apply to any given post, regardless of which category the post is nested in. In this way, you can think of categories as buckets that are used to group posts together, whereas tags provide a much looser relationship between posts.

 Link Categories

Link categories—the third taxonomy type that WordPress includes—are not necessarily a deprecated topic in WordPress, but are not particularly relevant for our discussion on taxonomies. What's more important is to recognize that they are officially a separate taxonomy type that happen to be included with core which you might see referenced in documentation from time to time. For more information on link categories, have a look in the Codex.[1]

Understanding the relationship between categories and tags in the context of taxonomy is central to developing a solid information structure for your website's content. The more thoroughly you plan how your WordPress site should function from the standpoint of content and information structure, the more successful your site will ultimately be.

A Word on Information Hierarchy

One of the most common mistakes made by both beginners and seasoned web developers alike when building a new website, WordPress or otherwise, is the lack of foresight to plan out the site's information structure and hierarchy. Especially when you are starting out, there's the romantic notion of sitting on a barstool somewhere, having a bright idea for a site, and then sketching ideas on a napkin for the next million-dollar online business model. Undoubtedly, this happens from time to time, but it's the exception to the rule. Ultimately, many of us become far too caught up in

---

[1] http://codex.wordpress.org/Taxonomies#Link_Category

the graphic design of a site, and then wonder why we end up with a watered-down product that fails to work as we intended.

Most effective websites are planned from an information hierarchy perspective, rather than from a design perspective. For our purposes, we'll define **information hierarchy** (or information structure) as the overall planned organization of the content on a given website. An effective information hierarchy takes various factors into account and puts them together to form a cohesive structure. These factors include the actual site content topics and how content should be presented. Will you be using pages and subpages for some types of content, or will it be posts added to categories and subcategories? What types of content should be searchable? Should some content be searchable on its own, without search entries from posts or pages elsewhere on the website? All these variables combine to create the information hierarchy of a given website.

When you begin putting together a site (or working with a client to put together their site), it's perfectly fine to ask questions about what the site should look like. However, it's far more important to ask what the site should do. What information is going to be on the site? How should users be able to interact with that information? Should the information be clustered together in one area of the site, or do we need more structure? Understand that there are no right or wrong answers to these questions, but it's important you ask them and seek genuine responses.

What you should attempt to end up with is a **content wireframe** for your website. Unlike layout wireframes, which show the overall design layout of a web page's basic components prior to it being fleshed out by a graphic designer, a content wireframe offers a comprehensive plan for your site's information hierarchy. We'll show you some examples of developed content wireframes in just a bit, but for now consider your responses to these basic considerations carefully. Take your time and be specific with your responses, and remember that regardless of how awesome WordPress or any other web development tool you happen to be using is, it's ultimately up to you to build your website intelligently.

Why Custom Taxonomies?

Part of your plan for the information hierarchy for your website is sorting out which content will be filtered into categories and posts, and which will be set up as pages. Organizationally, you'll also seek to figure out what you can label and cross-reference as tags. In truth, you can do a lot with WordPress pages, posts, categories, and custom post types, but using custom taxonomies is a fairly easy technique that provides more flexibility in how you organize your content. Using custom taxonomies is also more professional, as it provides the type of polish that clients tend to recognize and respect.

Throughout this chapter, we'll use a common example to highlight how to use custom taxonomies, and why they might be useful. We'll put together a WordPress site for a real estate company named Rutherford Real Estate, which wants to display properties organized by neighborhoods in several regions. Furthermore, Rutherford Real Estate has many sales agents working for it, all of whom

represent multiple properties in any given region or neighborhood. If Rutherford Real Estate sells property in three regions—each of which have several neighborhoods—and agents can sell properties in any region or neighborhood they choose, let's have a look at what a visual representation of the business might look like, in Figure 7.1.

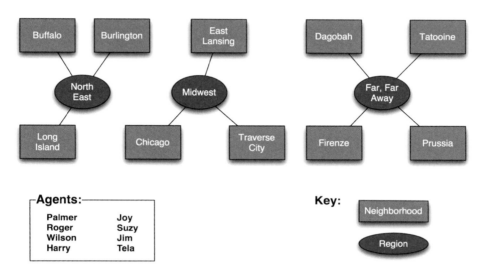

Figure 7.1. Regions and neighborhoods for Rutherford Real Estate

It's plain to see we're dealing with two types of information: hierarchical and nonhierarchical, with neighborhoods being hierarchical subsets of regions, and sales agents acting as free radicals that can attach to whatever they please. In WordPress terms, this means that we should be able to safely use categories for regions and neighborhoods, and tags for the agents. Now let's reframe our chart into a content wireframe that explains the information hierarchy for this business model in our website, in Figure 7.2.

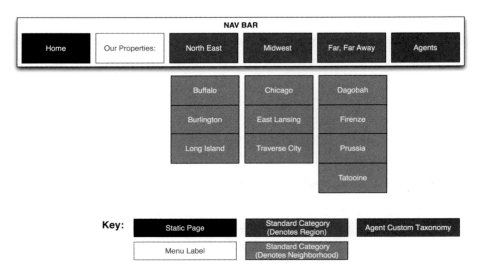

Figure 7.2. Content wireframe with category tags

That's more like it. Our taxonomy is starting to take shape. We've established that our three regions will be set up as categories, each having several related subcategories to handle the respective neighborhoods. Subsequently, individual posts will be used to handle individual properties, giving us a nice way to categorize our property listings for Rutherford Real Estate. We've also established that we'll be using tags to handle sales agents, as individual agents can sell properties in different regions, and there may be instances when several agents team up to represent one property in particular. Functionally, this should work well, and many developers will choose to simply stop here and proceed with development. However, with a bit of further planning, you'll be able to further customize WordPress functionality for Rutherford Real Estate. In the absence of this, a common default permalinking taxonomy that may be configured for Rutherford Real Estate might look like this:

```
/%category%/%postname%/
```

If we configured the site as described previously, this might render a permalink for a property titled "Farmhouse" in Traverse City to look like this:

http://www.esquandoloas.com/category/midwest/traverse-city/farmhouse

That's not bad. It certainly includes the category and post slugs that describe what the content is all about (a farmhouse in Traverse City that's located in the Midwest), but we could do even better from an SEO perspective. Custom taxonomies allow us to create a separate hierarchical structure with a more descriptive permalink that increases the relevance for search engines like Google, producing higher rankings. Consider a situation where we set up a custom taxonomy for our properties that could create a permalink that looked like this:

http://www.esquandoloas.com/properties-for-sale/midwest/traverse-city/farmhouse

This is semantically a much better permalink, as it instantly establishes to both search engines and real users that the content on this link is a property that's for sale, located in the Midwest (Traverse City, to be exact), and a farmhouse. Furthermore, if we set this up as a custom taxonomy, we create a whole new taxonomy to work with, leaving our original category taxonomy untouched and intact, which can be used for other purposes on the website—say blogging about news and events that support Rutherford Real Estate's sales efforts. By adding a custom taxonomy to handle properties, the new content wireframe might look like Figure 7.3.

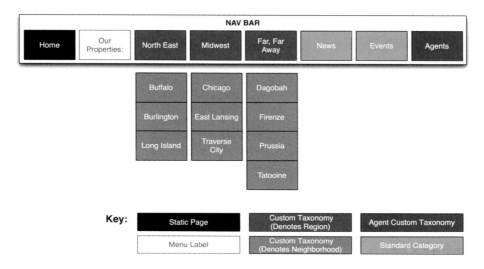

Figure 7.3. Our full content wireframe

Now we're cooking with gas. We have our custom taxonomy set up to work in a hierarchical manner, and we've also created a place to use our normal categories and tags for marketing purposes. In addition, we fully expect to set up our permalink taxonomies to reflect two different structures.

For our properties, we'll have permalinks that look like:
http://www.esquandoloas.com/properties-for-sale/midwest/traverse-city/farmhouse, while for our news and events, we'll have taxonomies that look like:
http://www.esquandoloas.com/category/events/marcos-crazy-estate-blowout-sale. Aren't we fancy?

There are two other really cool aspects of custom taxonomies: extensible functionality requirements and custom searching. Custom searching is fairly straightforward. Using custom taxonomies allows us to delineate content so we can create custom searching restrictions. Therefore, if we want to search the website and only return properties, we can restrict the parameters of the search to only pull from that taxonomy type (more on that in a bit). And when we consider custom taxonomies as a tool we can plug in at any time, we realize that we can extend WordPress in almost any direction we want, even if the site we're looking to extend is already in place and filled to the brim with existing content. We need do nothing more than establish the new type of content that we want to log within the site, create our taxonomies, and begin to use them.

Creating Custom Taxonomies

Now that we've discussed what custom taxonomies are and why we'd want to use them, let's go to the real heart of the matter: creating them and using them to our advantage.

Registering a New Taxonomy

Creating new taxonomies in WordPress is a relatively simple process, and WordPress provides us with a function that accomplishes the job: `register_taxonomy()`. You should always use the *init* action hook when calling `register_taxonomy()`, or else you will incur fatal errors, and nobody likes anything that includes the word "fatal", do they?

`register_taxonomy()` takes one required parameter and two optional but extremely useful parameters:

```
register_taxonomy( $taxonomy, $object_type, $args );
```

The *$taxonomy* parameter is required; it is simply the name of the taxonomy being used, and must exclude capital letters and spaces. It's extremely important to ensure that the name of the taxonomy is unique so that it avoids conflicts with plugins. Drawing from our Rutherford Real Estate example, when naming the taxonomy for sales agents, we'd be better served using "Rutherford-sales-agents" instead of "agents."

The *$object_type* parameter must be defined as either a predefined object that is built into core WordPress, or the slug name of a given custom post type that has already been created in the installation. The parameter is technically optional, but leaving it out (or explicitly setting it to *null*) will register the taxonomy without associating it with any objects. Therefore, the taxonomy will be unavailable for administration within the WordPress back end, and you'll have to manually register it using the *taxonomy* parameter (passed through *$args*) when registering a custom post type with `register_post_type()` or `register_taxonomy_for_object_type()`.

WordPress built-in post types that can be passed in as a valid value for the $object_type parameter are as follows:

- *post*
- *page*
- *mediapage*
- *attachment*
- *revision*
- *nav_menu_item*

The most commonly used of these built-in post types with custom taxonomies are *post* or *page*.

The $args$ parameter is an associative array of arguments that define and describe the taxonomy. While it is technically an optional parameter, the functions and switches that are managed within this array are essential for shaping taxonomies and making them do what you want. In fact, it's such an important aspect of understanding and managing taxonomies that we should delve deeper into this array.

The $args Array

The $args$ array (or arguments array, as we'll refer to it here) takes up to 12 different arguments, one of which is not recommended for use by core developers (the _builtin_ argument—see the Codex[2], which states it's just for documentation purposes). Each argument is optional, and individually handles important functionality switches for taxonomy registration, which can be useful for a variety of reasons. Let's look at them in detail.

label

This is a plural descriptive name for the taxonomy marked for translation that is overridden by $labels->name by default.

labels

This is an associative nested array of labels that define the text used within the taxonomy in and of itself. This nested array is important so we'll refer to it as the nested labels array argument, and cover this in more detail in the section of the same name.

public

This is a Boolean that describes whether or not the taxonomy should be exposed within the WordPress administrative back end; set to true by default.

show_in_nav_menus

This is a Boolean that describes whether or not the taxonomy should be made available for selection in the navigation menus in the WordPress administrative back end. It defaults to the value set in the _public_ argument.

show_ui

This is a Boolean that describes whether or not to display a user interface to manage different aspects of the taxonomy in the WordPress administrative back end. It defaults to the value set in the _public_ argument.

show_tagcloud

This is a Boolean that describes whether or not to allow the Tag Cloud Widget (which ships with core WordPress) to use information set within the taxonomy. It defaults to the value set in the _show_ui_ argument.

---

[2] http://codex.wordpress.org/Function_Reference/register_taxonomy

hierarchical

> This is a Boolean that describes whether or not the taxonomy will be hierarchical, and defaults to false. It's a principal argument, as it is the master switch that defines whether a custom taxonomy should work like a category or like a tag.

update_count_callback

> This is a function name that's used to update the count of the associated $object_type when it is updated.

query_var

> This defaults to the *$taxonomy* parameter value, and can be used to take either a string (as per the *$taxonomy* value) or a Boolean, which will often be *false* to prevent any queries. It's referenced in the next argument, *rewrite*.

rewrite

> Relatively advanced, this parameter can be passed either a Boolean or an array. It defaults to *true*, but you can pass a *false* value to prevent rewriting per the **mod_rewrite** module in Apache. If you pass the argument an array, these values can be passed:
>
> - *slug*: prepends posts with a custom slug, defaulting to the taxonomy's name
>
> - *with_front*: a Boolean that allows permalinks to be prepended, defaulting to *true*
>
> - *hierarchical*: a Boolean that allows hierarchical URLS

capabilities

> This array allows for user-group control by providing the ability to describe the exact capabilities that have access to use functions of the taxonomy. It is useful in determining who can use the taxonomy in the WordPress administrative back end. By default, users of roles with the `manage_categories` capability can manage, edit, and delete terms in a taxonomy; users with roles with the `edit_posts` capability can assign terms of a taxonomy to a post.

This sums up the arguments array, but as we noted earlier, we need to discuss the *labels* argument further.

The Nested Labels Array Argument

The array used for the *labels* argument is important for providing the text used throughout the WordPress administrative back end for all your taxonomy terms. These labels can and should be set up to be localized for eventual translation (see Chapter 11 for an explanation of localization). Let's have a look at what's available to be configured:

name   The general name for the post type, which is typically plural and overridden by `post_type_object->label`. When internationalizing this string

in preparation for localization, it's best to use the `gettext` context matching your post type. For more information on context translation with `gettext`, go to the Codex.[3]

`singular_name`	The name of one object of the post type, which defaults to the value of `name`. Using the `gettext` context translation type is useful here as well, and is described in the Codex.
`add_new`	The text used for adding a new term, and the default value is **Add New** for both hierarchical and nonhierarchical content types. This is another instance where it's worth using the `gettext` context translation type (and yes, you can refer to the Codex).
`all_items`	The all items text used in the menu, which defaults to the `name` label.
`add_new_item`	The text used when adding a new item to the taxonomy, which defaults to **Add New Post** or **Add New Page**.
`edit_item`	The edit item text whose default is **Edit Post** or **Edit Page**.
`new_item`	The new item text whose default is **New Post** or **New Page**.
`view_item`	The view item text whose default is **View Post** or **View Page**.
`search_item`	The search item text whose default is **Search Posts** or **Search Pages**.
`not_found`	The not found text whose default is **No Posts Found** or **No Pages Found**.
`not_found_in_trash`	The not found in trash text whose default is **No Posts Found in Trash** or **No Pages Found in Trash**.
`parent_item_colon`	The parent text, which is only used on hierarchical content types. This defaults to **Parent Page** or **Parent Post**.
`menu_name`	The menu name text, which defaults to the value of `name`.

That's all there is to `register_taxonomy()`, which frankly is an awful lot. Yet `register_taxonomy()` is really just a function that defines a lot about how we want our taxonomy to work. This is best understood by looking at a real-life example, so let's revisit Rutherford Real Estate.

Using `register_taxonomy()`

We've already set up the content wireframes for Rutherford Real Estate that define their information hierarchies. As you may recall, we want to create a new taxonomy to handle locations (regions and

---

[3] http://codex.wordpress.org/I18n_for_WordPress_Developers#Disambiguation_by_context

neighborhoods), as well as a separate taxonomy to handle sales agents who represent the properties in different regions. The locations taxonomy needs to be hierarchical, as specific neighborhoods (Chicago, East Lansing, and Traverse City) are subsets of the regions they are situated in (Midwest). Conversely, a sales agent named Palmer may represent a property in several neighborhoods, and in more than one region, so there is no hierarchical relationship with sales agents. The taxonomy that handles sales agents should therefore be loose in structure and act similarly to tags. Let's see what our code should look like to register our new taxonomies:

chapter_07/register-taxonomy.php

```php
<?php
//hook into the init action and call create_property_taxonomies
add_action( 'init', 'create_property_taxonomies', 0 );

//create two taxonomies, locations and sales agents
function create_property_taxonomies()
{
  // Add new taxonomy locations, make it hierarchical (like categories)
  $labels = array(
    'name' => _x( 'Locations', 'taxonomy general name' ),
    'singular_name' => _x( 'Location', 'taxonomy singular name' ),
    'search_items' =>  __( 'Search Locations' ),
    'all_items' => __( 'All Locations' ),
    'parent_item' => __( 'Parent Location' ),
    'parent_item_colon' => __( 'Parent Location:' ),
    'edit_item' => __( 'Edit Location' ),
    'update_item' => __( 'Update Location' ),
    'add_new_item' => __( 'Add New Location' ),
    'new_item_name' => __( 'New Location Name' ),
    'menu_name' => __( 'Locations' ),
  );

  register_taxonomy('location', post, array(
    'hierarchical' => true,
    'labels' => $labels,
    'show_ui' => true,
    'query_var' => true,
    'rewrite' => array( 'slug' => 'location' ),
  ));

  // Add new taxonomy for sales agents, NOT hierarchical (like tags)
  $labels = array(
    'name' => _x( 'Sales Agents', 'taxonomy general name' ),
    'singular_name' => _x( 'Sales Agent', 'taxonomy singular name' ),
    'search_items' =>  __( 'Search Sales Agents' ),
    'popular_items' => __( 'Prolific Agents' ),
    'all_items' => __( 'All Sales Agents' ),
    'parent_item' => null,
    'parent_item_colon' => null,
```

```
    'edit_item' => __( 'Edit Sales Agent' ),
    'update_item' => __( 'Update Sales Agent' ),
    'add_new_item' => __( 'Add New Sales Agent' ),
    'new_item_name' => __( 'New Sales Agent' ),
    'separate_items_with_commas' => __( 'Separate agents with commas' ),
    'add_or_remove_items' => __( 'Add or remove agents' ),
    'choose_from_most_used' => __( 'Choose from the most prolific sales agents' ),
    'menu_name' => __( 'Sales Agents' ),
  );

  register_taxonomy('agent','post',array(
    'hierarchical' => false,
    'labels' => $labels,
    'show_ui' => true,
    'update_count_callback' => '_update_post_term_count',
    'query_var' => true,
    'rewrite' => array( 'slug' => 'agent' ),
  ));
}
?>
```

This pulls together all that we've just covered on the `register_taxonomy()` function quite nicely—so let's pick it apart. First of all, we're creating a function called `create_property_taxonomies()`, which we're adding with the *init* action hook. Our new function begins by defining a `$labels` variable that consists of the nested labels array we discussed, and establishes all the text for the location taxonomy we'll define in our first `register_taxonomy()` function call. Notice that in keeping with standard coding practices throughout this book, we have set up the values in our labels array to be localized if required. Additionally, in the `register_taxonomy()` function we've defined the hierarchical parameter to be true, ensuring that locations will work similarly to categories.

Immediately after our first `register_taxonomy()` function call, we have reset the information in the `$labels` variable by adding a new array similar to the first, this time inserting the internationalized text variables that focus on the sales agents. We use the previous technique in pulling this array into the `register_taxonomy()` function that defines sales agents; however, notice that this time our hierarchical parameter is set to false, allowing the agents to operate as tags. We've also added the option *update_count_callback* with a string value of *_update_post_term_count* to our `register_taxonomy()` function. This ensures that the taxonomy behaves like a tag, and in instances where you add multiple items to the taxonomy separated by commas, the items are saved as separated values as intended, rather than one long, single item that makes no sense.

 Where Do I Register?

You can register new taxonomies anywhere you like, so long as you call it with the *init* action hook, but it's probably mainly called from a theme's **functions.php** file. While this technically works, seriously consider whether this makes the most sense for your users. If you tie your custom taxonomy

directly to the **functions.php** file in your theme, you essentially tie your clients' hands if they lack the technical awareness or available expertise to port the taxonomy registration into the subsequent **functions.php** file of the new theme. While every website has its own unique situations and circumstances, custom taxonomies should be viewed as a feature of the website's permalinking structure, not a feature of the current theme that is active on the site. Therefore, taxonomy registrations should be housed in a must-use plugin, ensuring that they stay with the website itself, regardless of whether or not the theme is swapped out at a later date.

Notice that in the screenshots and the previous code example, we're associating our new taxonomies with generic posts. In many instances (especially a real estate property), you may be looking to associate the taxonomy with a custom post type instead of a generic content type. In this case, you'd actually want to call the name of the custom post type or an array of instances of that post type in a hierarchical situation, as seen in this code chunk:

chapter_07/register-taxonomy-custom-post-type.php

```php
<?php

// Associating the $object_type with an array of instances of custom post type
  register_taxonomy('location',array('property'), array(
    'hierarchical' => true,
    'labels' => $labels,
    'show_ui' => true,
    'query_var' => true,
    'rewrite' => array( 'slug' => 'location' ),
  ));

// Associating the $object_type with a single instance of a custom post type
  register_taxonomy('agent','property',array(
    'hierarchical' => false,
    'labels' => $labels,
    'show_ui' => true,
    'update_count_callback' => '_update_post_term_count',
    'query_var' => true,
    'rewrite' => array( 'slug' => 'agent' ),
  ));
```

Regardless of how you set up your taxonomy, you'll see it in your WordPress administrative back end once it's registered, and thus have the ability to begin managing content therein. For Rutherford Real Estate, we have chosen to just associate our taxonomies with regular old posts. As a result, you can find our two new taxonomy types on the **Posts** submenu panel, as shown in Figure 7.4.

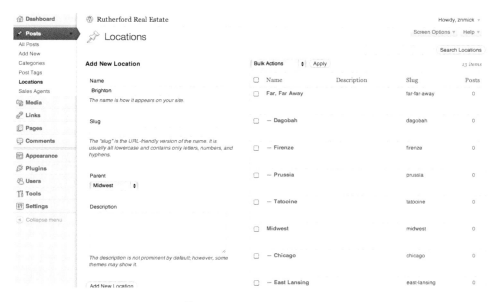

Figure 7.4. **Locations** taxonomy

Notice that the locations taxonomy management page looks identical to the categories management page; were we to have a look at the sales agents taxonomy page, we'd see an interface that likewise mimics that tag management page. Furthermore, since we've associated our new taxonomies with posts, when we go to add a new post or edit an existing post, we'll now see the appropriate meta boxes in the right-hand column, as seen in Figure 7.5.

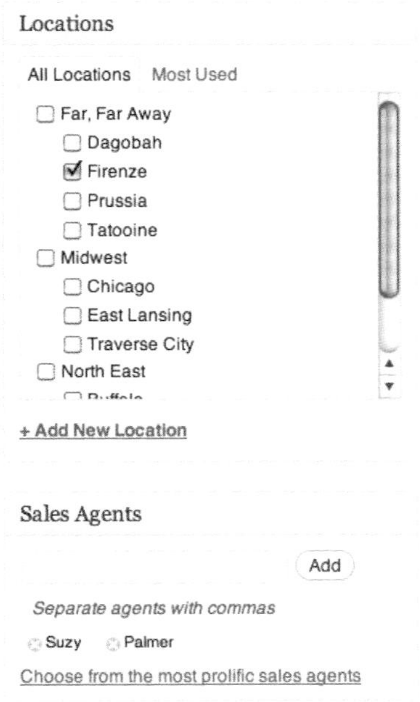

Locations

All Locations   Most Used

- ☐ Far, Far Away
  - ☐ Dagobah
  - ☑ Firenze
  - ☐ Prussia
  - ☐ Tatooine
- ☐ Midwest
  - ☐ Chicago
  - ☐ East Lansing
  - ☐ Traverse City
- ☐ North East
  - ☐ Buffalo

+ Add New Location

Sales Agents

Add

Separate agents with commas

Suzy   Palmer

Choose from the most prolific sales agents

Figure 7.5. **Locations** and **Sales Agents** meta boxes

We can use these meta boxes to mark our property's neighborhood—as well as the sales agents representing it—in the same way we utilize categories and tags. Overall, it's intuitive, easy-to-use stuff!

Using Our Custom Taxonomies

Once our custom taxonomies have been set up for Rutherford Real Estate and we've begun to put up properties on the site, we'll want to actually use the data and make it available for public consumption. There are several ways to integrate the data on your website, and it's all about creatively using the functions and techniques that WordPress provides you. Let's have a look at some of these methods now as we'd apply them to Rutherford Real Estate.

Take a look back at Figure 7.3 and that final wireframe we ended up with. When we begin coding our theme for Rutherford Real Estate, we'll set the menu up to manage **Home** as a standard static page, and both **News** and **Events** as standard categories that can be routinely linked to with standard nomenclature. Our three regions and their subsequent categories (as well as our **Agents** taxonomy), however, can be managed in several ways, and you're probably going to need some modifications to The Loop in order to make the magic happen. Technically, you could go into your **index.php** or **archive.php** template file and begin structuring The Loop with some complex conditional logic to get things moving in the right direction, or you could take advantage of WordPress's template hierarchy nomenclature as it applies to custom taxonomies.

Taxonomy Template File Hierarchy and Nomenclature

We've already discussed the notion of WordPress template hierarchies and nomenclature at length in Chapter 6, but WordPress does give us a template hierarchy nomenclature dedicated to custom taxonomies. This is seen in Figure 7.6.

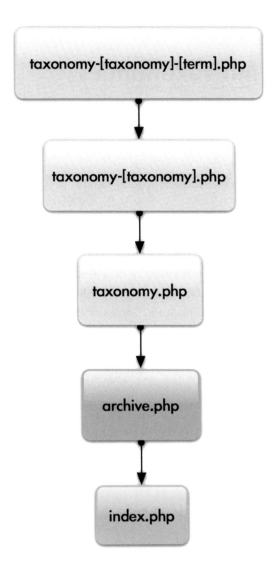

Figure 7.6. Custom taxonomy template hierarchy structure

Using this template hierarchy system automatically tells WordPress which visual blueprint should be used for any given taxonomy. This automatically simplifies the process of deciding which functional display logic we'll use for each of our taxonomy types by removing the conditional logic for us. At this point, the taxonomy nomenclature should be fairly straightforward, but let's review it briefly, just to be sure.

The most specific taxonomy template file is the top one, which in our example might look like **taxonomy-location-firenze.php**. If this file was created and populated, it would be the default file that WordPress would utilize when displaying information for the "Firenze" neighborhood. However,

if we were comfortable with all the neighborhoods and regions having display logic that worked in exactly the same way, we could add that display logic to the **taxonomy-location.php** file. Similarly, if we wanted our display logic for neighborhoods and agents to act the same way, we'd be fine using a file named **taxonomy.php**. From there, the nomenclature defaults into the general system, with **archive.php** and then **index.php** being the final defaults in that order. It's easy to see how this can allow you to customize the appearance of WordPress in conjunction with taxonomies (especially if you choose to work with custom post types as well), but exactly what type of functions are available in the context of these template files? We're glad you asked …

Customizing Output with Functions That Must Be Called in The Loop

Yes, we're back to the *meat* of WordPress again; after all, who doesn't love The Loop? We know that The Loop is the beating heart of WordPress, and in order to customize the display output and functionality it's often necessary to roll your sleeves up and plunge into the template files that manage logic in The Loop. With respect to custom taxonomies, there are several functions you can utilize to change the way The Loop pulls in post information.

query_posts()

Back in Chapter 3, we mentioned that you can use wp_query() to handle just about any queries you want within The Loop, but if you really want to customize your queries and pull from just a subset of all posts, in some instances you may need to use query_posts() instead. This is one of those instances. Let's say you would like to display a post for a specific taxonomy term. In our example, this may be a situation where you wanted to display all the properties that are being listed by our sales agent named Tela. In this instance, you could create a template called **taxonomy-agent-tela.php** and use the function call `<?php query_posts( array( 'agent' => 'tela' ) ); ?>` to list all properties that are currently being represented by Tela. You can actually pass in an array of parameters to define this as specifically as you'd like. For more information as to the parameters that are available to be passed into the query_posts() function, look in the Codex.[4] For more information on query_posts(), see this Codex page.[5]

get_the_term_list()

get_the_term_list() needs to be echoed in order to print to the screen, and returns an HTML string of the terms associated with a given taxonomy. For instance, in a situation where we might want to list all the individual properties located in our East Lansing neighborhood, using the function call `<?php echo get_the_term_list( $post->ID, 'east-lansing', 'Properties in East Lansing:', ' ', '' ); ?>` would generate a listing of all the properties we're looking for. For more information on using get_the_term_list(), see the relevant page in the Codex.[6]

---

[4] http://codex.wordpress.org/Class_Reference/WP_Query#Parameters
[5] http://codex.wordpress.org/Function_Reference/query_posts
[6] http://codex.wordpress.org/Function_Reference/get_the_term_list

`get_terms()`

In a situation where you need to retrieve an array of your custom taxonomy values to manipulate them in other ways, you can use the `get_terms()` function. In this way, `get_terms()` is very much a utility function with a wide variety of potential programmable uses. For more details and ideas on using this function, check out the Codex.[7]

Customizing Taxonomy Output outside of The Loop

The most useful and common way to customize the display of your taxonomy output outside of The Loop is through the use of the `wp_tag_cloud()` function. This core function creates a Tag Cloud, and one of the parameters it will take is a *taxonomy* parameter. Therefore, if we decided that we wanted to create a Tag Cloud which listed all our agents and then insert that tag cloud into our sidebar, we could place the function call `<? wp_tag_cloud( array( 'taxonomy' => 'agents' ) ); ?>` into the appropriate location, either in a widget or within the code for our sidebar display.

As you can see, custom taxonomies are useful features that are hidden in the depths of core Word-Press, and using them to your advantage can really provide the polish that makes your work superior to your competitors. It's not that hard to use custom taxonomies; it's more a case of understanding how to register them and then utilize the template hierarchy and a few loop functions to make all the pieces come together nicely.

Everything in Its Place

WordPress employs taxonomies to manage content loaded inside it. Taxonomies are methods of grouping similar individual instances of content together in meaningful ways. By default, WordPress comes with three types of taxonomies: categories, tags, and link categories. Categories are hierarchical by nature, while tags can be applied to any given piece of content, regardless of where it sits in the content structure, as a label to provide a relational categorization element to the content.

WordPress also gives you the ability to create custom taxonomies, and there are several reasons you might set them up, namely to:

- better organize the content on your website
- increase the search engine optimization of the permalinks throughout your website
- give the website a more professional, polished look and feel
- segment content so that it can be easily queried on its own
- institute entirely new functional requirements that a client may have for the website

---

[7] http://codex.wordpress.org/Function_Reference/get_terms

We illustrated custom taxonomies by looking at a practical example of setting up a taxonomy that could be used in managing properties for a fictional real estate company. We started out by explaining the process of creating a content wireframe to outline an intuitive information hierarchy for content in the site. We then implemented the ideas in that wireframe by registering what we felt was an intelligent taxonomy design in a must-use plugin. Afterwards, we discussed creating specialized page templates that took advantage of the WordPress template hierarchy structure and nomenclature to simplify our conditional logic. We then introduced The Loop functions that could be used to manipulate your new taxonomy data. Like anything else, taxonomies are easy to work with when you know how!

Image Galleries and Featured Images

Working with images draws many first-time users to content management systems. After all, everybody wants to be able to change text on their posts and pages, so users just learning what content management is all about are keen to know how they can work with images on their website. To this end, just about every modern content management system has some sort of mechanism in place to address images and image galleries, and WordPress is no exception. Let's have a look at some of the more advanced image manipulation tools that WordPress makes available to us.

Revisiting the Media Library and Media Settings

To briefly review what we discussed about images in WordPress in Chapter 2, users are able to upload images to WordPress in various locations. In the WordPress administrative back end, you can navigate to the **Media** subpanel and add new images by clicking on **Media** > **Add New**, or by editing a new or existing post or page and adding an image directly from the content editor. Either way, the image is uploaded into WordPress's media management area, known as the **Media Library**. The Media Library therefore provides you direct access to view and manage all images, audio files, videos, and additional media file types that have been uploaded directly to your WordPress installation. If you need to view or modify the metadata for any image that has been loaded to the site, you can do so in the Media Library.

Once an image has been uploaded into WordPress and thus the Media Library, it can then be inserted either into a post or page with specific formatting and sizing parameters. The formatting parameters are fairly straightforward—you can align images left or right, or center them, and you can also provide different values for vertical and horizontal spacing—but one element that even seasoned

professionals can miss is that WordPress allows you to insert a large, medium, or thumbnail version of the image. What's notable about this is that WordPress isn't just offering to apply an inline HTML or CSS style to your image to make it display in a particular dimension; it's actually a modified version of the image that has been scaled down by WordPress's image processing features. Let's explore image processing a bit deeper.

Configuring Image Processing in Media Settings

If you have been a web developer for more than five years, you have probably run into the situation more than once where clients wanted to upload images straight from their digital camera to their website, and such images were routinely way too large. Teaching clients to use image-resizing software is a task in itself that none of us necessarily signed up for, so ultimately it's preferable for the problem to be solved by the CMS you're using. Like many other content management systems, WordPress fixes this problem by actually processing the image upon its initial upload to the Media Library. What happens is that when an image is uploaded, WordPress assesses its dimensions and matches it against the sizing parameters that have been defined in the **Media Settings** subpanel, located at **Settings** > **Media Settings** and seen in Figure 8.1.

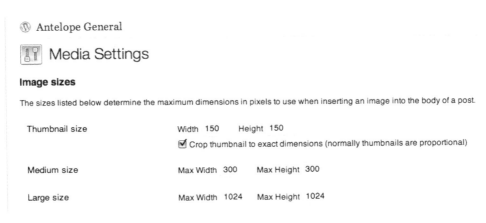

Figure 8.1. Setting image sizes

There are three different sizing parameters that you can set, and they are defined as follows:

Thumbnail size
> The thumbnail is a cropped version of the original image, and you can set it to be cropped to specific sizes. By their very nature, thumbnails are not necessarily meant to include the entire image, but rather a portion of it that represents the image as a whole. Thumbnails are often clickable, and WordPress's gallery shortcode (which we'll discuss in a bit) uses thumbnails by default to build image galleries.

Medium size

A medium-size image is the full image that has been downsized to meet a uniform image size. WordPress will take the larger of the image's width or height and scale the image proportionally to the medium image setting's **Max Width** or **Max Height**.

Large size

This is identical to the medium-size image, with the predictable exception that the **Max Width** and **Max Height** dimensions are larger but still designed to fit within the context of the website design.

WordPress then creates the appropriate new, smaller images that relate to the originating image. In instances where the original image being uploaded is smaller than one of the medium or large image sizes defined, that particular large or medium sizing is simply not created. For example, let's say you are uploading an image named **anna.jpg** with dimensions of 1,000 pixels by 1,500 pixels. In this instance, and assuming we used the settings in the screenshot, WordPress would ultimately store four versions of the image for eventual use on the site:

- **anna.jpg** (original)
- **anna-150x150.jpg** (thumbnail size)
- **anna-200x300.jpg** (medium size)
- **anna-682x1024.jpg** (large size)

However, were we to upload a different image named **readicculus.jpg** whose original dimensions were 376 pixels by 126 pixels, only three versions of the image would be stored for eventual use:

- **readicculus.jpg** (original)
- **readicculus-150x126.jpg** (thumbnail size)
- **readicculus-300x100.jpg** (medium size)

In this instance, there's no need to have a large image created, as the large size dimensions are inherently bigger than the original image. Note also that because the original image's height of 126 pixels is smaller than the default thumbnail height of 150 pixels, the thumbnail height size just defaults to 126 pixels. WordPress makes no attempt to add additional pixels in order to make an image fit.

Finally, it's important to reiterate that *WordPress only runs image processing upon the initial upload of the image.* This means that if you have a bunch of images loaded out to the Media Library and decide to change the dimensions of your thumbnails (perhaps to facilitate a theme change), the thumbnails won't be automatically reprocessed to match your new settings. To do this, you'll either need to re-upload your images with the new settings applied (which is an unattractive option), or you can use a plugin to assist you in regenerating your specifically sized images. There are plenty

of plugins available within the WordPress Plugin Directory that do this for you, but one that's worth looking at in particular is AJAX Thumbnail Rebuild.[1]

AJAX Thumbnail Rebuild is a handy utility because it will let you rebuild all the set size images (thumbnails, medium-size, and large-size) on your site at the same time in a resource-efficient way. Many thumbnail rebuilding plugins will run off a single script that tells the server to resize the images all at once, and in situations where you have a lot of images to resize, the script may time out on some servers. For this reason, AJAX Thumbnail Rebuild is useful as it fires the script individually for each photo, thus keeping the script execution time to a minimum.

The [gallery] Shortcode

For all the cool functionality that can be built into shortcodes (see Chapter 5 or Chapter 9), it's mildly surprising that WordPress core developers fail to make more use of them to introduce enhanced functionality within the system. That said, core WordPress comes preloaded with exactly one shortcode: [gallery]. The gallery shortcode is often overlooked by developers because, quite frankly, many of us are yet to realize it's there and available to use. There is a multitude of popular image gallery plugins out there and in heavy use, but the gallery shortcode institutes some really cool functionality right out of the box, and is a hidden gem in the WordPress toolkit.

As is implied by its name, the gallery shortcode can be used to insert a photo gallery directly into a post or a page where the [gallery] tag is added in the content editor. The shortcode itself fires a core WordPress PHP script that constructs the gallery for you, and pulls all the images that are either embedded within the post or page, or are otherwise attached to the post or page. This is an important distinction, as it is entirely possible to "attach" images to a particular post or page without actually embedding them directly in the content. In order to do this, go to the **Media Library**, click open the **Screen Options** at the top of the screen, and make sure to check the **Attached to** checkbox, as seen in Figure 8.2.

---

[1] http://wordpress.org/extend/plugins/ajax-thumbnail-rebuild/

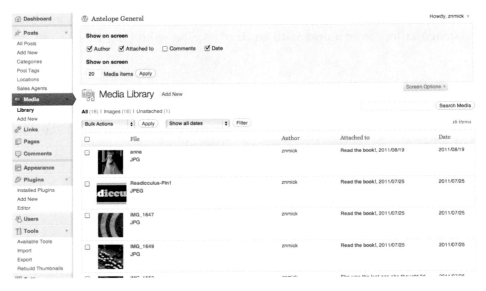

Figure 8.2. Attaching images

This will show you what page or post any given image is attached to for the purpose of your image galleries, and will let you select a page/post if the image is unattached. Using the Media Library in this instance is an easy way to manage which images are located within which image galleries on any given post or page.

Common Uses of [gallery]

Simply inserting the [gallery] shortcode into a page or post will automatically grab all the images attached to that page/post and create an image gallery, which is formatted into three rows using the thumbnail as the clickable link to view a larger version of the image. You can control these default gallery characteristics by passing the shortcode options, which is done similarly to passing parameters to a PHP function. The syntax of any shortcode (and thus the [gallery] shortcode) is the following:

```
[gallery option1="parameter1" option2="parameter2" option3="parameter3"]
```

Therefore, you can control the gallery's appearance and output by working with the several built-in options. Like many functions, several of these are frequently used, while others are for more specialized purposes. Let's have a look at the most popularly used options:

columns

This option determines the number of columns that should be built into the image gallery by triggering the insertion of a break tag at the appropriate location. This option defaults to 3.

id

This specifies the ID of the post, and defaults to the current post ID that the shortcode is inserted into. This is useful if you want to insert the image gallery from a different page or post onto

your current post; for instance, if you were editing a post with an ID of 42, and you wanted to insert the image gallery from a post with an ID of 84, you would use this option.

size

By default, the image that is used for display within the gallery itself is the thumbnail image. However, if you want to use a different image for gallery display, you can choose the size setting with this option. Values for this option are limited to *thumbnail* (which is the default), *medium*, *large*, and *full*.

Pulling all this together, let's say we were looking to insert a two-column image gallery for all the images in post 197, and we wanted to use the medium-sized images for the gallery thumbnails. In this instance, we'd insert a shortcode that looks like this:

```
[gallery columns="2" id="197" size="medium"]
```

Piece of cake, right? You'll rarely need to use any other options with the [gallery] shortcode, but there are a few more tricks you can do with it. Let's look at some of its more advanced uses.

The Psychology Behind ID

Wondering what we mean when we're talking about ID? If you're unsure, don't sweat it … it's not insanely intuitive. In WordPress, every post, page, and piece of media is given a unique ID that identifies it from everything else inside WordPress. IDs start with the number 1, and increase sequentially. You can find out what a given page or post ID is when you're in the WordPress back end by rolling your cursor over the link to edit the post and looking at the trailing numerical value, or by actually clicking to edit a post and looking for the value in the same location. Alternately, if for some reason you don't have pretty permalinks enabled, the ID will be the number listed in the link of your post or page. Likewise, when you go to the **Media Library** and roll over or click on a given piece of media, you'll be able to find the `attachment_id` the same way.

Specialized Uses of [gallery]

There are eight more options at your disposal to play with when you tinker with the [gallery] shortcode. Let's have a look at them now.

orderby

This option lets you specify the item used to sort the display thumbnails. It defaults to *menu_order*, but also takes *ID* and *RAND* (which means random) as values.

order

This option lets you specify the sort order used to display thumbnails, and takes ASC or DESC (ascending or descending) as values.

itemtag

This is the name of the tag used to enclose each item in the gallery, and it defaults to *dl*.

icontag	This is the tag used to enclose each thumbnail icon in the gallery, defaulting to *dt*.
captiontag	This tag is used to enclose each caption in the gallery, and defaults to *dd*.
link	This option can be set to *file* if you like, which will cause each image to default directly to the image file rather than the attachment's permalink; this will essentially give the attachment its own page on your site.
include	This option is used to provide a list of comma-separated attachment IDs, which means that the gallery will explicitly only include the images specified. This option cannot be used in conjunction with the *exclude* option, and its format looks like:

```
[gallery include="42,89,229"]
```

exclude	This option provides a list of comma-separated attachment IDs, but this time the gallery will explicitly *exclude* the images specified. This option cannot be used in conjunction with the *include* option, and the format looks like:

```
[gallery exclude="55,72,111"]
```

Taking all these options into account and looking at how to use them together, let's say that we wanted to change the gallery markup to use <div>, <span>, and <p> tags. We'll specifically exclude several files from our gallery, which we'd like to be five columns wide. In this instance, we'd use the following implementation of the shortcode:

```
[gallery columns="5" itemtag="div" icontag="span" captiontag="p" exclude="4,12,19"]
```

For the most part, this is all fairly intuitive stuff once you realize that the [gallery] shortcode is around and available to be worked with at all. However, what's also kind of cool is that WordPress has a built-in visual editor to manage [gallery] shortcode options.

Working with [gallery] in the Content Editor GUI

After you insert the [gallery] shortcode into the visual content editor and save your post or page, the visual editor will no longer display the shortcode (although you'll still be able to work with it via the HTML view of the content editor). In the visual editor, you'll find a large light blue box that denotes the existence of the gallery. If you roll your cursor over this box, you'll see two buttons show up in the upper left-hand corner of the box in much the same way you see them when looking to edit an existing image. The box on the right can be used to delete the gallery, but clicking on the box to the left will bring up a lightbox with options for working with and managing the gallery. The screenshot seen in Figure 8.3 shows the images we're using for our sample gallery, and gives us

plenty of options to work with them. We'll now briefly go through the visual options describing what you can do here.

Figure 8.3. Content editor graphical user interface

At the top of the dialog box you'll see a visual representation of all the images in the gallery. Here, you can either numerically change their order by changing the numbers in the boxes on the right, or you can just drag and drop them into your preferred order (which is a whole lot easier and a bit more rewarding). You can also click the **Show** button to display and modify the characteristics of any given image. Clicking the **Show** button will also allow you to remove an image from your gallery,

or make it the featured image for your page or post. Furthermore, at the bottom of the dialog box are controls to change what the thumbnails link to, decide how you want to order your images, and govern the number of columns you want the shortcode to create on your behalf. When you finish making your modifications, be sure to save your gallery settings and changes, as well as your page or post to ensure that the gallery changes you've made are actually committed.

Firing the [gallery] Shortcode from a Template

If you are a theme developer and like the idea of the [gallery] shortcode, but would like to harness it with a little more control, you may choose to fire it directly from within the template. A simple way of doing this is to echo the shortcode with the do_shortcode() function directly within a page template inside your theme like this:

```php
<?php echo do_shortcode('[gallery columns="4"]'); ?>
```

Obviously you can use whatever [gallery] shortcode options you'd prefer for your theme. If you want to make the gallery a bit more dynamic, perhaps because you're actually looking to create a series of galleries throughout your theme, you could also use a filter hook to add appropriate galleries with code similar to the following:

chapter_08/dynamic-galleries.php

```php
<?php
  $gallery_shortcode_feature = '[gallery id="' . intval( $post->post_parent ) .➥
    '"]';
  print apply_filters( 'the_content', $gallery_shortcode_feature );
?>
```

Lightboxes

All right, let's be honest: galleries are cool and all, but WordPress's default options of either viewing an image in an attachment page, or viewing it in its raw format on its own … well, they're a bit vanilla. To this end, lightboxes have become a popular solution as a mechanism to scroll through image galleries without leaving the thumbnail area. A **lightbox** is an overlay that darkens everything on a site (usually with some amount of translucency that allows you to still make out the site in the background) and displays an element on top of the site. Usually lightboxes are used to display images, but you can display almost anything with them—videos, opt-in boxes, external HTML pages, whatever you want.

In general, lightboxes are crowd-pleasers. They're easy to implement, and garner a lot of "oohs and aahs" from your clientele, but it's typically a good idea to ensure that you really want to use them. How about a quick pros and cons list?

The pros list is obvious. First and foremost, a lightbox makes it much easier for most of your users to view your galleries. They can click on an image, which instantly pops up in a handy inline screen right in the browser. Well-constructed lightbox scripts also have solid, intuitive, and easy-to-use navigation, which makes it easy for your user to flip through an entire gallery quickly and with style. And of course, let's not forget that last word, style. Simply put, lightboxes are just really sexy, and an easy way to add a bit of bling to any website.

As for the cons, the biggest one is that lightboxes are built in JavaScript. While it's becoming more rare, occasionally you'll find a user who's deactivated JavaScript in the browser for some reason, and the gallery just fails to work in that instance. Of course, you could make the counterargument that users who choose to deactivate JavaScript should be used to such situations, but that's really a different discussion altogether. Furthermore, you may want to consider the user experience of flipping through photo galleries on mobile devices. Where the screen is very small, lightboxes may be a poor choice. However, some scripts have solid deprecation that handle mobile devices well. Overall, you want to be certain that any lightbox script you choose avoids overriding mobile device default image handling.

So if you are sold on the concept of using a lightbox for your galleries at this point, the next question is naturally about how to do it. You have two options here: you can either code a script right into your theme using the `wp_enqueue_script()` function (see Chapter 9 for more information as to its usage), or you can adopt the easier route of just using one of several readily available plugins. Note that if you are a theme developer, you'll probably want to pass on using a plugin and build your script into your theme. However, if you are just setting up a site for a client or for yourself, a plugin is often the easiest and most flexible way to go. There are tons of them available in the WordPress Plugin Directory.

Working with Featured Images

Playing with galleries is lots of fun for end users, but if you are a theme developer and are looking to make use of WordPress's built-in image-handling functions to your advantage, you're probably a lot more interested in working with featured images. The featured image functionality that's built into WordPress allows you to use an image to represent each page or post for use somewhere on the website. Often the image is just displayed in a cropped format next to the post's excerpt, but it could be displayed anywhere, and theme developers find it quite handy.

Enabling Support for Post Thumbnails

The first point you want to realize about featured images is that they are synonymous in the WordPress world with the term **post thumbnail**. Originally introduced in WordPress version 2.9, post thumbnails are now more commonly referred to as featured images. So while we refer to them as featured images, all the WordPress function documentation refers to them as post thumbnails, which is only a little bit confusing.

Post thumbnails are actually a theme feature defined in WordPress, so they need to be activated within the theme to gain access to their full functionality and user interfaces. Hence, the first step is to add theme support for post thumbnails by adding the following code to your **functions.php** file:

chapter_08/add-theme-support.php

```php
<?php

if ( function_exists( 'add_theme_support' ) ) {
  add_theme_support( 'post-thumbnails' );
}

?>
```

As you can see, in this code we've ensured that our theme will remain compatible with WordPress installations older than 2.9 by checking to see if the function `add_theme_support()` exists before we go ahead and initiate it. Afterwards, simply adding the post thumbnail support as we've done here is enough to add the post thumbnail user interface for both page and post content types. If, for whatever reason, you only want to add post thumbnail support for either pages or posts, replace the `add_theme_support()` function with the appropriate selection as listed in this code:

chapter_08/add-theme-support-posts-OR-pages.php

```php
<?php

add_theme_support( 'post-thumbnails', array( 'post' ) );
  // Add support individually for posts
add_theme_support( 'post-thumbnails', array( 'page' ) );
  // Add support individually for pages

?>
```

Once you have your theme supporting post thumbnails, you have a whole set of template tags and other functions available to use in your theme's template files. These include functions and tags such as:

- `has_post_thumbnail()`
- `the_post_thumbnail()`
- `get_the_post_thumbnail()`
- `set_the_post_thumbnail_size()`

We'll talk about some of these functions shortly, but if you'd like to read more about what's available to you as a theme developer in reference to post thumbnails, have a look at the Codex.[2]

---

[2] http://codex.wordpress.org/Post_Thumbnails

Functions Are Fine

Throughout this book, we focus heavily on choosing the correct location to code any functionality into your site. In most situations, we suggest that you should be placing your site's functionality in plugins to keep it independent of the theme, so that the site doesn't break if you change your theme. However, in this particular case all your code can quite comfortably be embedded into your **functions.php** file, as post thumbnail support tends to be much more about display logic than it is about general site logic. There are instances where you can make the case that this isn't so, and that's when it's permissible to embed the functionality in a must-use plugin, but **functions.php** will often work just fine for these purposes.

Sizing Your Post Thumbnails

Once you've enabled post thumbnails in your theme, you'll need to determine what size you want the post thumbnails to be wherever you happen to be using them in your theme. You have two options here: you can either choose to use the default thumbnail size as specified within the **Media Settings** screen in the back end, or you can go your own way and fix the size for your own purposes at that location in your theme. While keeping the size editable in WordPress may seem like a good idea at first, from the perspective of a theme developer, we'd like to keep as much of the theme's functionality as bulletproof as possible. Therefore, it's typically wiser to grab the post thumbnail size right inside the code and work from there. To do this, you'll use the `set_post_thumbnail_size()` function, which takes the following parameters:

```php
<?php set_post_thumbnail_size( $width, $height, $crop ); ?>
```

These parameters are equivalent to:

$width   the post thumbnail width in pixels

$height   the post thumbnail height in pixels

$crop   A Boolean that determines if the image will be cropped. This defaults to *false*, meaning that by default your image won't be cropped, but rather resized proportionately to fit inside the size set in the first two parameters.

What's important to note here is that you essentially have two choices for how you display featured images. If you omit the *$crop* parameter or explicitly set it to *false*, your image will be resized proportionately to fit inside that space. Therefore, if you have a thumbnail size of 150 pixels wide by 150 pixels tall, but your featured image actually has a dimension of 200 pixels wide by 300 pixels tall, your image will be displayed with a width of 100 pixels and a height of 150 pixels. On the positive side, you'll be able to see the whole image, but it may not necessarily look uniform with the rest of your post thumbnails. Your other option here is to set the *$crop* parameter as *true*, which

will simply chop the appropriate amount from the left and right sides, or from the top and bottom of the image, ensuring a uniform look with all featured images on the website.

Adding Different-sized Post Thumbnails

Another handy tool you can use in relation to post thumbnails is to actually add your own custom thumbnail types with their own respective sizing. This can be useful in slightly complex theme designs where you may want to use several sizes of the post thumbnail in different places across the site. For example, you may like to use a large, uncropped featured image for the first two posts in your post listing pages, and then have smaller, cropped post thumbnails for the remaining eight posts on that page. To make this happen, use the add_image_size() function, which takes the following parameters:

```php
<?php add_image_size( $name, $width, $height, $crop ); ?>
```

The parameters are equivalent to:

$name   the new image size name, which can be called as a handle by the_post_thumbnail()

$width   the post thumbnail width in pixels

$height   the post thumbnail height in pixels

$crop   A Boolean that determines if the image will be cropped. This defaults to *false*, meaning that by default your image won't be cropped but rather resized proportionately to fit inside the size set in the first two parameters.

If we wanted to automatically create these custom image sizes for the larger featured image (we'll call it *featured-image* in our function) and our smaller cropped versions (we'll call those *small-crops*), we could use the following code in our **functions.php** file to make it happen:

```
                                                          chapter_08/custom-image-sizes.php
<?php

add_image_size( 'featured-image',  424, 9999 );
  // uncropped featured image fixed to 424 pixels wide with no height restriction
add_image_size( 'small-crops',  150, 100 , true );
  // cropped image fixed to 150 x 100 pixels wide

?>
```

Remember, thumbnail images are only created during the initial image upload, so be sure to take account of that fact. Finally, when we want to use either of our new custom image sizes in our theme, we can call the_post_thumbnail() and pass it the image size handle like this:

```php
<?php the_post_thumbnail( 'featured-image' ); ?>
```

All of which brings us to the fun part: actually implementing our featured images in our themes.

Post Thumbnail Implementation in Themes

Once we have everything prepped and ready to go with our post thumbnails, actually implementing them in our custom themes is a breeze. To do this, we'll make use of two functions: `has_post_thumbnail()` and `the_post_thumbnail()`. Both these functions should be used in your theme's template files within The Loop in order to work correctly.

`has_post_thumbnail()` is a simple Boolean function that's used in a conditional PHP loop, returning a value that describes whether or not a post has a post thumbnail associated with it. If it does, you can use the `the_post_thumbnail()` function to display the thumbnail in that location. Let's look at a simple version of this script in action:

chapter_08/if-post-thumbnail.php

```php
<?php

if(has_post_thumbnail()) {    // Does the post have a thumbnail?
  the_post_thumbnail();    // If a thumbnail exists, display it
} else {
  // Do something else here in place of a post thumbnail
  }

?>
```

This is just a simple `if`/`else` statement that degrades gracefully to whatever action you'd like it to in the event that a post thumbnail is absent. When it's present, using `the_post_thumbnail()` you can either print it out directly to the screen, or you can pass it back to your PHP code to perform a task with it using `get_the_post_thumbnail()`. The functions are very similar, so we'll take a brief look at each one beginning with `the_post_thumbnail()`, which takes the following parameters:

```php
<?php the_post_thumbnail( $size, $attr ); ?>
```

The parameters are defined as:

$size   This is the image size that you want to use in the thumbnail, with acceptable values being *thumbnail*, *medium*, *large*, *full*, or the name of the handle that you create with the `add_image_size()` function. Alternately, you can pass in an array to describe the size you want; for example, `the_post_thumbnail( array( 150, 150 ) )`.

$attr This is an array of attributes most commonly used to assign alignment classes. For more information on available attributes, see the Codex.[3]

By simply adding this function in your conditional logic, you'll be able to print out your post thumbnails where you want them. However, if you need to pass the thumbnail to another PHP script, you'll use the `get_the_post_thumbnail()` function, which takes the following parameters:

```
<?php get_the_post_thumbnail( $id, $size, $attr ); ?>
```

The parameters are defined as:

$id This is the post ID for the post or page of the thumbnail you're looking to retrieve, and is a required value.

$size This is the image size that you want to use in the thumbnail, with valid values being *thumbnail*, *medium*, *large*, *full*, or the name of the handle that you create with the `add_image_size()` function.

$attr This is an array of attributes most commonly used to assign alignment classes. For more information on available attributes, see the Codex.[4]

Note that because you can pass in an *$id* parameter, you can use `get_the_post_thumbnail()` outside The Loop, if you wish. With this type of flexibility available, the creative use of these two functions will allow you to do practically whatever you'd like to do with the featured image functionality in WordPress.

Got the Picture?

There are a lot of opportunities for advanced image manipulation in WordPress, and we covered a substantial amount in this chapter. We started off by revisiting the notion of uploading images to a central **Media Library** in your WordPress installation, and explained why that matters in the context of working with WordPress galleries. We also revisited the **Media Settings** section of the WordPress administrative back end, discussing what the different image sizes are all about, and how (and when) they are used. In addition, we noted that while WordPress does process images to create the image sizes that are defined within the **Media Settings** area, this image processing is only done upon the initial upload of the image. If you want to resize images that have already been uploaded to the Media Library, you'll need to make use of one of any number of available plugins found in the WordPress Plugin Directory.

After that, we moved on to talk about the sole shortcode that core WordPress gives us to play with: the [`gallery`] shortcode. Because it's the only shortcode that comes pre-rolled in WordPress, it's

---

[3] http://codex.wordpress.org/Function_Reference/the_post_thumbnail#Parameters
[4] http://codex.wordpress.org/Function_Reference/get_the_post_thumbnail#Parameters

commonly overlooked by both novice and seasoned WordPress developers alike, but you can do all sorts of cool stuff with it. We covered all the basic options for WordPress galleries, as well as how to change them both manually within the context of the shortcode and via the graphical user interface that appears once you save a gallery in a page or post.

Addressing the needs of professional theme developers, we talked a bit about how to effectively fire both individual and dynamic galleries directly from your page templates, before discussing the use of lightboxes as mechanisms to create a better viewing experience for users looking through your galleries. Finally, we talked about featured images, which are the same thing as post thumbnails (in WordPress, the two terms are synonyms). Post thumbnails are really easy to use, and need to be enabled as a theme feature in the **functions.php** file. We discussed using built-in image sizes, as well as creating new ones for customized purposes, before going into a brief explanation about how to actually display post thumbnails in your theme, or pass them into your PHP logic for use in a script.

In a way, you could say that all the post thumbnail functionality integrated into WordPress is a form of application programming interface. This leads us quite nicely into our next chapter—WordPress APIs!

The WordPress API

Learning how to intimately work with the most fleshed-out portions of WordPress can be a detailed, arduous task, but as you get pretty hardcore with some of the handstands you'd like WordPress to perform on your behalf, you may well find the need to go to the most low-level functions WordPress has to offer. To this end, the WordPress API offers some avenues to really fine-tune your installation.

Developers differ in their ideas of what an API is because, in practice, it's often presented as a tool that performs a very specific function. Since most of us pick up new concepts as we go on an as-needed basis, we tend to learn how to work with a particular API, and then assume that all APIs are used for that particular purpose. Usually, the term API is used in relation to providing an interface within a particular software program that other external programs can use to form a common language and communicate data between one another. When you make your website talk to Facebook, for example, you are mainly using the Facebook API. Likewise, providing an interface for websites to use a particular merchant account vendor is often done using the API terminology. Whether this is your exposure to APIs, or otherwise, you probably already have a fair idea of its definition.

While most of us know that the acronym **API** stands for Application Programming Interface, in reality it is a catch-all term that describes a group of ideas rather than a single function. The term can be used to refer to an entire interface, a single function, or a set of complete interfaces that serve different functions. Therefore, the term API is defined by the context of its use. APIs can be language-dependent, making them more convenient to use in an environment where the language is constant, or language-independent, where their functionality can be accessed by a variety of programming languages; the latter is more appropriate for web services and hence, more common for what we need to do. In fact, the **WordPress API** itself is defined as "the plugin/theme/add-on interface created

by the entire WordPress project." Put that way, you could make the case that everything we have already covered in this book—as well as anything you'll ever find in the Codex—is all the WordPress API, but that's a little too broad. So let's now ask the million-dollar question: what exactly is the WordPress API, aside from *everything*?

Glad you asked. There's actually a page on the WordPress API in the Codex.[1] For our purposes, we're going to be talking about the WordPress API in terms of these more specialized, compartmentalized aspects of WordPress that you can individually tap into and manipulate to fine tune different aspects of your WordPress website. We're also going to extend the conversation a little bit with some other functions that, while not officially listed here within the WordPress API, enable you to do all sorts of really cool and interesting things. Seriously, this is the stuff that separates the figurative men from the boys in the WordPress world. Let's get it on!

A Quick Review of the APIs Covered So Far

So if you've been paying attention, you probably remember seeing the term API thrown around in several places throughout this book already. We've already covered some of the more commonly used APIs in detail in Chapter 5, so we'll just review them here. If you want to learn more about how any of them work, flip back to Chapter 5 and have a look. Otherwise, jump ahead and start digging into the new stuff.

Widgets API

The Widgets API is the collected set of PHP functions that manage the creation, registration and usage of functions of sidebars (or widgetized areas) and widgets inside WordPress. Within any given WordPress installation, the Widgets API can be located in **wp-includes/widgets.php**. An additional detailed explanation of the Widgets API can be found in the Codex.[2]

Plugins API

The Plugins API essentially deals with actions hooks and filter hooks. For the most part, it's a safe bet to assume that the entirety of Chapter 5 in and of itself documents the Plugins API, minus the areas that specifically discuss the Widgets API and Shortcodes, which we'll talk about next. For additional information on the Plugin API, take a look in the Codex.[3]

Shortcode API

The Shortcode API is the collected set of PHP functions that create macro codes, which can be used to insert complex functionality inside post content, and we call these macro codes **short-codes**. As heavily documented in Chapter 8, WordPress includes one major shortcode that adds photo gallery functionality to any given post or page —[gallery]—but we can make our own

---

[1] http://codex.wordpress.org/WordPress_API's
[2] http://codex.wordpress.org/Widgets_API
[3] http://codex.wordpress.org/Plugin_API

quite easily. We briefly discussed shortcodes in general in Chapter 5, but we'll study them in detail now.

Shortcodes under the Microscope

Shortcodes are written in a format very similar in appearance to WordPress filters where we add and name a shortcode, and then associate it with a handler function that actually executes the logic being called within the shortcode:

```
add_shortcode( 'shortcode-name', 'shortcode-handler-function' );
```

Shortcode handler functions commonly accept two parameters (and for some very rare uses, a third that we won't discuss as it'll just confuse the notion):

- $atts: an array of attributes
- $content: content enclosed within the opening and closing tags

As the second parameter above suggests, there are actually two different forms in which you can create shortcodes—enclosing shortcodes, and self-closing shortcodes. The [gallery] shortcode is an example of a self-closing shortcode. In this form, the shortcode's functionality is entirely self-contained, and merely adding the shortcode and any of its necessary parameter values will cause the shortcode to properly function when added to post content. For instance, let's take this self-enclosed shortcode as an example:

```
[gallery id="55" columns="4"]
```

If we inserted this shortcode into the post content of any given post or page, WordPress would automatically go out and grab all of the images associated with posts with the numerical ID of 55 and add them to a gallery that is set up to display in four vertical columns.

Enclosing shortcodes, on the other hand, require the use of an opening and closing tag in order to work properly. Let's look at a fictitious example of an enclosing shortcode:

```
[helping-friendly-shortcode]We want you to be happy.[/helping-friendly-shortcode]
```

In the instance of enclosing shortcodes, we are taking a particular text string (in this instance, We want you to be happy.) and planning on placing code on either side of it to encapsulate it in the final output HTML that will be read by a browser. Let's look at some actual code examples to see how all this works in practice. We can begin by looking at the code for a simple self-closing shortcode; the same shortcode that we looked at in Chapter 5:

chapter_09/shortcode-example.php

```php
<?php

function thank_you_mr_miner() {
  return 'You can feel good about Hood.';
}

add_shortcode( 'mrminer', 'thank_you_mr_miner' );
?>
```

In this example, we're creating a shortcode that can be called by typing [mrminer] into any post or page. When WordPress parses out the content, it'll fire the shortcode's handler function and output the text You can feel good about Hood. where the shortcode is added. Simple stuff, right?

 Return, Don't Echo

A common mistake made with shortcodes is attempting to output your shortcode results using an echo instead of a return. Keep in mind that anything that is echoed will be output to your browser, but it won't be displayed in the correct location you intend it to. Returning the value will produce the desired results.

Now let's take it a step further, and investigate enclosing shortcodes:

chapter_09/enclosed-shortcode-example.php

```php
<?php

function readicculus( $atts, $content = null ) {
  return '<span class="helping-friendly-book">' . $content . '</span>';
}

add_shortcode( 'helping-friendly-shortcode', 'readicculus' );
?>
```

All right … so this is a little bit more complicated, but not too bad really. The first thing you'll note is that our handler function now has two parameters being passed into it: *$atts* and *$content = null*. At the moment, we haven't defined any attributes to be passed into the handler function, so it's blank. However, *$content = null* essentially acts like a switch to let WordPress know that this shortcode is designed to act as an enclosed shortcode rather than as a standalone self-closing shortcode. The return code is actually a string that concatenates the $content we have encapsulated within our shortcode tags in-between the opening and closing text strings we have hard coded here. Now let's look at what this shortcode does:

```
[helping-friendly-shortcode]We want you to be happy.[/helping-friendly-shortcode]
```

Were we to add this shortcode into a post or page, the HTML output in association with it would look like this:

```
<span class="helping-friendly-book">We want you to be happy."</span>
```

We're making some headway here; however, let's say we wanted to pass an attribute into this shortcode now, giving us the ability to modify our CSS or JavaScript behaviors depending on the class being referenced in the <span> tag. We'd need to create an array that contained a default value for each attribute our shortcode can receive; that way, if we don't pass the attribute in with the shortcode, the shortcode itself still has all the information it needs to operate correctly. Consider the following code block:

```
                                        chapter_09/enclosed-shortcode-attribute-example.php
<?php

function readicculus( $atts, $content = null ) {
  extract( shortcode_atts( array(
      'class' => 'helping-friendly-book',
      ), $atts ) );

  return '<span class="' . esc_attr($class) . '">' . $content . '</span>';
}

add_shortcode( 'helping-friendly-shortcode', 'readicculus' );
?>
```

We've now given ourselves the ability to pass in an attribute for class. If we choose not to do so, our output will be exactly as we saw above, defaulting to the helping-friendly-book class. However, let's say we use the following form of the shortcode in our post or page:

```
[helping-friendly-shortcode class="magazine"]We want you to be happy.➡
  [/helping-friendly-shortcode]
```

In this instance, we've replaced the default helping-friendly-book attribute with our new one, magazine, causing a new output when rendered to HTML:

```
<span class="magazine">We want you to be happy.</span>
```

All in all, it's fairly simple when you break it down into bite-sized pieces.

One last point is that the shortcode parser uses a single pass on post content, which means that by default you cannot fire separate shortcodes inside of enclosed shortcodes. Like anything else though, there is a workaround if you feel you need to give yourself the ability to do this. The solution is to encapsulate your *$content* tag with the do_shortcode() function, as shown below:

```
                                    chapter_09/doshortcode-enclosed-shortcode-attribute-example.php

<?php

function readicculus( $atts, $content = null ) {
    extract( shortcode_atts( array(
        'class' => 'helping-friendly-book',
    ), $atts ) );

    return '<span class="' . esc_attr($class) . '">' . do_shortcode($content) .➥
        '</span>';
}

add_shortcode( 'helping-friendly-shortcode', 'readicculus' );
?>
```

By structuring your shortcodes in this way, you'll essentially be able to fire shortcodes within shortcodes, should the need arise.

 do Us a Favor

> The `do_shortcode()` function is an extremely useful function. Using this function, you can easily execute any shortcode you like from directly within any of your theme's template files. For more information on the specifics of its usage, check it out in the Codex.[4]

As you can see, shortcodes can be extremely powerful, and you can use them in innovative ways to increase the usability and functionality of your WordPress installation. For more detail on the Shortcode API, have a look in the Codex.[5] Now let's move on and look at some genuinely new stuff in the WordPress API.

The Dashboard Widgets API

First up to the plate is the Dashboard Widgets API, a great place for us to start because of its similarity to action hooks, filter hooks, and the way in which we interact with the Shortcode API. We briefly touched on the use of Dashboard widgets in Chapter 2, but the Dashboard Widgets API gives you the facility to easily register your own. Let's have a look.

The main new function we'll be playing with here is `wp_add_dashboard_widget()`, which takes three required parameters and one optional parameter:

```
wp_add_dashboard_widget( $widget_id, $widget_name, $callback,➥
    $control_callback = null )
```

---

[4] http://codex.wordpress.org/Function_Reference/do_shortcode
[5] http://codex.wordpress.org/Shortcode_API

Here's how the parameters are defined:

$widget_id	an identifying slug for your widget, which can be used as the CSS class and the key in the array of Dashboard widgets
$widget_name	the actual name the Dashboard widget will display in its heading
$callback	the name of the function you create, which will display the actual contents of the Dashboard widget
$control_callback = null (optional)	the name of the function you create, which will handle submission of widget form options

Furthermore, in order to run the function, you'll need to call it with the wp_dashboard_setup action hook, telling WordPress to initiate your widget functionality into the Dashboard. Therefore, the complete code for a simple Dashboard widget might look like the following:

chapter_09/dashboard-widget.php

```php
<?php

// Create the function to output the contents of our Dashboard Widget
function underoverground() {
  // Display whatever it is you want to show
  echo "Don't forget to turn the Earth so both sides get their share of➡
      darkness and of light.";
}

// Create the function used in the action hook
function add_underoverground() {
  wp_add_dashboard_widget('not_so_fast', 'Not So Fast', 'underoverground');
}

// Hook into the 'wp_dashboard_setup'
add_action('wp_dashboard_setup', 'add_underoverground' );
```

Working from the bottom up, we've used the *wp_dashboard_setup* action hook to call our new function add_underoverground(), which invokes the necessary wp_add_dashboard_widget() function to create the actual Dashboard widget instance. And what goes in that instance? The code that is fired by our referenced function—underoverground(). Therefore, the code above will result in a Dashboard Widget being installed with a heading of **Not So Fast** and the text-based contents of Don't forget to turn the Earth so both sides get their share of darkness and of light. Pretty cool, huh?

Removing Dashboard Widgets

The Dashboard API does a few other actions that we have no room to cover here, but one topic that comes up rather often in the development community is how to customize the Dashboard experience for users by default. Users can, of course, always navigate up to **Screen Options** in the upper right-hand corner of the Dashboard and uncheck any Dashboard widgets they want to remove from view; however, sometimes users have no business seeing some of the types of Dashboard widgets available by default in a standard WordPress installation. If this pretty well describes your situation, then don't fear: the Dashboard Widgets API has your back, providing a method to remove default Dashboard widgets you don't want to see. Here's how you do it.

You'll be working with the `remove_meta_box()` function, which you can read about in more detail in the Codex.[6]

First of all, recognize that your default widgets are named in the following manner:

Main column

- `$wp_meta_boxes['dashboard']['normal']['core']['dashboard_right_now']<br/>`

- `$wp_meta_boxes['dashboard']['normal']['core']['dashboard_recent_comments']<br/>`

- `$wp_meta_boxes['dashboard']['normal']['core']['dashboard_incoming_links']<br/>`

- `$wp_meta_boxes['dashboard']['normal']['core']['dashboard_plugins']<br/>`

Side column

- `$wp_meta_boxes['dashboard']['side']['core']['dashboard_quick_press']<br/>`

- `$wp_meta_boxes['dashboard']['side']['core']['dashboard_recent_drafts']<br/>`

- `$wp_meta_boxes['dashboard']['side']['core']['dashboard_primary']<br/>`

- `$wp_meta_boxes['dashboard']['side']['core']['dashboard_secondary']<br/>`

What you'll want to do is tap into the `wp_dashboard_setup` action hook and create a new function that removes the Dashboard widgets of your choice. Just mimic the pattern following to remove whatever Dashboard widgets you need to. Your code might look like this:

---

[6] http://codex.wordpress.org/Function_Reference/remove_meta_box

chapter_09/remove-dashboard-widget.php

```php
<?php

// Create the function to remove default Dashboard widgets
function peace_out_dashboard_widgets() {
  remove_meta_box( 'dashboard_right_now', 'dashboard', 'normal' );
  remove_meta_box( 'dashboard_incoming_links', 'dashboard', 'normal' );
  remove_meta_box( 'dashboard_quick_press', 'dashboard', 'side' );
  remove_meta_box( 'dashboard_recent_drafts', 'dashboard', 'side' );
}

// Hook into the 'wp_dashboard_setup' action
add_action('wp_dashboard_setup', 'peace_out_dashboard_widgets' );
```

This code stops four default Dashboard widgets from displaying within a WordPress installation: the **Right Now** widget, the **Incoming Links** widget, the **Quick Press** widget, and the **Recent Drafts** widget.

For more information as to how work with the finer points of the Dashboard Widgets API, have a look in the Codex.[7]

The HTTP API

If you are an experienced PHP coder, you've no doubt come across situations that have required you to make an HTTP request in PHP. You may have used cURL[8] or fopen()[9] or something else, but what you're bound to have noticed is that there's more than one way to make an HTTP request in PHP. And what makes the game fun is that not all servers support the same methods—occasionally, some servers don't support any methods at all (gotta love that!). HTTP requests can range from simple GET requests that are looking to poll the latest tweets from Twitter to slightly more advanced POST requests where you might need to pass a few parameters like a username and password to retrieve the most recent Facebook status of a particular user.

WordPress officially recognizes five methods to send an HTTP request in PHP, and refers to them collectively as **transports**. The HTTP API was developed specifically to support all these transports, providing a universal method of handling them within WordPress. In this way, WordPress is able to assess which transports are available on any given server, and automatically use the most appropriate one when making its general HTTP requests.

WordPress provides four helper functions that retrieve URLs in different ways, which you can use to interface directly with the HTTP API classes located in **wp-includes/http.php**. These functions and their uses are as follows:

---

[7] http://codex.wordpress.org/Dashboard_Widgets_API

[8] http://curl.haxx.se/

[9] http://au.php.net/manual/en/function.fopen.php

wp_remote_get()

retrieves a URL using the GET HTTP method

wp_remote_post()

retrieves a URL using the POST HTTP method

wp_remote_head()

retrieves a URL using the HEAD HTTP method

wp_remote_request()

retrieves a URL using either the default GET or a custom HTTP method that you specify; this is useful when you need to send basic authentication headers with a URL request

All these functions return a WP_Error class upon failure, so you need to check for WordPress errors after using them.

chapter_09/error-check.php

```php
<?php

$whatchutalkinboutwillis = wp_remote_get('http://esquandolas.com');

if( is_wp_error( $whatchutalkinboutwillis ) )
    // Deal with your error here

?>
```

Other helper functions that work with the HTTP API deal with retrieving only specific portions of a response, and in this instance the functions actually do the error testing on your behalf:

wp_remote_retrieve_body()

retrieves only the body from a given response

wp_remote_retrieve_header()

retrieves a single HTTP header from a given response

wp_remote_retrieve_headers()

retrieves all HTTP headers from a given response

wp_remote_retrieve_response_code()

gives you the number code for a given HTTP response; positive responses should be 200, but failed responses could be within the 300-400 range

wp_remote_retrieve_response_message()

retrieves the response message based upon the response code

Finally, these functions are stackable within themselves, so the following is perfectly acceptable; it will return only the body of the URL http://esquandolas.com, checking for WordPress errors along the way:

```
$whatchutalkinboutwillis = wp_remote_retrieve_body( wp_remote_get➡
  ('http://esquandolas.com') );
```

For more detailed information on the HTTP API, look in the Codex.[10]

The Database API

The Database API is actually a collection of three APIs that combine to manage the plugin, theme, and add-on interactions with WordPress's database and the stored values within. These APIs include the Options API, the Transients API, and the Metadata API. Let's look at each one in turn.

The Options API

The Options API is composed of a set of functions that provide a standardized way to create, access, update, and delete options and values within the database, without the need to utilize SQL statements, which may become obsolete in later versions of WordPress or MySQL (WordPress's database of choice). All the data managed through the Options API is stored in the **wp_options** table within the database.

The Options API's four functions provide a fairly predictable functionality:

`add_option()`
> adds a new option to the database for use throughout the installation via the `get_option()` function; it takes no action if an option of the same name has already been added

`delete_option()`
> removes an existing named option and its associated value from the **wp_options** table in the database

`get_option()`
> returns an existing option from the database if it exists

`update_option()`
> updates a named option and its associated value, and adds it if the option is yet to exist

For more detailed information on the Options API, look in the Codex.[11]

---

[10] http://codex.wordpress.org/HTTP_API
[11] http://codex.wordpress.org/Options_API

The Transients API

The Transients API is very similar to the Options API, with the exception that the Transients API allows you to store data in the database temporarily that will expire and be deleted after a set period of time. This allows WordPress a mechanism to store cached data in the database, although caching plugins have the ability to force WordPress to store transient values in memory rather than in the database, inherently speeding up any WordPress installation. For this reason, you should never assume that transient data is automatically stored within the database, and hence permanent data should never be stored with the Transients API at all.

The Transients API offers functions that imitate the Options API, with the exception that the add and update functions are traded out for a set function as described here:

set_transient()   sets or updates the value of a transient

get_transient()   returns an existing transient value if it exists

delete_transient() deletes a transient value

For more detailed information on the Transients API, look in the Codex.[12]

The Metadata API

The Metadata API provides a standardized mechanism for storing, retrieving and manipulating metadata such as custom fields on posts for various WordPress object types in the **wp_commentmeta**, **wp_postmeta**, or **wp_usermeta** tables. This essentially makes it possible to add and manipulate custom data to comments, posts, or users at will.

The Metadata API offers four functions which mimic the Options API functions exactly, assume that a dedicated MySQL table exists for the $meta_type you specify as listed above, and are described below:

add_metadata()   allows for metadata to be added to any kind of WordPress object

delete_metadata()   deletes metadata for a particular object

get_metadata()   returns the existing metadata from the database for a specific object if it exists

update_metadata()   updates the metadata of a certain object within the database and adds it if it doesn't exist

For more detailed information on the Metadata API, look in the Codex.[13]

---

[12] http://codex.wordpress.org/Transients_API

[13] http://codex.wordpress.org/Metadata_API

The Rewrite API

The Rewrite API is an advanced API and should be dealt with and used with caution. It is a set of four functions that essentially helps WordPress developers tap into the `WP_Rewrite` class to programmatically specify new, custom rewrite rules for use with WordPress's pretty permalinks. It is dependent upon the availability of the **mod_rewrite** Apache module, meaning that its usage is necessarily predicated upon the installation being run on a Linux platform. Each function that makes up the Rewrite API is typically called within the *init* hook, meaning they are run during WordPress's initialization process. Furthermore, permalinks will usually need to be refreshed within the **Settings > Permalinks** page in the WordPress back end before the rewrite changes will take effect. The code for the Rewrite API is housed in **wp-includes/rewrite.php**. Let's take a look at these functions:

add_rewrite_tag()

This is used to make WordPress aware of custom `querystring` variables in conjunction with `add_rewrite_rule()`. It takes two required parameters—a tag name, and a regular expression to parse the tag name for use in the rewrite URL. The function call must be made on *init* or earlier, otherwise the tags are not available for use by `add_rewrite_rule()`. There are a lot of advanced tasks you can do with `add_rewrite_tag()`, but they're beyond the scope of this book. For more information on using `add_rewrite_tag()`, see its page in the Codex.[14]

add_rewrite_rule()

Commonly used in conjunction with `add_rewrite_tag()`, `add_rewrite_rule()` searches for custom rewrite tags and uses them to insert individual values into a particular rewritten URL. For example, if a page employing a custom page template about veterinary records took two custom rewrite variables—pet type and pet name—as defined by `add_rewrite_tag()`, a requested URL that looked like http://esquandolas.com/vetrecords/dog/mcgrupp could be interpreted to actually mean http://esquandolas.com/index.php?p=42&pettype=dog&petname=mcgrupp. Like `add_rewrite_tag()`, there are a lot of advanced actions you can complete with `add_rewrite_rule()` that are beyond the scope of this book. For more information on using `add_rewrite_rule()`, see its page in the Codex.[15]

add_rewrite_endpoint()

This is used to add custom endpoints to the end of your URLs in a format like /trackback/.

add_feed()

This is used to add new feed types.

---

[14] http://codex.wordpress.org/Rewrite_API/add_rewrite_tag
[15] http://codex.wordpress.org/Rewrite_API/add_rewrite_rule

For more detailed information on the Rewrite API, look in the Codex.[16] Additionally, you'll find a wealth of information and resources by looking at the page on `WP_Rewrite`, WordPress's class for managing rewrite rules. The `WP_Rewrite` class documentation is located in the Codex.[17]

Other Functions and Tools

This concludes our discussion of the WordPress API as defined in the Codex, but take note that there are several other APIs described in the Codex worth exploring. For now, we're going to move on to some interesting, useful functions and tools that you should aim to really understand.

register_activation_hook()

The `register_activation_hook()` function allows you to register a custom activation hook when you activate a plugin, and is useful when your plugin needs to take a specific action upon activation. The function takes two required parameters:

```
register_activation_hook ( $file, $function );
```

The parameters are defined as follows:

$file   the path to the main plugin file inside the **wp_content/plugins** directory
$function   the function to be called within the plugin file when the plugin is activated

A corresponding function exists that reverses the process in `register_deactivation_hook()`. We'll take a closer look at the `register_activation_hook()` and `register_deactivation_hook()` functions in action with our next noteworthy function that handles the regular scheduling of events.

wp_schedule_event()

If you are familiar with Linux, you'll no doubt be familiar with cron. In Linux, cron is a program that allows you to schedule scripts to run automatically on a schedule. It's a handy tool that essentially gives you the ability to automate just about any routine task you'd like such as backing up a directory, sending emails in batch, or anything else you can dream up. WordPress provides us with a series of functions that could probably be referred to as the Cron API, but for our purposes we'll focus on the `wp_schedule_event()` function.

`wp_schedule_event()` utilizes cron-like functionality to fire events on a regular schedule within WordPress themes, plugins, and core files. In fact, WordPress makes use of this function to check for plugin and general WordPress updates once every 12 hours, as well as publish scheduled posts. While `wp_schedule_event()` doesn't utilize cron itself, it's located within the **wp-includes/cron.php**

---

[16] http://codex.wordpress.org/Rewrite_API
[17] http://codex.wordpress.org/Function_Reference/WP_Rewrite

file, and there's actually a function within that file named wp_cron which does most of the heavy lifting.

Most developers regularly use wp_schedule_event() in their plugins, and the function works by scheduling a hook to be executed by WordPress at a specific interval that you as the developer define. The action triggers whenever a user visits the site if the initial scheduled time has passed, and takes three required parameters and one optional parameter:

```
wp_schedule_event( $timestamp, $recurrence, $hook, $arg );
```

The parameters are defined as follows:

$timestamp	the first time that you want the event to occur in a UNIX timestamp format
$recurrence	the frequency in which the event should occur, where possible values are hourly, twice daily, or daily
$hook	the name of the action hook that should be executed
$args (optional)	any arguments that should be passed to the hook functions

To see the wp_schedule_event() function in action, let's consider the code that we'll add to a plugin file:

chapter_09/schedule-event-plugin.php

```php
<?php

// Register our custom activation hook
register_activation_hook(__FILE__, 'roggae_activation');

// Add custom action hook and call our custom function
add_action('hourly_turning_event', 'hourly_earth_turn');

// Define the function associated with our custom action hook
function roggae_activation() {
  wp_schedule_event(time(), 'hourly', 'hourly_turning_event');
}

// Define our function that will do something on a scheduled basis
function hourly_earth_turn() {
  // code that turns the Earth every hour
}

// Clean scheduler upon plugin deactivation
register_deactivation_hook(__FILE__, 'roggae_deactivation');

function roggae_deactivation() {
  wp_clear_scheduled_hook('hourly_turning_event');
}
```

Firstly, take note that we are telling WordPress to register our custom action hook upon the *activation* of our custom plugin by using the `register_activation_hook()` function we discussed before. Notice that at the bottom of the code block, we clear out the values of the hook so that we can eliminate it altogether when we deactivate the same plugin.

As you can see, our scheduled event is written to allow WordPress to turn the Earth ever so slightly every hour, on the hour. We do this by creating a function in our plugin (`roggae_activation()`, in this case), which calls `wp_schedule_event()` and provides it with the necessary parameters. In our example, we're telling WordPress we'd like to execute the `hourly_turning_event` action hook (which fires the functionality we've defined in our `hourly_earth_turn()` function) every hour, on the hour. This is beginning from the exact timestamp that was created when we initially activated our plugin. After all, it's incumbent on us to ensure that every portion of the Earth receives its fair share of darkness and light, and it would become tiresome to try to remember to do all that on our own!

In all seriousness, `wp_schedule_event()` and its similar supporting functions are incredibly powerful, and for the most part rather underutilized. To learn more about it and other cron-type functions in WordPress, have a look at the Codex page.[18]

wp_enqueue_script() and wp_register_script()

We all know that JavaScript is an extremely popular client-side scripting language that gives us easy access to insanely cool GUI elements that make our websites visually stunning. However, if you've ever tried to manually work with different JavaScript libraries on the same website, you're acutely aware that, despite their inherent sexiness, JavaScript libraries rarely play nicely with one another. Just go ahead and try to load out jQuery and script.aculo.us on the same site; it might work, and, then again, it might not. Still, all too often you'll find theme developers hardcoding JavaScript libraries into the <head> code of their websites to make their interface elements work as intended. This is just fine for the initial theme developer, but what about plugin developers who want to use different JavaScript libraries, or even if the same theme developer finds it handy to use another version of the same library in other locations on the same site? As usual, WordPress comes to the rescue with a useful and shockingly underused pair of functions: `wp_enqueue_script()` and `wp_register_script()`.

By using `wp_register_script()`, you can safely register and save JavaScript libraries to be called by `wp_enqueue_script()` later on when needed. `wp_register_script()` is always called with an *init* action, and takes one required parameter as well as four optional parameters:

```
wp_register_script( $handle, $src, $deps, $ver, $in_footer );
```

The parameters are defined as follows:

---

[18] http://codex.wordpress.org/Category:WP-Cron_Functions

$handle	This is the unique name of the script that will be later used when called by `wp_enqueue_script()`.
$src (optional)	This is the URL to the script, a required parameter when not using a default script that ships with core WordPress (see the Codex for a listing of scripts that are included with core WordPress).[19]
$deps (optional)	This is an array of dependencies the script has, which defaults to false if the script has none. This parameter is required only where WordPress does not ship with the script.
$ver (optional)	This is a string defining the version number of the script, if it has one.
$in_footer (optional)	Scripts are normally loaded into the <head> section of the code, but if you need the script to be queued with `wp_footer()`, this Boolean can optionally be set to true.

Once a script has a registered handle as defined by `wp_register_script()`, it can then be utilized by `wp_enqueue_script()` for use in a plugin or theme (or core function). `wp_enqueue_script()` queues scripts in the proper order based on their explicit dependencies, and thus allows you to use any of WordPress's built-in script libraries or external scripts you need to manually load. `wp_enqueue_script()` takes the same required parameter and four optional parameters that `wp_register_script()` takes:

```
wp_enqueue_script( $handle, $src, $deps, $ver, $in_footer );
```

The parameters are defined as follows:

$handle	It's the unique name of the script defined by `wp_register_script()`.
$src (optional)	This is the URL to the script, a required parameter when not using a default script that ships with core WordPress (see the Codex for a listing of scripts that are included with core WordPress).
$deps (optional)	This is an array of dependencies the script has, which defaults to false if the script has no dependencies. It's a parameter that's required only where WordPress does not ship with the script.
$ver (optional)	This is a string defining the version number of the script, if it has one.

---

[19] http://codex.wordpress.org/Function_Reference/wp_enqueue_script#Default_scripts_included_with_WordPress

$in_footer (optional)   Scripts are normally loaded into the <head> section of the code, but if you need the script to be queued with the wp_footer(), this Boolean can optionally be set to true.

wp_enqueue_script() is added to the *init* action hook, and should only be called when needed (that is, wrapped in an if (!is_admin()) {} statement so that it doesn't interfere with administrative scripts if it's meant to be used for the outwardly facing areas of the website). Likewise, if the script is being used for a plugin admin screen, it can (and should) be restricted to only being shown on that particular section of the admin area.

 ### Avoid Script Clashes

It's vital to remember that you should only run scripts where they're necessary. If you run scripts in the background where they're unnecessary, you can find yourself experiencing incompatibilities and collisions with other libraries. A script that you actually need to use could be found to be competing with the JavaScript library you have carelessly left running in the background, causing all sorts of unanticipated issues on the page.

For more information on how wp_register_scripts()[20] and wp_enqueue_script()[21] work, look at the relevant sections in the Codex.

A corresponding set of functions to wp_register_scripts() and wp_enqueue_script() exist dealing with stylesheets. For these purposes, \wp_register_style()[22] and wp_enqueue_style()[23] work to manage stylesheets in exactly the same way that scripts can be managed, although the sly functions are more commonly used to ensure that stylesheets are not loaded before any necessary dependencies are loaded. For more information on these two functions, reference the section called "Dissecting a Plugin: Antelope General Social Media Links" in Chapter 5, or check the Codex.

BackPress

Last but certainly not least, let's say you're looking to build a brand new web application independent of WordPress, but would love to take advantage of many of the tools and feature sets included within core WordPress. If this sounds interesting to you, BackPress may just be what you're been looking for.

Licensed under the GPL2 license, BackPress[24] is the WordPress code back end presented as a PHP library, which allows you to build scalable web applications independent of the WordPress CMS.

---

[20] http://codex.wordpress.org/Function_Reference/wp_register_script
[21] http://codex.wordpress.org/Function_Reference/wp_enqueue_script
[22] http://codex.wordpress.org/Function_Reference/wp_register_style
[23] http://codex.wordpress.org/Function_Reference/wp_enqueue_style
[24] http://backpress.org

While you need to roll your own database and implementations for the code, BackPress provides you with access to many of the valuable features WordPress provides, including:

- logging
- user roles and capabilities
- database connections
- HTTP transactions
- object caching
- formatting
- XSS and SQL injection protection
- taxonomies
- options management

If you are a web developer looking for a fabulous framework to begin your web application development with, remember to say please and thank you to the kind folks at backpress.org.

A Box Full of Tools

The WordPress API is a set of compartmentalized functions that serve to provide programmable interfaces into different aspects of core WordPress. After reviewing the Widgets API and Plugin API, and providing a bit more detail on the Shortcode API (all of which we explored in detail in Chapter 5) we explored the majority of the remainder of the WordPress API. This includes the Dashboard Widgets API, the HTTP API, the Database API (itself a set of three APIs managing WordPress's database layer—the Options API, the Transients API, and the Metadata API), and the Rewrite API.

We also looked at some really useful functions not officially listed within the WordPress API, but essential when seeking to unveil sophisticated functionality within WordPress. Notably, we covered the wp_schedule_event() function, which creates a mechanism in WordPress to automate the processing of routine tasks like batch email functionality, as well as the wp_enqueue_script() and wp_register_script() functions, which allow us to safely load and use different JavaScript libraries in our plugins and themes. Finally, we took a brief look at BackPress, a PHP library available with the GPL2 license that allows you to utilize much of WordPress's core functionality in your own separate web applications

10

Multisite: Rolling Your Own Network

So far in this book, we've delved deep into the WordPress universe and pulled back the curtain to show how the most fundamental elements of the core WordPress installation are put together and operate. Now, we're going to look at one of the newest and most exciting additions to core: Multisite. Its capabilities allow you to extend the CMS in a way that will let you host and manage your own centralized network of WordPress websites, much in the same way that Automattic manages the free wordpress.com service. So you can literally leverage a single WordPress installation to managing dozens, hundreds, or even thousands of individual WordPress websites. It's one of the most popular up-and-coming features within core, and well worth the effort of learning.

Once you understand and master it, Multisite has a host of practical purposes. For individual developers and marketers who handle a large number of WordPress sites, Multisite can save significant time and aggravation by centralizing plugin management in particular; after all, if you have a thousand websites and need to upgrade the same plugin on each one, it's a lot easier and faster to do it once than a thousand times, right? Communities can also find Multisite helpful by enabling their users to manage their own blogs themselves, much like wordpress.com does. Finally, there are several examples of business models that use Multisite to target specific industry vertical markets, and provide valuable syndicated content services in any number of creative ways. The notion of a self-hosted multisite concept is still in the early stages of development when compared to other content management concepts in the web development community, but like anything else, its uses are much more dependent upon the imagination of the developers working with it than any technical limitations.

A Brief History of Multisite

Before we examine the specifics of Multisite, it's a good idea to investigate its background so that you have a better understanding of its functionality. In the early days of WordPress, there were two distinct projects that were actively maintained: WordPress, and WordPressμ. Pronounced "WordPress M-YOU," μ was also called WordPress Multi-user; it was built to be a standalone version of WordPress that featured the ability to create multiple blogs, which could be accessed by many users with different administrative privileges. While μ shared much of the same codebase as core WordPress, it was ultimately far less popular, so when changes were made to core WordPress, they weren't necessarily added immediately to μ. This resulted in a feature set that was perpetually lacking and generally behind the curve, causing μ to have a reputation as a dodgy framework that worked as expected only some of the time.

In order to correct the situation with μ, the powers that be wisely chose to discontinue the standalone project and instead factor its functionality into core WordPress, beginning with the major release of WordPress 3.0 in March 2010. Since that time, Multisite, as it came to be known, has been actively developed within the core WordPress feature set, although it is deactivated by default in a standard WordPress installation. The point you should understand is that Multisite doesn't need to be installed, but merely enabled within an existing core WordPress installation. Let's take a look at how.

 Change Is Good

It's pertinent to note that Multisite is a WordPress feature that is truly in an evolutionary development cycle within core WordPress at this time. As this book is based upon WordPress 3.2, the Multisite functionality discussed within this chapter reflects the 3.2 implementation. While conceptually the same as its previous iterations, the visual presentation and functionality of Multisite as implemented in 3.2 is significantly different from its implementation in 3.1, which was similarly different from the 3.0 implementation. While it's unclear how much the implementation will shift in future major releases, it's a reasonable assumption that the implementation in future releases will continue to be augmented and refined.

Enabling Multisite

For the amount of functionality that you are instantly afforded, it's surprisingly easy to enable Multisite in WordPress. The trickiest part is that because you're creating individual websites that each need to operate as a unique entity, you'll have to create a specific namespace for each one to operate in. Multisite offers you two methods of doing this: creating sites via subdomains, or via subdirectories. Utilizing one of these will give you a clean website installation in its own unique namespace that looks like one of these examples:

- subdomain namespace: http://marco.esquandolas.com
- subdirectory namespace: http://www.esquandolas.com/marco

Now you might be thinking that this is all well and good, but you're better off avoiding namespaces that look like either format; you want a unique domain to be used here instead of a subdomain or subdirectory. Never fear, there's a plugin to help you do that, but we need to walk through the initial process first.

Location, Location

While it's common among many web developers to give WordPress its own directory as a matter of rule, Multisite precludes you from this practice because of the routing it needs to define and manage for its network sites. Therefore, in order for Multisite to operate at all, WordPress itself must be installed in the public HTML directory the website propagates to. Put differently, the site URL and the WordPress URL as defined in **Settings** > **General** must be set to the same location in order to use Multisite.

Enabling Multisite can be up to a four-step process, with several of the steps being optional or skipped altogether, depending on whether you're setting up the site from scratch or converting an existing site to Multisite, as well as whether or not you're going to be using subdomains. Let's have a look at the process.

Step 1: Back up WordPress

Understand that when you set up a network with Multisite, by definition you'll be updating your WordPress files. At the risk of losing your data, it's a wise idea to back up your WordPress installation before you begin any work, especially if you're going to be enabling Multisite on an existing live WordPress site. If you're enabling Multisite on a fresh WordPress install, this is an unnecessary step.

Step 2: Set up wildcard subdomains if you'll be using a subdomain namespace with Multisite

If you are setting up Multisite to create new sites in subdirectories instead of on subdomains, you can skip this step and move straight to step 3.

In order to set up Multisite to create new network websites on unique subdomains, you'll first need to have a cursory knowledge of DNS, as well as the confidence and the necessary server permissions required to make a few changes to the DNS records that manage your web server. **DNS** is an acronym that stands for Domain Name Service, and in this context consists of a set of text-based rules that reside on your web server. These rules direct types of traffic that are associated with your domain name, such as email, web service, file transfer protocols, and the like, and serve as a master record that describes everything about where information physically goes and how it acts in relation to your domain name. If you've never been introduced to DNS before and it sounds like a serious topic, your intuition is serving you well—it's heavy-duty stuff, and not something you want to mess with unless you genuinely feel comfortable doing so. If the whole notion scares the living esquandolas out of you, go talk to your server administrator to see if they'll help you out, or find another qualified individual to perform these modifications.

In order for Multisite to work properly, we need to create a wildcard entry for subdomains. **Wildcard subdomains** are domains that haven't been specifically defined within the DNS tables, and setting them up alleviates the need to make individual DNS entries for each subdomain that Multisite creates. There are a couple of ways to set up wildcard subdomains, and it's a two-step process. On your Linux web server, you'll first need to be certain that Apache (the software that enables web serving capabilities) is configured to accept wildcards. To do this, open up the **httpd.conf** file or the include file containing the VHOST entry for your web account, and add in the following line:

```
ServerAlias *.esquandolas.com
```

It should go without saying, but you need to replace the domain name with your own. After this, you'll want to add the following DNS record to your server:

```
A *.esquandolas.com
```

It's worth mentioning that many hosting providers offer their clients one of several standardized control panels to assist them in managing their Linux web servers, and these control panels have their own steps and processes that users must go through in order to make modifications. Arguably, the most widespread of these control panels is cPanel, as seen in Figure 10.1.

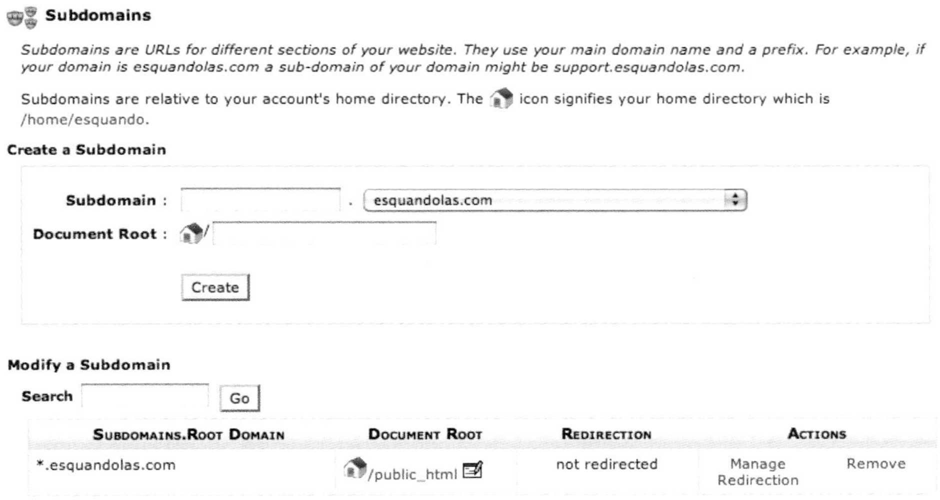

Figure 10.1. Creating your wildcard subdomain in cPanel

cPanel boasts the easiest method by far of enabling subdomains for Multisite; all you need to do is add a subdomain entry named "*" on the domain you're enabling Multisite on, and ensure that you point the subdomain to where your **wp-config.php** file is located. For a more detailed

explanation of how to similarly enable subdomain Multisite with other common control panels, take a look at the Codex page.[1]

 Check Your Plan

Be careful to take note that many cheap hosting providers do not allow their clients to set up wildcard DNS entries like we've just done. If you're uncertain whether this applies to you and your hosting plan, contact your hosting provider before you attempt this step.

Step 3: Allow Multisite in wp-config.php

Next, open up your **wp-config.php** file in a text editor, and where it says /* That's all, stop editing! Happy blogging. */, add the following line of code above it:

```
define('WP_ALLOW_MULTISITE', true);
```

This line of code is all that's needed to let WordPress know you plan to enable Multisite. It creates a new submenu item called **Network Setup** in the **Tools** subpanel of the **Admin** menu in the WordPress administrative back end.

Step 4: Install a network

Now that we've allowed Multisite on our WordPress install, it's time to go ahead and create a network. Be certain to deactivate all your plugins before you activate Multisite, or you'll receive an error telling you that all plugins must be deactivated before proceeding. So long as you're all set and good to go on the plugin front, navigate to **Tools > Network Setup** and you'll see the **Create a Network of WordPress Sites** screen, as shown in Figure 10.2.

---

[1] http://codex.wordpress.org/Create_A_Network#Specific_Configurations

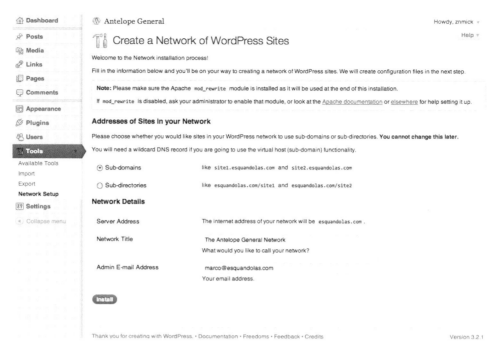

Figure 10.2. Creating a network of WordPress Sites

This is the place where we'll define whether we'll be using subdomains or subdirectories within Multisite, as well as name our network and provide an admin email address. Once you are satisfied with your entries, click the **Install** button … WordPress will do its thing, and then display a new screen providing a set of three instructions, as displayed below in Figure 10.3.

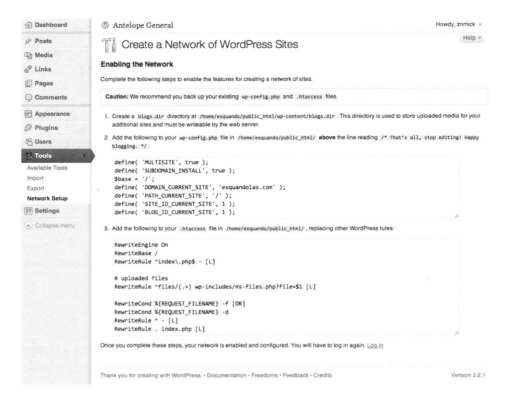

Figure 10.3. Customizing a directory for your network

As described by the onscreen instructions, you'll need to manually create a **blogs.dir** directory in the **wp-content** directory that is writable by the server, and then manually copy the code blocks provided into your **wp-config.php** and **.htaccess** files, respectively. Complete this step, and then log out of WordPress. Congratulations; you've just enabled Multisite in WordPress!

Multisite in Action

Now that we have successfully enabled Multisite in our WordPress installation, let's log back in and have a look around. Upon logging into WordPress with Multisite enabled and running, you'll initially not notice much difference at all, with the exception that there is now a **My Sites** submenu item listed in the **Dashboard** submenu panel. However, something else has changed, and that is the introduction of a new user role—a super administrator (which we'll also refer to as a super admin or a network admin). A super admin is an administrator who looks after all the network management systems and processes on a given WordPress Multisite installation. As the user who initially created the Multisite installation, you are granted super admin status (although you'll be able to spread this out to additional users later on if you so choose).

Logged into WordPress now as a super admin, some further investigation will yield a new menu item in the drop-down menu listed next to your name in the upper right-hand corner of the screen, as evident in Figure 10.4.

Figure 10.4. Now you're a network admin!

The key factor to recognize here is that with Multisite enabled, WordPress will provide you with two entirely separate administrative control panels to work with: the **Site Admin**, and the **Network Admin**. The **Site Admin** control panel looks almost identical to the WordPress you have come to know and love, and is designed to provide all the management functionality necessary for a website installed on the network. The main difference is the **My Sites** submenu item in the Dashboard subpanel, which gives you options to navigate to the Site Admin Dashboards that you have administrator access to within the network. You'll notice that the **Network Admin**, on the other hand, has a variety of options that a network administrator can work with. Go ahead and click on the **Network Admin** link and have a look around.

The Network Admin Dashboard

You'll notice in Figure 10.5 that the **Network Admin** area appears similar to the **Site Admin**, but there are several visual clues you can latch onto that will confirm you're in the right place.

Figure 10.5. Your new **Network Admin** dashboard

Your main indicator is the name of the network that you created; in this instance, the Esquandolas Network, which differs from the Antelope General website that we installed the network onto. A subtle color change might be a suitable visual cue to remind the administrator that the area they're

operating in is, indeed, an administration area entirely separate from the **Site Admin** area. Then again, as we've previously stated, Multisite is a feature set in evolutionary development, and it's reasonable to think that this distinction might be made clearer in the future.

In addition to the network name at the top of every screen in the **Network Admin** area, you'll also notice a slightly different **Admin** menu layout. We've expanded each of the top-level menus in our screenshot, and you'll see that they collectively hold a significant amount of new functionality that is essential for managing Multisite. Before we dig into each area one by one, notice that the Dashboard in the **Network Admin** area does include a new widget that you won't find on the **Site Admin** screen, giving you quick links to create new sites and new users, as well as search for existing sites and users (which become quite handy as the volume of sites and users grow in your network).

The Sites Submenu

The **Sites** submenu is fairly straightforward, as you can see in Figure 10.6, provides the **All Sites** and the **Add New** submenu items.

Figure 10.6. Adding a new site as the network admin

Clicking on the **Add New** submenu item brings you to the **Add New Site** screen. In the screenshot above, you'll notice we are using the subdomain method of creating new websites within our network. In order to create a new site, you'll need to define only three parameters:

1. the subdomain zone that the site will be created on (or the name of the subdirectory if you have selected subdirectory installation)
2. the title of the website
3. the primary administrative email

Here we've created a site called the Doniac Schvice, a sample network site that we'll be referring to for the duration of this illustration. Click on the **Install Site** button, and you'll see the new site loaded when you click the **All Sites** submenu option, as in Figure 10.7.

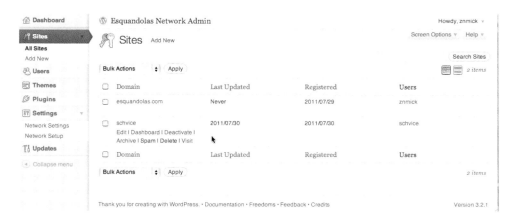

Figure 10.7. Our new site in the **All Sites** submenu

There are several points to take note of here. First of all, the label for the network site you just created is the name of the subdomain (or subdirectory) you just provided. Secondly, a new user with the same subdomain (or subdirectory) name has been automatically created for you. In this instance, Multisite has created **schvice** for us, associating the email address of mike@esquandolas.com that we provided while adding the site. This user is given the role of administrator by default, although it's pertinent to note that they are only able to administer settings on the site that they have been added to, in this instance **schvice**. Finally, rolling over an individual network site reveals a contextual menu similar to those we've seen elsewhere in WordPress. However, what you may find interesting are some of the submenu items that seem more likely to be found in posts rather than in network site administration. The **Edit**, **Dashboard**, **Delete**, and **Visit** options are all self-explanatory (and we'll dig much deeper into **Edit** in a moment), but **Deactivate**, **Archive** and **Spam** require a bit more explanation.

As we'll see in more detail in the **Network Admin Settings** menu, Multisite gives us the ability to create network websites in a manner that has shades of WordPress's built-in commenting system. Depending upon how Multisite is configured, new blog sites can actually be set up automatically without the intervention of an administrator. While this practice has relevant uses, it carries with it the inherent danger of automated **splog** (or "spam blog") creation. Splogs are unwanted blogs created either manually or by means of an automated script, and are typically packed full of content or affiliate links designed to fool search engines into providing a higher ranking to a particular website. Splogs are every bit the problem that comment spam can be on individual blogs themselves, and to this end Multisite gives you the ability to mark a particular network site instance as **Spam**, deactivating and removing it from the WordPress installation.

The final options in the contextual submenu in **All Sites** are **Archive** and **Deactivate**. Archiving and deactivating network site instances are very similar, and both are reversible (deleting a network website is not a reversible action). Either archiving or deactivating a network website will cause the website to no longer be outwardly visible on the Web, but deactivating a website will cause the site to no longer be accessible or manageable by site administrators either. Archived sites can be

managed by administrators. Network administrators have the sole ability to reactivate deactivated sites, while site administrators can unarchive their sites to make them once again visible on the Web. Plenty of tricky fun to be had here, right? Just wait … we're about to learn that there's a whole lot more than meets the eye to what at first seems to be some fairly light functionality.

Individual Network Site Settings

Every network site truly is its own individual entity, complete with its own content and privacy rules, visual design, and user base. When you click on the **Edit** submenu item in the contextual menu we've just described (or click on the name of the site you want to edit), you'll be greeted by a screen that says **Edit Site:**, and then the name of the site you are working on. In our case, it reads **Edit Site: schvice.esquandolas.com/** as seen in Figure 10.8.

Figure 10.8. Editing the settings for an individual site

It's useful to note that these are some of the most low-level settings offered for direct manipulation within WordPress, and as such none of them are to be toyed with.

 The High and the Low

If you are new to low-level/high-level terminology, here's a quick description. It's reasonably well understood that the higher-level a particular feature is, the more is being automatically done for you in the background. High-level functionality is designed to take the guesswork out of whatever it is you are doing, and typically caters to tasks that can be completed quickly by batching certain repetitive processes, or to less-experienced users who don't have the knowledge base to do certain things. Examples of high-level functionality include the visual editor provided within WordPress, or the WordPress administrative back end itself. Low-level functionality, on the other hand, involves functionality that's happening deeper within the code, closer to where the logic is actually being executed. Low-level functionality affords more options and a higher level of flexibility in how you

can make something happen, but it's also much, much easier to permanently break things with low-level tools, so it's worth offering you a firm warning before you wade too deeply into anything with those characteristics. Don't be afraid to look around, but proceed with caution and respect.

In the **Network Admin** area, the **Edit Site:** screen is broken up into four tabs, beginning with the **Info** tab. There's no good reason to modify the **Info** tab in any way, but it's useful for understanding when the site was registered and last created. Matters become a bit more interesting when you click on the **Users** tab, as you'll see in Figure 10.9.

Figure 10.9. Editing individual site users

The **Users** tab looks much like the standard **Users** screen in the regular **Site Admin** area, but you'll notice that there are actually two ways to add users to a network site. Because we're working within the context of a website network, users who have already been registered on a different website within the network can be added here as well, and assigned any role of your choosing. Perhaps enacted as a security feature, WordPress doesn't provide a username input box here that is smart enough to pull from an Ajaxed list of users already defined within the database, but rather forces you to input a specific username upon adding the user. There are, of course, plugins available that modify this default functionality, but it's worthwhile mentioning the basic way it works here. The second way to add users reflects the way users are added and managed throughout the rest of WordPress, enabling you to create new users and assign roles as you would anywhere else.

Next up is the **Themes** tab, and marks our first introduction in Multisite to the notion of something being network enabled. Let's take a moment to explain this concept. Both themes and plugins can be defined as **network enabled**, which means that they are automatically available for use by any given site administrator within every single website throughout the network. However, themes and plugins differ in that network administrators are able to upload individual themes to the network and then enable them for specific sites within the network. Plugins that are uploaded to the network must either be network enabled or inactive altogether. Furthermore, once Multisite is enabled, plugins can only be installed in the **Network Admin** area, which by definition means that the only users who can actually install new plugins are super admins. Site administrators, therefore, cannot upload new plugins themselves, but can activate and deactivate plugins that have been made available for use on their site. If you are a bit confused, don't sweat it—this one is a bit of a mind bender, but Figure 10.10 below might help you understand it better.

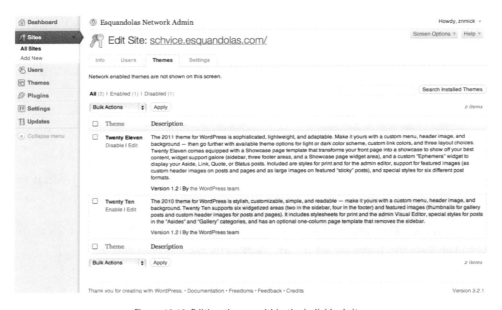

Figure 10.10. Editing themes within the individual sites

In the **Themes** tab, we see two themes that are available for us to work with: Twenty Eleven and Twenty Ten. We've enabled Twenty Eleven here, which won't actually activate the theme on the http://schvice.esquandolas.com network site, but rather makes the theme available to the individual site administrator to activate and make live on their network site. Furthermore, notice the line of text above the themes which states that "Network enabled themes are not shown on this screen." This lets us know that while we've enabled Twenty Eleven for use on schvice.esquandolas.com, we very well may see other options that we choose to use for our theme as well. For instance, if our network administrator has marked two other themes—Twenty Twelve and Twenty Thirteen—as network enabled, then ultimately the site administrator for schvice.esquandolas.com will have three themes available to work with: Twenty Eleven, Twenty Twelve, and Twenty Thirteen.

After you have read the above paragraph a few times and stopped your head from spinning, you may find yourself asking the question: "Okay, so where do the themes come from that I'm seeing in the **Themes** tab?" It's a great question, and the answer is that the themes that are made available to you within the **Themes** tab are the disabled themes that have been loaded into the Network Admin Themes Manager, as seen in Figure 10.11.

Figure 10.11. Themes that have been installed in your network

If this all seems like a long, strange, winding road, we're here to tell you that yeah, it is. Have we mentioned that Multisite is in an evolutionary development cycle?

Finally, we can click on the **Settings** tab, depicted in Figure 10.12, which provides extremely low-level access to the specific features set up for each network site.

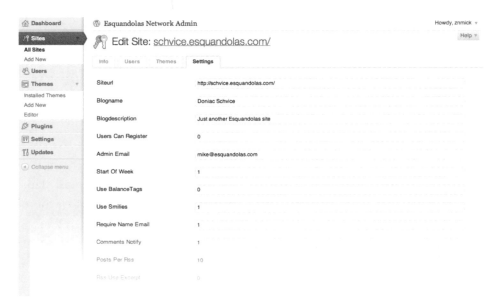

Figure 10.12. Editing the settings in an individual site

The options and parameters that are available to be set correspond directly to the record for the network site, as listed in the installation's database, and you'll notice that some of the options listed here are actually Booleans (where **0** equals no or false, and **1** equals yes or true). If you feel comfortable playing around in here, you can use this screen to quickly override some global Multisite settings, which brings us to the **Settings** subpanel of the **Admin** menu in the **Network Admin** area.

The Settings Submenu

Although it's not the next option sequentially in the **Admin** menu, if you look towards the bottom of the **Admin** menu and expand the **Settings** panel, you'll see two options: **Network Settings** and **Network Setup**. **Network Setup** is there for reference purposes only, and is the same screen that we saw when initially enabling Multisite in our WordPress installation; this asked us to create a **blogs.dir** directory in **wp-content**, and install specific code chunks into both **wp-config.php** and your **.htaccess** file. **Network Settings**, however, is the primary screen that controls most of the master settings functionality for the entire Multisite installation. This is a screen with many options, but we'll break each down for you here in Figure 10.13, complete with screenshots, starting with **Operational Settings**.

Figure 10.13. Operational settings for your network

This defines the name of the network as well as the network administrative email. This is fairly straightforward, so let's move down to **Registration Settings**, seen in Figure 10.14, where things get a bit more interesting.

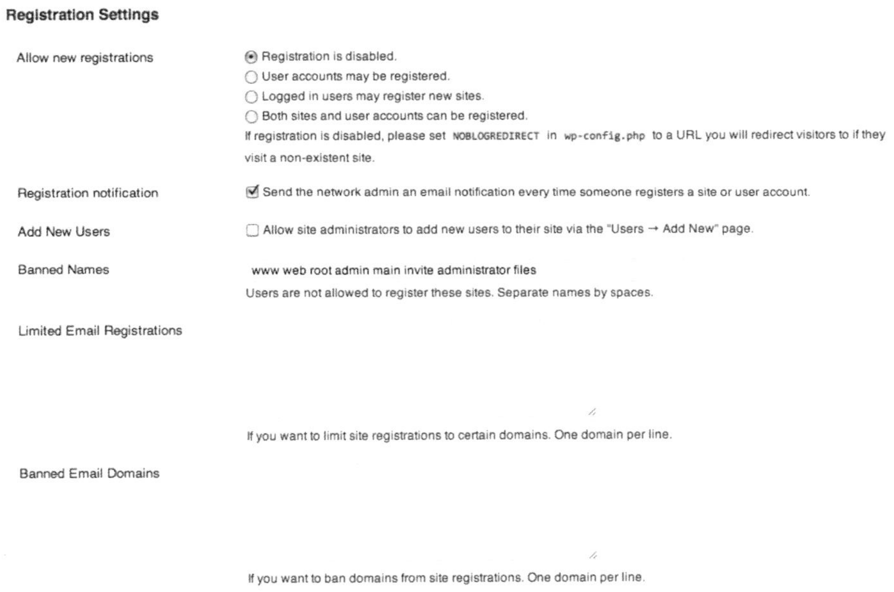

Registration Settings

Allow new registrations
- Registration is disabled.
- User accounts may be registered.
- Logged in users may register new sites.
- Both sites and user accounts can be registered.

If registration is disabled, please set `NOBLOGREDIRECT` in `wp-config.php` to a URL you will redirect visitors to if they visit a non-existent site.

Registration notification
☑ Send the network admin an email notification every time someone registers a site or user account.

Add New Users
☐ Allow site administrators to add new users to their site via the "Users → Add New" page.

Banned Names
www web root admin main invite administrator files
Users are not allowed to register these sites. Separate names by spaces.

Limited Email Registrations

If you want to limit site registrations to certain domains. One domain per line.

Banned Email Domains

If you want to ban domains from site registrations. One domain per line.

Figure 10.14. Registration settings for your network

Registration Settings defines who can create a new user or new site, and where those sites can be created. While it looks harmless, it's really one of the most crucial aspects of Multisite configuration. Let's break down each option, one by one:

Allow new registrations deals specifically with who can create new users and websites via the front-facing public portal of the Multisite installation. It refers to users who are visiting and interacting with the network, rather than site administrators.

- **Registration is disabled** essentially locks down the Multisite installation. Any existing sites or users that have been created are allowed to remain intact, but under no circumstances can anybody create new user accounts or network sites while this option is selected. It's ideal if you're paranoid about security, spam, and splogs.

- **User accounts may be registered** allows new users to register themselves but not necessarily create new sites. This option is good if you want to allow users to register and interact with one another via WordPress's built-in commenting system on existing websites within the network.

- **Logged in users may register new sites** allows users who are logged in to create their own sites, but does not necessarily give users the ability to register on the network themselves. This is an excellent option to use where you want to define a set of users that you as an administrator trust with creating websites, but want to stop short at opening your site registration to the public.

- **Both sites and user accounts can be registered** is almost identical to the way the website network on wordpress.com is run, and opens up the front-end registration page that would be accessible at http://esquandolas.com/wp-signup.php. Users have the ability to register themselves, and then create new site/s that they can manage. This is obviously the most permissive of all the different user and site creation options, and has the potential to be exploited if not configured and monitored properly.

Registration notification is a checkbox that sends the network admin an email notification every time a user registers a site or email account. This is a handy tool to use in the early stages of populating a network with users and sites, but can become unwieldy as the volume increases.

Add New Users is a checkbox that allows site administrators to add new users within their own **Site Admin** area by navigating to **Users** > **Add New**. Again, this is a useful switch that you can flip on or off depending largely upon how much you trust the site administrators working within your network. Every network is different, and don't be afraid to make security restrictions that you deem appropriate to your particular situation.

Banned Names refers specifically to subdomains or subdirectories that you will under no circumstances allow to be created in your network. WordPress lists the defaults that you will probably want to make sure are listed, but you may find that there are others that you want to add as well. For example, due to the combination of the method that permalinking structures are set up with in WordPress as well as the very nature of Multisite, routing collisions can occur when you create a page on your primary site and then and allow a network site of the same name to be created.

To better understand the potential problem here, let's look at an example. Consider a situation where you use a Multisite network configured to work with subdirectories to create a network website called running. The URL for that website might be called http://esquandolas.com/running, which is all well and good; however, what if we already had a **Running with the Antelopes** page on the primary directory that already had a slug entitled running. This would create a permalink collision, and in this instance the network site would be given routing priority and actually override the page originating within the primary site, creating a situation where people just can't find out how to run with the antelopes … and nobody wants that.

The solution to this is to be sure to take care to add the individual slugs of pages within your primary site to the **Banned Names** box, thus avoiding the possibility of anybody using one of those names in the first place. Who knows—in the future, maybe Multisite will be smart enough to be able to at least give us the option to dynamically pick up the page slug listing from the primary site and automatically restrict the ability to create network sites in those namespaces.

In the event that you're happy to allow site registrations from anybody who uses an email address with a particular domain name, you can just add the domain name in the **Limited Email Registrations** dialog box, and you'll be set to go. This is useful, for example, if you are an organization with your own domain name and want to allow only your employees with a corporate email address to create their own sites. In this instance, you'd just add your corporate domain name (or domain names, if you use several for your corporation). Subsequently, users who registered on the network under their corporate email addresses would have site creation authority, while other users would not.

Banned Email Domains have the exact opposite effect as **Limited Email Registrations** do. Using **Banned Email Domains**, an administrator can specifically restrict the authority to create new network sites from users who are using specific domain names. This is a useful option if you'd like to restrict users who create a veil of anonymity by originating from free email hosting services.

New Site Settings, as seen in Figure 10.15, are next to the plate, and supply the verbiage templates that users will see upon initially registering as both a user as well as creating a new site. Network administrators who are sensitive to the ambience and sense of community they want to create and nurture among the members of their network are well advised to pay attention to this area in particular, as the tone and content of the verbiage provided in this space provides the initial impression your user will receive of your network as a whole. After all, networks are typically put together for one of two reasons: either to consolidate the management of a set of websites and make things easier for technical staff, or to create and nurture an online community. If your intent falls within the community side of things, then you'll find that this is one of those "separating-the-men-from-the-boys" type of aspects that many organizations fall completely flat on. Pay attention to this—it's a detail, to be sure, but it's an awfully big detail.

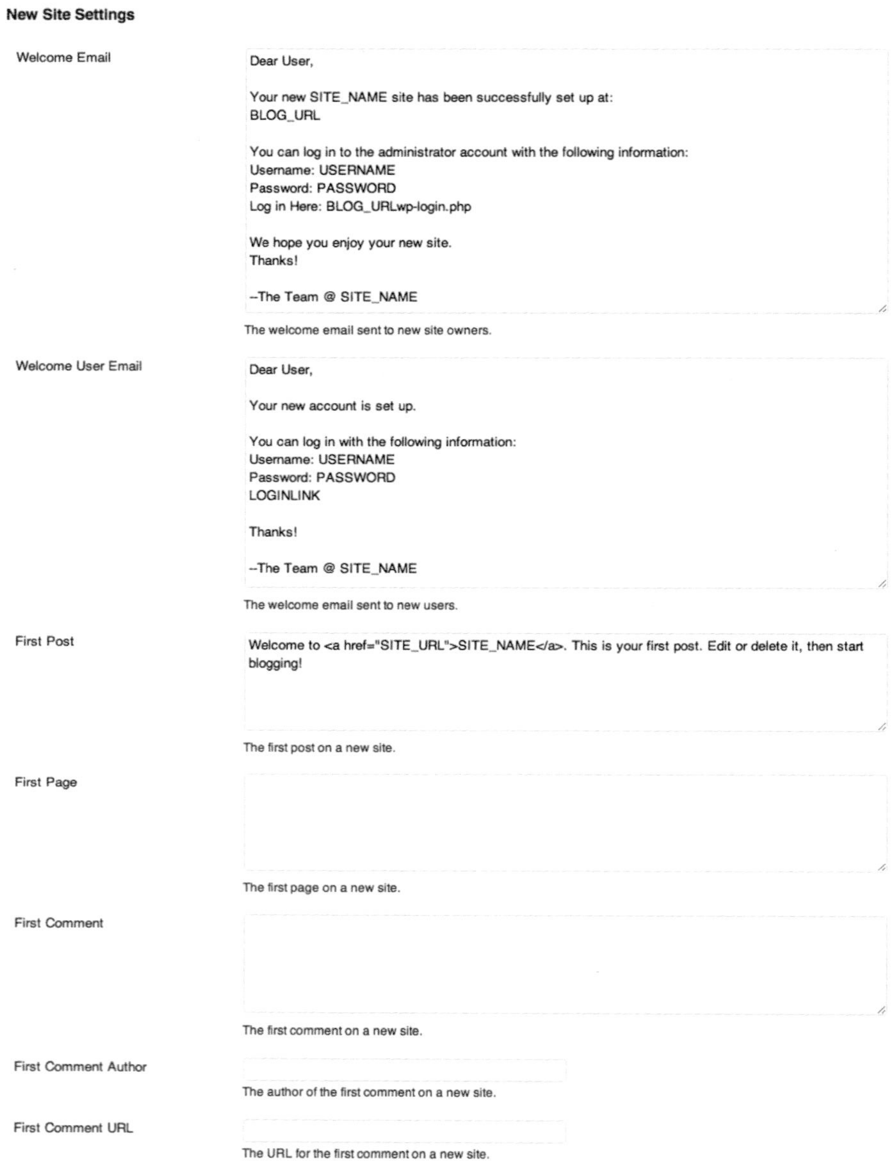

New Site Settings

Welcome Email	Dear User, Your new SITE_NAME site has been successfully set up at: BLOG_URL You can log in to the administrator account with the following information: Username: USERNAME Password: PASSWORD Log in Here: BLOG_URLwp-login.php We hope you enjoy your new site. Thanks! --The Team @ SITE_NAME

The welcome email sent to new site owners.

Welcome User Email	Dear User, Your new account is set up. You can log in with the following information: Username: USERNAME Password: PASSWORD LOGINLINK Thanks! --The Team @ SITE_NAME

The welcome email sent to new users.

First Post	Welcome to <a href="SITE_URL">SITE_NAME</a>. This is your first post. Edit or delete it, then start blogging!

The first post on a new site.

First Page	

The first page on a new site.

First Comment	

The first comment on a new site.

First Comment Author	

The author of the first comment on a new site.

First Comment URL	

The URL for the first comment on a new site.

Figure 10.15. Verbiage templates that you can modify to suit your needs

In this screenshot, we've included the default text associated with each of the templates. You can (and should) make changes to all of them, adding your own text to personalize your user's experience. As you'll note in **First Post**, HTML is allowed here.

Most of these templates should be self-explanatory, but we'll give you a heads-up on the nuances of each. **Welcome Email** is, of course, the email that will be sent out to the site admin email address any time a new site is registered. Notice that the email includes the variables SITE_NAME, BLOG_URL, USERNAME, and PASSWORD. If you've ever worked with **Mail Merge** inside word processors, hosted

newsletter services, or other programs of the sort, you'll recognize these types of variables as tags that will be replaced by actual user information. It's unnecessarily to include them, but your user will probably appreciate it if you do. You'll find similar variables in the **Welcome User Email** (sends out a welcome email to a user), as well as **First Post**, which defines the text for the initial post on the website.

First Page, **First Comment**, and **First Comment Author** are all left blank. WordPress has default content that it inserts into these spaces; however, your own entries here will trump WordPress. Finally, **First Comment URL** is just the slug that's associated with the first comment, and defaults to comment-1.

The last section of the **Network Settings** page contains **Upload Settings** and **Menu Settings**, and can be seen in Figure 10.16.

Figure 10.16. **Upload Settings** and **Menu Settings**

The **Media upload buttons** checkbox options do nothing more than display the different icons that provide a visual cue as to the different types of media that can be uploaded. However, if you have played with the media upload and media library functionality within WordPress at any length, you know that these buttons actually all go to the same upload screen, and what is far more important is that **Upload file types** text box listed further on within the same section. The file types are based upon the file extension associated with each file, and delineated from one another by a single space between each one. While you can technically add new file types to your heart's content, the ones that are added by default are generally a pretty good indication of what is appropriate. If you value having a running, non-compromised web server, do yourself a favor and try to stay away from **.exe**, **.doc**, and **.docx** files as a rule of thumb.

Site upload space and **Max upload file size** are handy controls to pay attention to as well. Uploaded files are almost always media files, and media files can get pretty big, eating up space on your web server and slowing your system down. It's generally considered a poor practice to expand either of these values too high, or uncheck the **Site upload space** parameter altogether.

Finally, **Menu Settings** deals solely with whether or not you want to allow site administrators the ability to activate or deactivate plugins that have been approved for use and made available to individual sites by network administrators. It's important to note that site administrators never have the ability to add, delete or modify plugins on their own, and this authority must instead be managed strictly by a network administrator.

The Users Submenu

Well, that was a mouthful, huh? There really is a lot to Multisite, but the good news is that we've covered the bulk of the menu options. From here on, the rest of the configurable options in the **Network Admin** area are fairly self-explanatory, with the exception of a few items that are worth pointing out. Let's start by clicking on the **All Users** submenu item in the **Users** subpanel seen in Figure 10.17.

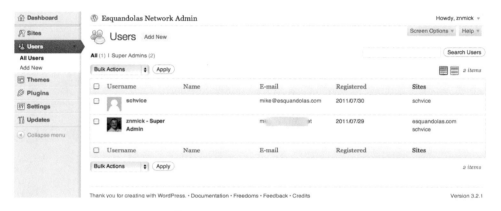

Figure 10.17. Looking into **All Users**

In general, users look, act, and feel very similar to users within the context of a typical standalone WordPress site. Aside from the notion of a network administrator (or super admin as denoted in Figure 10.17), the roles are identical in the core installation. What is useful to point out, however, is that users are not automatically added to every site, but rather are associated with individual sets within the network. In the **Users** screen, columns exist that list all of the sites a particular user is associated with, as well as the date that the user was initially registered on the network.

The Themes Submenu

The **Themes** subpanel predictably deals with themes that have been uploaded to the network. We've already discussed themes in detail in the context of Multisite, but for a theme to be initially available within any given network site, it must first be uploaded into the **Themes** subpanel by clicking on the **Add New** submenu item in the menu, or at the top of the **Themes** listing page. Once installed, any given theme can be network-enabled, which means that it's available for use by default throughout every site on the network. Themes that aren't network-enabled can still be made available

on a site by visiting the **Themes** tab of that site's **Edit Site:** screen, accessible in the **Sites** > **All Sites** listing.

For a more comprehensive discussion of themes within Multisite, refer back to the the section called "Individual Network Site Settings" on the **Themes** tab of the **Edit Site:** screen earlier in this chapter.

The Plugins Submenu

In the context of Multisite, plugins are similar to themes in that they can be installed and network-enabled, thus becoming available to site administrators throughout the network. The **Plugins** screen can be seen in Figure 10.18.

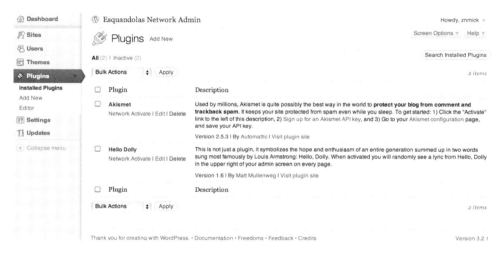

Figure 10.18. Network plugins

By network-enabling a plugin, network administrators can effectively determine which plugins are suitable for use within the network; however, it's worth noting that not all plugins will work when network-enabled. If a plugin is coded incorrectly, it can run into problems when used in conjunction with Multisite.

It's useful to note that just as they are with standard WordPress, must-use and drop-in plugins are also available for use within Multisite, enabling the ability to force the use of specific plugins throughout the network as well as the firing of specific scripts at specified times during the loading of Multisite in general. For more information on these types of plugins, refer back to the section called "Must-use Plugins" in Chapter 5 and the section called "Drop-in Plugins" in Chapter 5.

The Updates Submenu

Last but not least in the **Network Admin** area is the **Updates** subpanel. Arguably the most useful aspect of Multisite in general, the functionality controlled in this subpanel is the figurative engine that drives Multisite from a functional perspective. It's also the main reason you might be interested in

using it if you are looking to centralize the management of a multitude of WordPress sites rather than attempting to build a community.

Updates is essentially a two-step process. Clicking on the **Available Updates** submenu item will list all the available theme, plugin, and core WordPress updates that are available to be downloaded and used. When you're ready to make your upgrades, click on the **Update Network** submenu item that will bring you to a screen with an **Update Network** button. This function works by calling the update script of each site individually and automatically, so that the individual network sites update themselves one by one.

As always, save yourself a headache and have some mechanism to back your sites up before you touch this with a 10-foot pole.

Useful Plugins Within Multisite

We've covered the basics of Multisite functionality as included with core WordPress, but there are several notable plugins that add useful functionality, making Multisite more relevant in the real world. While not an exhaustive list by any stretch of the imagination, here's a few that support Multisite and are worth taking a look at:

WordPress MU Domain Mapping[2]

Allows users to map their subdomain or subdirectory network nomenclatures to specific domain nomenclatures. In this way, you can take a specific domain and map it to any given network site, permanently altering your root permalinks to reflect unique domain names instead of subdomains or subdirectories.

Role Scoper[3]

Role Scoper is a killer plugin that allows you to extend user roles in many different ways. Aside from giving you the ability to define groups and assign them specific roles, it also gives you the opportunity to assign roles and restrictions to specific posts, pages, or categories.

Cimy User Extra Fields[4]

Cimy User Extra Fields allows you to create additional user fields to your heart's content, complete with form validation that's configurable by an administrator to verify that fields are all properly filled.

Troubleshooting Multisite

As we've previously mentioned, Multisite is a WordPress feature set that has recently been the subject of a rapid evolutionary development cycle, and chances are that this will continue with

---

[2] http://wordpress.org/extend/plugins/wordpress-mu-domain-mapping/
[3] http://wordpress.org/extend/plugins/role-scoper/
[4] http://wordpress.org/extend/plugins/cimy-user-extra-fields/

new major WordPress releases. As a result, there are nuances worth paying attention to. While by no means comprehensive, this next section should give you a general idea as to some of the more common issues.

Enabling Multisite

While enabling Multisite is easy enough in an ideal environment, it's not quite the painless, foolproof process that installing WordPress is. We've already covered a few situations where enabling Multisite is not possible, but there are several others. If you find yourself having issues, chances are that one of these reasons may be the culprit, so you'll need to circle the wagons and come up with a different approach.

Multisite has no support on subdomains in instances where the WordPress URL is defined as:

- localhost
- IP address, as opposed to a domain name

Multisite is not supported in subdirectories in the following circumstances:

- WordPress is installed on a non-Linux server that does not support **.htaccess** and **mod_rewrite**.

- Due to issues with the way that the permalinking system is set up, a WordPress installation has been set up for a time span that covers more than a single month (this is an issue that is slated to be corrected in a subsequent release).

Routing Issues in Subdirectory Multisite Installations

The other place where we tend to see issues crop up as a result of Multisite in subdirectory installations is in permalink routing collisions between the primary site hosting the network functionality and the network site themselves. Let's look at the two most common ones.

- On the primary site, an extra taxonomy label of **/blog/** is automatically created to avert routing collisions in subdirectory Multisite installations. This only pertains to the category and post structure, and not pages. However, if you create a page with a slug of blog on the main site, you'll find an issue where the page is superseded and fails to display due to the inherent permalink collision. As of the time of writing, there is no solution for this permalinking collision issue, aside from being aware of it and simply avoiding it.

- We touched on this earlier within the chapter, but there's also the issue of creating named pages whose slugs are labelled identically to network sites within the installation. To avoid this issue, be sure to manually add the individual slugs of pages within your primary site to the **Banned Names** box in the **Network Settings** screen. This is accessible via **Settings** > **Network Settings**, and will avoid the possibility of anybody using one of those names in the first place.

You're Multiskilled

Multisite enables you to consolidate the management of multiple WordPress sites into a single installation, and is an extremely useful tool that appeals to two primary user groups: people who want to streamline the management of multiple WordPress sites, and people who are interested in developing diverse communities of blogs the way Automattic maintains on wordpress.com.

Beginning its life as a separate project in the WordPress universe, Multisite was merged into the WordPress core as of the major 3.0 release. While an incredibly feature-rich set of functionality, Multisite is currently in a heavy stage of development as a core WordPress component, and is not enabled by default in any given WordPress installation. However, if you are willing to roll up your sleeves and get dirty with Multisite, its benefits are potentially extremely rewarding.

Going Global with Themes and Plugins

With the worldwide success of WordPress, it's easy to understand why it's useful to be able to seamlessly translate plugins, themes and WordPress itself into other languages. However, that doesn't necessarily make it easily adopted, and for good reason. Localization (or internationalization, as it is sometimes referred to) is not a new concept, nor is the notion of doing business internationally. However, what we're beginning to see now amounts to a perfect storm for WordPress.

Initially a blogging platform popular among a niche of independent amateur journalists, WordPress' growth has been fueled by its widespread adoption within the SME (small to medium-sized enterprises) market in the past few years. As of the time of writing, WordPress is being run by roughly 14.5% of all websites on the Internet, easily outpacing its closest competitors, Drupal and Joomla. The reasons for this are varied:

- Since the social media explosion of the late 2000s, being online has become a way of life for professionals throughout the world. Online services and software that are functional and easy to use have exploded in popularity, and WordPress is arguably the easiest CMS available to nontech people.

- WordPress is painfully easy to set up. Like many other CMSs, WordPress can be installed via a one-click installer like Fantastico or SimpleScripts. However, if you want to install WordPress manually, your time investment won't be more than five minutes or so.

- WordPress is incredibly flexible, as we've seen with plugins that are easy to use and install, essentially future-proofing the system. This has caused the typically frugal SME market to gain confidence and feel comfortable investing time and financial resources in WordPress websites.

■ We're seeing a shift in the business climate, with many parts of the world decentralizing and moving away from a typical corporate structure. This is fueling a more independent-thinking SME market.

■ When properly set up and configured, WordPress has shown itself to be extremely attractive to search engines, often gaining organic ranking with ease where other CMSs fail (more on this in Chapter 12).

Understandably, localization has been the source of confusion for many a WordPress developer. After all, we're web developers, not linguistic experts, and it's a lot easier to just apply labels to fields in our programs in plain English. Plus, the idea of trying to figure out how to translate text strings into other languages on our own (much less having somebody else do it for us) might induce mild nausea in even seasoned developers who've never had the need or inclination to do so before. But trust me, it's really not all that bad, and it can significantly increase the usefulness as well as the user base of your custom WordPress plugins and themes. Let's break it down into bite-sized pieces, starting with the foundations.

The Basics of Internationalization and Localization

Let's examine that aforementioned development nausea just a bit. The way many of us learned to code, keeping language considerations in mind when coding a PHP program was, at best, rather academic. The majority of commercial coding projects have targeted scopes with defined audiences, so it's often been reasonable to assume we can proceed without regard to translation. However, since WordPress plugins and themes ultimately become more functional when a user can employ them in their own language, we need a systematic way to correct this issue.

Enter **i18n**—another fun acronym to tuck under your belt. Named for the fact that there are 18 letters between the i and the n in the word *internationalization*, i18n describes the notion of creating software systems that are designed to be translated into other languages. The process of actually translating that software into a specific language is referred to as localization or **L10n** (can you guess how many letters are between the L and the n in the word *localization*?).[1] WordPress utilizes a specific framework to handle i18n called GNU gettext—the de facto standard system that is used in nearly all open-source software. GNU gettext is really just a library of PHP helper functions. Since it is coded right into core, WordPress has the hooks necessary to allow you as a developer to define text string variables in your themes and plugins, as well as a standardized system to provide translations for each string in an unlimited number of languages.

---

[1] The "L" in L10n is generally upper-cased to distinguish it from "i," which, when upper-cased, looks almost exactly the same.

Anatomy of a Localization Process

In general terms, the localization process is fairly straightforward. Conceptually, there are three key components to the process for either a theme or a plugin:

- GNU gettext markers in your theme or plugin that tell WordPress which strings to translate

- a function linking the markers in your theme or plugin to a file that provides a translation key

- a file that provides a translation key, essentially creating a one-to-one relationship between translatable strings, and what the translation should be for a given string

Let's talk in a bit more detail as to what each of these three components do.

GNU gettext Markers Tell Which Strings to Translate

In this first component, we need to let WordPress know which strings we want to translate. This is done directly in the output code of your theme or plugin by wrapping a specific string with a PHP function that identifies the type of localization you want, and then running your original string through a filter that will return the correct version. While there are an array of functions that exist within gettext that allow you to define or output localized strings in different ways (you can see a more thorough description of them in the Codex[2]), there are really only two localization functions you'll use the majority of the time:

`__( 'string', $domain )`	This is a double underscore, and returns a localized string.
`_e( 'string', $domain )`	This is an underscore "e" that prints out a localized string directly to the browser.

Note that both `__()` and `_e()` take two parameters, a string and a domain. In this context, a domain is strictly a unique identifier; the label that is attached to a specific translation file (many developers commonly recommend that this be the unique plugin name). This relationship is defined in the second component.

A Function Linking Markers to a File with a Translation Key

Secondly, within your theme or plugin, you'll need to create a relationship between the strings you want to translate and a translation file that provides a key for the string translation. This is done using the PHP function `load_theme_textdomain()` for themes, or `load_plugin_textdomain()` for plugins.

In the case of theme localization, you'll use `load_theme_textdomain()` in your **functions.php** file. The function takes two parameters, which follows:

---

[2] http://codex.wordpress.org/I18n_for_WordPress_Developers#Marking_Strings_for_Translation

```
load_theme_textdomain( $domain, $path )
```

- *$domain*: a unique identifier assigned to your custom translatable strings
- *$path*: the path to your translation key file within the theme

Theme localization is connected to the WPLANG constant in **wp-config.php**, but we'll discuss this in more detail in a bit.

Plugin localization works very similarly to theme localization, but with a few differences. Set within the core PHP files of the i18n-enabled plugin, load_plugin_textdomain() takes *three* parameters:

```
load_plugin_textdomain( $domain, $abs_rel_path, $plugin_rel_path )
```

- *$domain*: a unique identifier assigned to your custom translatable strings

- *$abs_rel_path*: an optional, deprecated function as of WordPress 2.7, which you can default to false or just omit—it's nothing to worry about

- *$plugin_rel_path*: the relative path to your translation key file. If you fail to define this path, it will default to the root directory that the file is in. While this is by definition an optional parameter, it's best practice to keep your language translation files separate from your logic files, so you'll usually want to specify a value here.

In both these instances, *$domain* is the unique identifier that we referred to in the first component. It serves only to define a relationship between the strings in the code that require translation, and the third component, the translation key.

A File Providing a Translation Key

In this third component, GNU gettext offers us a systematic way of providing a mechanism to create one-to-one string translation relationships between individual default strings and their respective translations, and then feeding those various string translations to WordPress in an efficient manner. This is done through .**PO** and .**MO** files.

A .**PO** file is a file that provides a human-readable and editable translation key for a specific language. For instance, if your theme or plugin was written in English and you had translations readily available for French, German, and Pirate English, you would have three corresponding .**PO** files—one for each of the languages. When a specific string translation is made, it happens in this file.

While .**PO** files are human friendly and easily editable, they are not ideal for WordPress to use while processing translation in practice. Instead, WordPress will use an .**MO** file for its actual translation. .**MO** files are compiled files that can be automatically generated for you when you use helper tools

like Poedit (see the section called "Introducing Poedit"). Each **.PO** file has a corresponding **.MO** file that is updated each time the **.PO** file is updated.

The final file pertinent file type is the **.POT** file, or **.PO Template** file. A **.POT** file is an exact copy of any of the **.PO** files in a localization instance, with the exception that it is void of any translations. Making **.POT** files available to translators allows them to easily create translations for your themes and plugins into their own native language using helper tools.

Putting the Pieces Together

So now that we know the main components in a localization process, let's have a visual look at how they work together in WordPress. Consider the diagram in Figure 11.1.

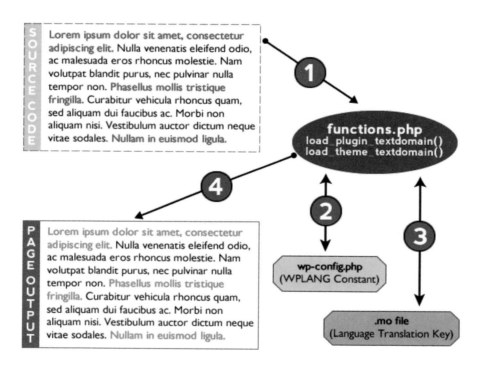

Figure 11.1. Localization in action

We'll start with the program's source code. When a browser initially moves to call a specific page, the translation process is initiated when it recognizes the __() and _e() functions in the source code wrapping text strings. WordPress recognizes these functions because GNU gettext is built into its core, and automatically seeks to translate them. Your **functions.php** file has already been loaded here, and WordPress is able to use the load_plugin_textdomain() or load_theme_textdomain() functions in the **functions.php** file to identify and connect the strings to a library location (depicted in Step 1 in Figure 11.1). load_plugin_textdomain() or load_theme_textdomain() then retrieve the locale information from the WPLANG constant set in **wp-config.php** (Step 2 in Figure 11.1) and retrieve the proper **.MO** file associated with the locale (Step 3 in the Figure 11.1). If the properly

named **.MO** file exists, the functions output the translated strings to the browser (Step 4 in Figure 11.1). If a properly named **.MO** file does not exist, or for any strings that do not have translated entries within the **.MO** file, the default verbiage is instead output to the browser. Finally, the **.MO** file is a compiled version of a **.PO** file, which is human editable. Likewise, **.PO** files have template files that allow translators to easily modify strings in your program into other languages.

Now let's dig a little deeper and take a look at some real code, shall we?

Localizing a Theme

When you are localizing a theme, you'll usually only be addressing text strings that appear in different places of your theme. Let's have a look at some basic HTML code that has a few strings in it:

chapter_11/html-unlocalized-example1.php

```
<!DOCTYPE HTML>
<html>
<head>
<meta http-equiv="Content-Type" content="text/html; charset=UTF-8">
<title>Localization Sample</title>
</head>

<body>
  <p>My name is Mick.</p>
  <p>I have a dog named Lacie.</p>
  <p>My dog's name is Lacie, but we call her Bug.</p>
  <p>Sometimes, we call her Buggers.</p>
  <p>Lacie has a black coat.</p>

</body>
</html>
```

Not much to see here, really. We just have five different strings of text entered into an HTML document in a pretty generic way. However, we can localize this page by simply wrapping each of the strings with the _e() function:

chapter_11/html-localization-example1.php

```
<!DOCTYPE HTML>
<html>
<head>
<meta http-equiv="Content-Type" content="text/html; charset=UTF-8">
<title>Localization Sample</title>
</head>

<body>
  <p><?php _e( 'My name is Mick.', 'our-very-unique-domain' ); ?></p>
  <p><?php _e( 'I have a dog named Lacie.', 'our-very-unique-domain' ); ?></p>
```

```
<p><?php _e( 'My dog\'s name is Lacie, but we call her Bug.',➡
            'our-very-unique-domain' ); ?></p>
<p><?php _e( 'Sometimes, we call her Buggers.', 'our-very-unique-domain' );➡
    ?></p>
<p><?php _e( 'Lacie has a black coat.', 'our-very-unique-domain' ); ?></p>

</body>
</html>
```

This is a bit more interesting now. We've wrapped each text string with _e() and set our textdomain constant for the localization. Note that we use a constant called our-very-unique-domain. It really doesn't matter what you call this domain so long as it's unique to you, and that you initialize the relationship with the same unique name.

Be Consistent

You absolutely *must* use the same domain throughout the context of your theme or plugin in order for the localization process to work. Mismatched names will break the link, causing the translation to not work correctly (or at all).

How do we initialize the relationship within **functions.php**? Let's look at the code:

chapter_11/initialize-functions-dot-php-localization.php

```php
<?php
load_theme_textdomain( 'our-very-unique-domain', TEMPLATEPATH.'/languages' );

$locale = get_locale();
$locale_file = TEMPLATEPATH."/languages/$locale.php";
if ( is_readable($locale_file) )
    require_once($locale_file);
?>
```

As you can see, on line one we've fired up load_theme_textdomain() and specified that our language translation files will live in the **languages** folder of our theme. So far, so good, but now we see bunch of stuff that talks about locale. Theme localization depends on the WPLANG constant in **wp-config.php** that defines the locale. The locale is a combination of both a country and a language code specified by the GNU gettext framework—you can look up country and language abbreviations in the gettext manual[3]. Open up your **wp-config.php** file and look to see if you have a custom WordPress locale defined; if you don't, go ahead and define it now. For example, if you are using German as the main language for your site, you would see (or manually add) a line in your **wp-config.php** file like this:

```php
define ( 'WPLANG', 'de_DE' );
```

---

[3] http://www.gnu.org/software/gettext/manual/

With the WordPress locale set, (in this case *de_DE*), our code above will now seek to find a German localization file called **de_DE.mo** in the **languages** directory of our theme. Therefore, the files in our sample theme directory might ultimately have a structure that looks like Figure 11.2.

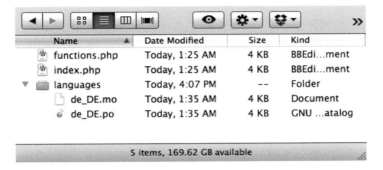

Figure 11.2. Theme-localized file structure

Localizing a Plugin

Localizing a plugin is similar to localizing a theme. Let's take it from the top by looking at a simple plugin that is yet to be localized:

chapter_11/plugin-unlocalized-example1.php

```php
<?php
/*
Plugin Name: Our Sample Plugin
Plugin URI: http://www.sitepoint.com/our-sample-plugin
Description: Sample localization code demonstration
Version: 1
Author: Mick Olinik
Author URI: http://www.sitepoint.com
License: GPL2
*/

add_action( 'init', 'olin_osp_init' );
function olin_osp_init() {
  add_action( 'admin_menu', 'olin_osp_menu' );
}

function olin_osp_menu() {
  add_options_page( 'Our Sample Plugin Options', 'Our Sample Plugin',➥
    'manage_options', 'our-sample-plugin', 'olin_osp_settings' );
}

function olin_osp_settings() {
?>
<div class='wrapper'>
  <h1>Our Sample Plugin Settings</h1>
  <!-- Imagine there is some really exciting functionality happening here -->
```

```
</div>
<?php
}
?>
```

Again, there's little to see here. We're simply registering our plugin with WordPress, creating an **Admin** menu for our users, and then adding an **Admin** page to modify the settings of our sample plugin. However, when we move to localize the plugin, we'll want to make some key changes. Let's look at the same plugin with correctly localized code:

chapter_11/plugin-localization-example1.php

```php
<?php
/*
Plugin Name: Our Sample Plugin
Plugin URI: http://www.sitepoint.com/our-sample-plugin
Description: Sample localization code demonstration
Version: 1
Author: Mick Olinik
Author URI: http://www.sitepoint.com
License: GPL2
*/

add_action( 'init', 'olin_osp_init' );
function olin_osp_init() {
  add_action( 'admin_menu', 'olin_osp_init' );
  load_plugin_textdomain( 'our-very-unique-domain', false, dirname➡
    ( plugin_basename( __FILE__ ) ) . '/languages/' );
}

function olin_osp_menu() {
  add_options_page( sprintf( __( '%s Options', 'our-very-unique-domain' ),➡
    'Our Sample Plugin' ), 'Our Sample Plugin', 'manage_options',➡
    'our-sample-plugin', 'olin_osp_settings' );
}

function olin_osp_settings() {
?>
<div class='wrapper'>
  <h1><?php _e( 'Our Sample Plugin Settings', 'our-very-unique-domain' ); ?>
  </h1>
  <!-- Imagine there is some really exciting functionality happening here -->
</div>
<?php
}
?>
```

Our first task is to initialize the localization, and it's conceptually the same for plugins as it is for themes. In the *init* action we are using within our plugin, we'll add the load_plugin_textdomain()

function. As you can see, we're identifying our unique *textdomain* as well as the location of the translation files—in this case the **languages** folder within the plugin. Then, we can go about our business as usual preparing strings to be localized within our code, just as in the case of themes. The files for **Our Sample Plugin** might ultimately look like Figure 11.3.

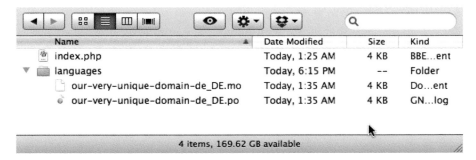

Figure 11.3. Plugin localization file structure

A Word on .MO File Nomenclature

In looking at Figure 11.3, you may notice that the nomenclature for our **.MO** files has changed within a plugin as opposed to how we labeled it in our theme. When looking for compiled **.MO** translation files, WordPress looks for a different syntax for theme localizations than it does for plugin localizations. With theme localizations, you'll want to name your **.MO** file in the format of **locale.mo**. For example, in translating your theme to German, your theme translation file in the **languages** directory within your theme should be named **de_DE.mo**. On the other hand, if you're localizing a plugin, WordPress will seek the translation file in your specified **languages** directory within your plugin in the format of **pluginname-locale.mo**. In this instance, the plugin name corresponds directly to the *textdomain* you assigned to the localization in your plugin. Keeping with the previous examples, our translation file would thus be named **our-very-unique-domain-de_DE.mo** if we were translating that plugin into German.

Introducing Poedit

Poedit is a popular open-source tool that you can download and install on your Windows, Apple, or Linux computer to help you create and maintain all the files you'll need. Poedit will automatically sort through all the source code you have in your plugin or theme, and return all strings that you've defined to be localizable through the _e() or __() functions. Then, it's just a matter of going through each string and providing a translation for a specific language. Let's get started by downloading and installing Poedit.[4]

---

[4] http://www.poedit.net/download.php

Creating a .POT File

To localize our own plugin or theme, we'll need to create a **.POT** file. To refresh your memory, a **.POT** file is just a **.PO** file that doesn't have any definitions—it merely defines the strings that need to be translated. By default, Poedit looks for **.POT** files to open and work off of when a translator first seeks to localize our code, but since we don't have one yet we'll need to make it first. To do this, fire up Poedit, click **File** and then select **New catalog** as in Figure 11.4.

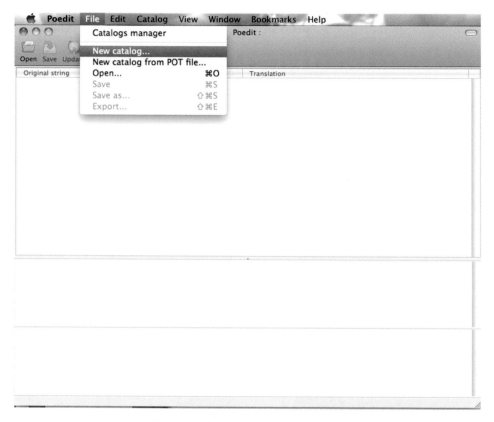

Figure 11.4. Creating a new catalog in Poedit

When creating a new catalog, the first place you'll be brought to is the **Project info** tab, as seen in Figure 11.5. You can fill this in as completely as you like, but all that is really required is to give our new catalog a project name. Give it a name, and then click on the **Paths** tab.

Figure 11.5. **Project info** in Poedit

Now we need to create the path to our translation file. This path is relative to the file or files being translated. Since we consider it best practice to create a separate directory for your language translations, we prefer adding ../ for the path as we've done in Figure 11.6. Once you have your path set, click the **Keywords** tab to continue on.

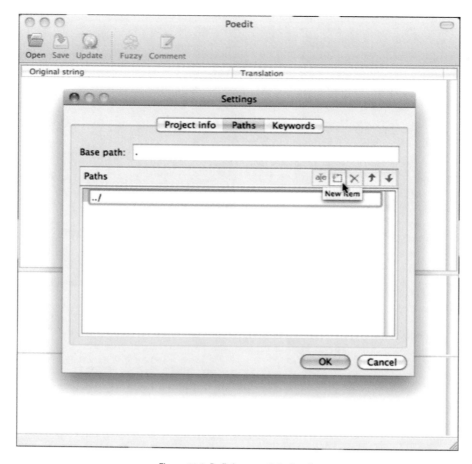

Figure 11.6. Defining a path in Poedit

In the **Keywords** tab, we need only to define the GNU gettext elements that we used to prepare our strings for localization within our code. Again, __ and _e are the most common gettext functions that are used, but if you happened to use _n, _x, or any other gettext functions, you will need to define them all here. It's good to remove the functions you don't need, and so we'll remove each of the functions we're not using, as in Figure 11.7.

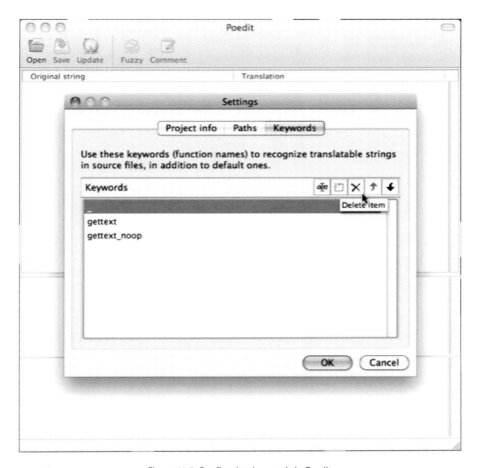

Figure 11.7. Configuring keywords in Poedit

This is a standard **Keywords** configuration that will suit the purposes of our discussion very well. We've added only __ and _e because these are the functions being called in our code. Make your additions and then click **OK**, as shown in Figure 11.8.

Figure 11.8. Adding keywords in Poedit

Upon clicking **OK**, we'll be prompted to save our configuration as a new **.PO** file. Before you save your file, be sure to navigate to the correct location according to what you set in the **Paths** tab of your catalog. Poedit will use the location you save your file to as a point of reference when it searches for the files to which you've added your localization strings. In our example, we've added a path of ../, so we'll want to save the new **.PO** file in a subdirectory where our files are located. While any subdirectory will do, it's best to be descriptive by using labels such as **languages** or **lang**. Save the **.PO** file with a name appropriate to your purpose. Just to be creative, we used **appropriate-name.po**, as you can see in Figure 11.9.

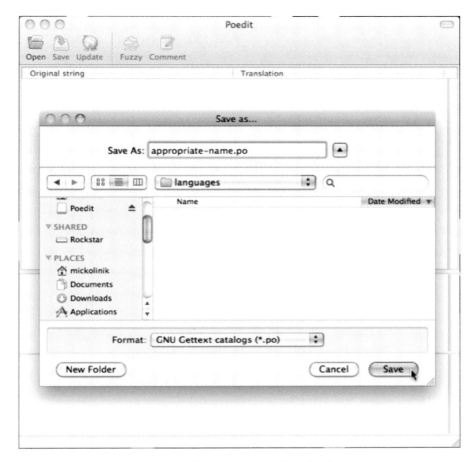

Figure 11.9. Creating a new .PO file in Poedit

Upon saving the file, Poedit uses the path parameter that you set to find and index any files it sees. At this point, Poedit checks all of the files available against the list of gettext functions you defined in the **Keywords** tab and returns a list of translatable strings to you. Figure 11.10 shows a short list of strings revolving around me (Mick Olinik) and my dog, Lacie. Click **OK**, and you have a blank .**PO** file with a few string definitions.

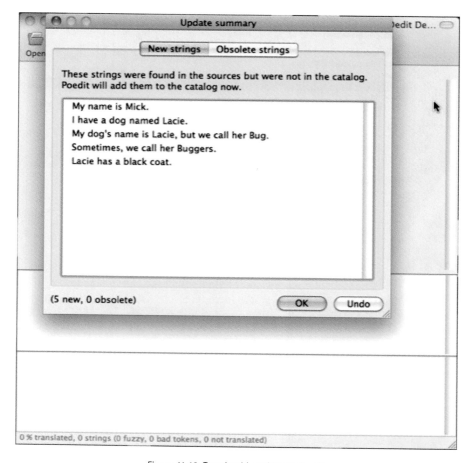

Figure 11.10. Translatable strings in Poedit

This is the tricky part—and *essential for creating a .**POT** file with Poedit*. Before you do anything else here, *save the file a second time*. The reason this is necessary is that when Poedit initially creates the .**PO** file, it saves the file first and then imports the translatable strings. If you fail to save the file a second time and close it, you'll end up with a blank .**PO** file that has no translatable strings, thus defeating the purpose. Once you save your .**PO** file a second time as in Figure 11.11 (with your translatable strings added), close the file and quit Poedit. Don't worry—we'll be right back.

Figure 11.11. Saving the file a second time

Now navigate to your directory structure where you've saved your **.PO** file. You'll notice you actually have two files available: a **.PO** file that you created, and an **.MO** file that Poedit automatically compiled for you when you saved the **.PO** file. Because we first want to create a template file, we don't need the **.MO** file—go ahead and delete it. Then, just rename the **.PO** file to a **.POT** file. When you're done, you'll end up with just one **.POT** file in your **languages** directory as highlighted by the arrow in Figure 11.12.

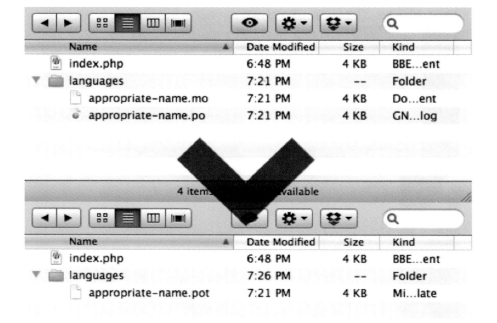

Figure 11.12. .**POT** file in Poedit

Translating Our .POT File

If all you are aiming to do is to set up your theme or plugin so that it can be easily localized by others, congratulations! At this point, you are all set, and you can move on with your life. So long as you include your shiny new .**POT** file in the correct directory, anybody will be able to work with and translate your theme or plugin into an infinite number of languages. That said, let's assume you want to actually do a few translations. Get started by firing Poedit back up and instead of selecting **New catalog**, select **New catalog from POT file**, as in Figure 11.13.

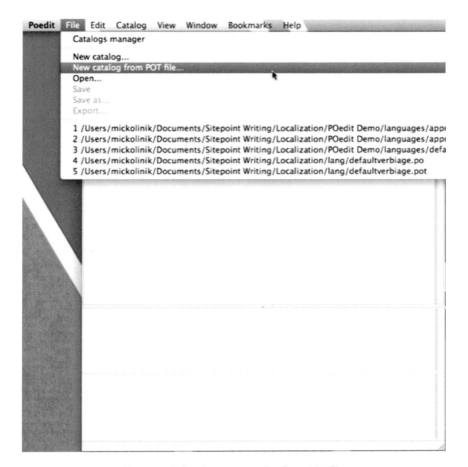

Figure 11.13. Creating a new catalog from .POT file

Go ahead and find the .POT file you just created, open it, and then click OK to the subsequent catalog settings (they are the exact same ones you set yourself). Poedit will then ask you what you'd like to save your new .PO file as. Give it an appropriate name and save it as shown in Figure 11.14.

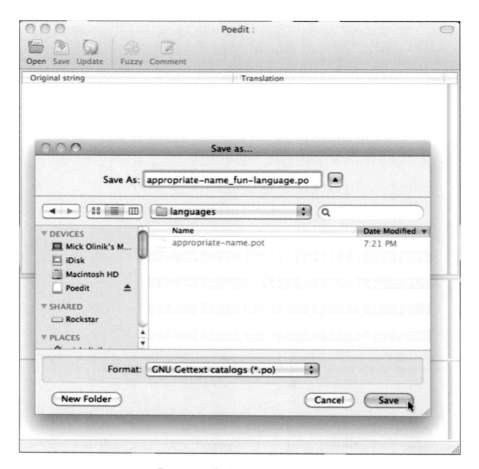

Figure 11.14. Saving your new **.PO** files

It's clear sailing from here on. Just click on the string you'd like to translate in Poedit, and type a translation into the box on the bottom of the Poedit window as shown in Figure 11.15.

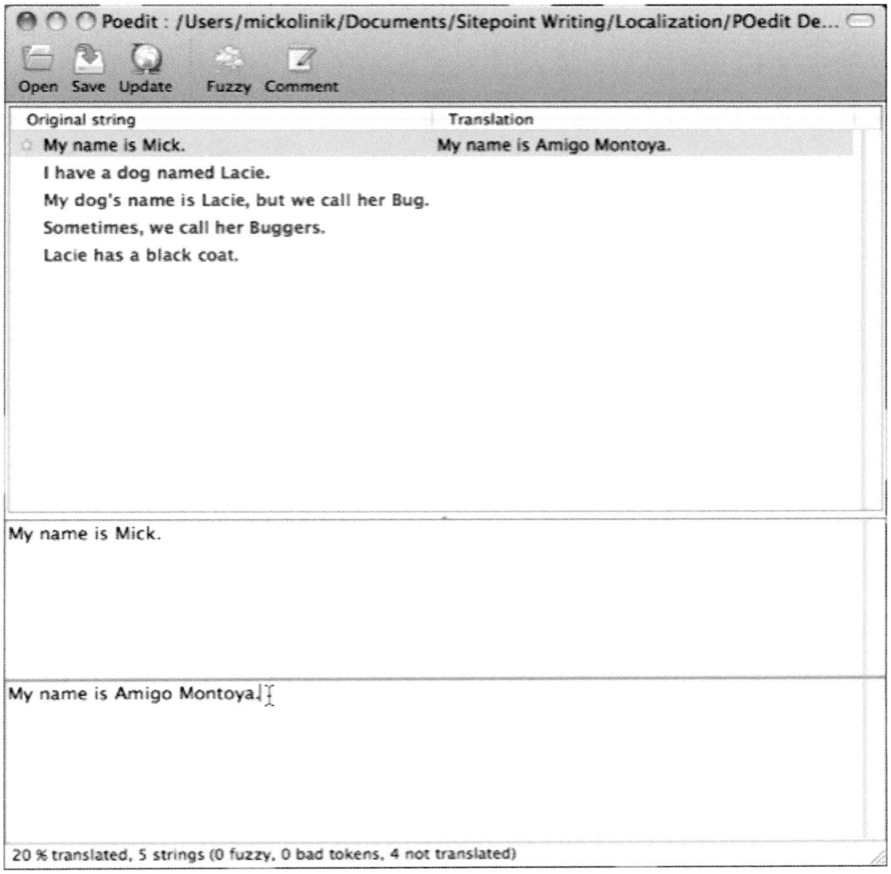

Figure 11.15. Translating your strings

We'll wash, rinse, and repeat this procedure until all the strings have been translated. Editing strings is just as easy ... click on the string you want to edit, as in Figure 11.16, and make your modifications. Remember, each time you save a **.PO** file, a new .MO file will be compiled for you. It is the .MO file – not the **.PO** file – that WordPress will actually use when doing translations.

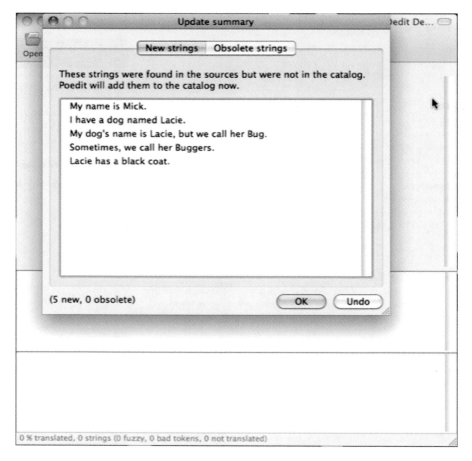

Figure 11.16. Translations for all our strings

Another Way to Generate a .POT File

Tools like Poedit are really useful, but if you are planning on submitting your plugin to the Wordpress Plugin Directory, there's an easier way to create a **.POT** file. Instead of going through all the hassle involved in saving and resaving a file in Poedit, you can choose to have your **.POT** file created automatically after your plugin has been accepted into the directory. Simply log in as an administrator for your plugin, and click the **Get POT** button underneath **Committers**, and a **.POT** file will be generated for you to download. Since this is only useful if you're submitting your plugin to the directory, we've included it here, as seen in Figure 11.17, as an *extra* way to get the job done, not the *only* way.

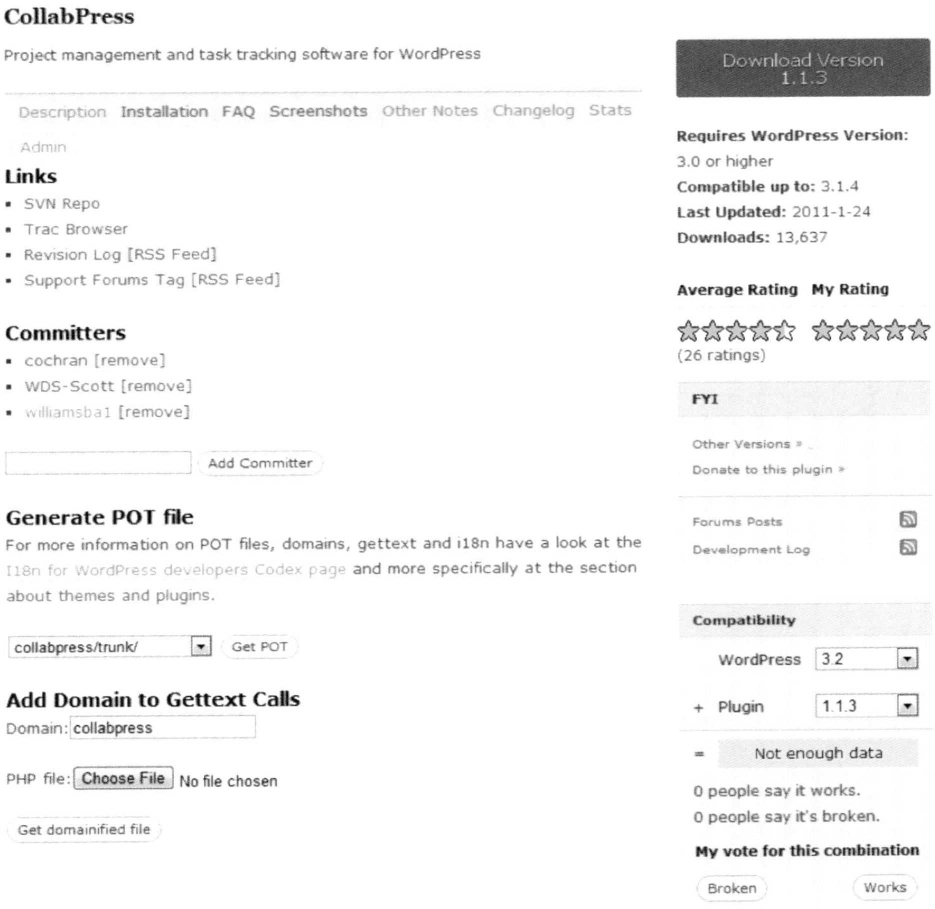

Figure 11.17. Plugin **Admin** screen showing a **Get POT** button

Is There an Easier Way Than Localization?

Funny you should ask that. There's a pretty cool tool that's been in development for some time now called WPML.[5] It's a premium plugin and well worth the investment. WPML greatly reduces the amount of time and effort it takes to localize your theme or plugin, at least within the context of a single website. All you need to do is identify your localization strings properly within your plugin or your theme by wrapping them in __() or _e() tags. Once you make your string identifications, WPML takes over, eliminating the hassle of setting up **.PO**, **.MO** and **.POT** files and sorting out how to add them to your files and themes.

When you initially run WPML on your WordPress site, WPML acts like Poedit and scans through all your theme and plugin files in search of translatable strings. Upon creating a list of strings, WPML asks which languages the website should be translatable to and automatically creates the

---

[5] http://wpml.org

necessary **.PO** and **.MO** files needed to support each. After that, WPML provides a really slick interface inside the WordPress backend that gives you options to translate strings as well as whole posts and pages. Even better, it creates unique, translated permalinks so that your posts and pages can be indexed in multiple languages by default! Finally, WPML integrates a translator management system. This lets you hire professional translators to do translation work directly on your site. Alternately, you can use WPML's management system to assign specific members of your own staff to do translation in a particular language.

Of course, WPML isn't the only game in town; as with most types of functionality in WordPress, there are several other plugins that you can use to accomplish the same purpose. At the time of this writing, the biggest competitor to WPML is qTranslate,[6] and it has quite a solid following. While we won't get into a feature comparison of the two, qTranslate is worth looking into, and is the translation plugin of choice for several popular plugins such as Google XML Sitemaps, which has released a specialized version to work with qTranslate, aptly named Google XML Sitemaps With qTranslate Support.

Installing WordPress in Your Own Language

So far we've discussed localizing themes and plugins in detail, but what if that's more than you're looking for, and you instead want to know how to install WordPress itself in a different language? After all, it's good to be able to localize themes and plugins, but it sure would be useful if we could make WordPress display in the language of our choosing, right? Well, there's a good reason that we've waited until now to talk about this, as we'll be able to utilize the localization concepts we've already covered to help it all make sense.

Thanks to the widespread use of WordPress across the globe, WordPress has already been translated into many languages for you, so you don't have to mess around with the heavy lifting. For your convenience, a complete listing of available languages and links to their repositories is available within the WordPress Codex.[7] As for installing the language of your choice, you can either install it manually, or you can look to see if the language translation team has a separate set of instructions that may be easier to work with (in some instances, you may be able to install WordPress with your preferred language already loaded and preconfigured). For our purposes here, we'll show you how to do it manually from a regular old English installation:

1. Download the **.MO** file for your language of choice. Again, you can find links to these files in the Codex.[8]

2. Next, open up your **wp-config.php** file in a text editor and locate `define('WPLANG', '');`, replacing the second parameter with the extension defined by your **.MO** file. For instance, if you were

---

[6] http://www.qianqin.de/qtranslate/

[7] http://codex.WordPress.org/WordPress_in_Your_Language

[8] http://codex.WordPress.org/WordPress_in_Your_Language

looking to use the British variant of English and downloaded the **en-GB.mo** file, you'd change this to `define ('WPLANG', 'en-GB');`. Conversely, if you were looking to translate WordPress to German and downloaded the **de_DE.mo** translation file, you'd change the line to read `define ('WPLANG', 'de_DE');`.

3. Once you have modified your `define ('WPLANG', '');` appropriately, save **wp-config.php**.

4. Now navigate to either **wp-content** or **wp-includes** and create a new folder called **languages**. So long as you create the **languages** directory in one of these two locations, WordPress will recognize it and look for your translation file there. Can you take a wild guess at what comes next?

5. If you guessed that we'll need to add our **.MO** translation file to the **languages** folder, congratulations—you win the gold star!

That's all there is to it. Next time you log in to your WordPress admin area, you'll find it all pretty and new in the language you've enabled. Very cool stuff!

World Tour Complete

With WordPress's continued increase in popularity and representation throughout the world, you're fooling yourself as a developer if you don't consider localization in everything you create for and with WordPress. In this chapter, we've touched on several aspects of localization, including:

- why localization is now more important than it ever has been, and why you should care

- the difference between internationalization and localization

- an explanation of how the process works, in theory as well as in practice

- a description of the three main types of files you're going to deal with in the process: **.MO**, **.PO**, and **.POT** files

- a detailed breakdown of how to use Poedit to create **.POT** files

- a walk-through of how to translate text strings with Poedit and save them as your own **.PO** files

- a description of plugins that can be used to help the localization process in your WordPress sites

- an overview of the process involved in running WordPress in languages other than English

With the global market we now have available to us, it'll be fun to dig into marketing and search engine optimization with WordPress in our next chapter. After all, we have so many new locations to explore!

12

SEO, Marketing, and Goal Conversion

Since the inception of the World Wide Web in the mid 1990s, search engine marketing has often proved to be a confusing, expensive, frustrating, and ultimately disappointing endeavor for many web developers, search engine marketers, and business owners. While well-intentioned developers and search engine marketers have done their best to provide solid onsite and offsite search engine optimization (SEO) solutions to business owners, results have been sporadically successful, frequently poor, or entirely nonexistent. It's a problem that has perpetuated itself repeatedly over the course of the history of the Web, creating a quagmire of frustration among business owners and developers alike. So why has it been so difficult to find a reliable solution?

Why SEO Is So Difficult

A qualified search engine professional would be able to talk to you for hours explaining why search engine optimization and marketing services have historically been hit-or-miss, but we'll boil it down for you.

SEO Is a Moving Target

SEO is really all about gaining **organic search rankings** (naturally occurring, "free" rankings gained for a specific keyword) in search engines like Google (and henceforth in this chapter, we'll just refer to all of these engines as "Google".) Google uses numerical formulae called algorithms to compute the relevance (and hence the ranking) of any given web page publicly available on the Web. What's pertinent to realize here is that Google is a private company; while its public image tends to be rather altruistic, its existence is predicated upon exactly one motive: making money. Google does

this by ensuring its users receive the most relevant results possible to any given query based upon an extremely complex set of criteria. If you follow the logic through, the more relevant the search results, the more trusted Google becomes and hence the more commercially valuable advertisement space is on its **SERPs**, or Search Engine Results Pages. Therefore, when Google identifies a way to hone its search algorithms to provide results that are more relevant to its users, it's financially induced to make the relevant refinement. And Google is very good at identifying and implementing refinements. Because of this, SEO tactics that worked on a given website last month or last week may not necessarily work today, and what works today will almost certainly not be as effective in the future.

The Google Search Algorithm Is Private

Here's where the real fun starts. While it's totally understandable that Google would do everything in its power to increase the financial value of its primary asset in search relevancy, it's also obvious that ranking very high in those search results for a specific set of keywords is extremely valuable for our clients as well (after all, isn't that why you are even reading this chapter?). The financial rewards associated with ranking on the first page for lucrative keywords can be astounding and literally make or break the economic success of many different types of business. It's because of this indisputable fact that the search engine marketing industry exists at all, and the volume of money in play within the marketplace has driven the industry to become fiercely competitive.

Early on in the search engine marketing game, the methodology that search engines used to rank web pages wasn't necessarily a closely guarded secret, even if they weren't officially made public. Engines that lacked manual submission and ranking processes by definition relied on a formulaic algorithm that could be easily manipulated if you understood the weighting of the formula. This resulted in the development of **black-hat** search engine techniques that were specifically designed to trick search engines into providing higher rankings for specific web pages by unfairly stacking the deck in their own favor through continued exploitation of various search engine algorithms.

As a direct result of this threat, search engines such as Google began to closely guard the secrecy of their algorithms, and now rarely provide straight answers as to the weight of the relevancy granted to any given factor of the equation—or whether something is, indeed, a factor at all. The search engines securing the privacy of their search algorithms, combined with frequently modifying their makeup has been a massive win for the consumer; returning highly relevant search results makes the Web a more useful tool for users across the globe. However, it's also introduced and perpetuated a cloudy haze concerning exactly how you go about achieving high rankings for any given web page. This ever-lingering mystery is the root of much of the confusion and consternation associated with search engine optimization and marketing.

Shades of Gray

The notion of black-hat tactics has over time come to refer to the negative end of the appropriateness and legality of all common search engine marketing techniques, with obviously clean and appropriate techniques being labeled **white-hat**, and techniques that fall somewhere in the middle of appropriate and shady acquiring the moniker of **gray-hat**.

Sharks Patrol These Waters

As consumers in the Information Age, we have come to expect and demand answers to the most pressing of questions at the drop of a hat. After all, anybody can "google" something and instantly have dozens of answers at their fingertips.[1] Sure, those answers are often entirely wrong, but it's easy enough to read through the results to gain an understanding of what something means.

The problem is that because Google doesn't actually publish its search algorithm (and for good reason), no concrete answer exists to the question of how to give a web page a high ranking for a particular keyword. Because of the ambiguity inherent in the marketplace, search engine marketers are forced to operate with a measure of conjecture when working with clients, and this conjecture opens the door to unscrupulous behavior. While not all search engine marketers engage in this type of behavior, there is certainly a subset of organizations and individuals within the profession that use black hat and gray hat techniques to attempt to game the system and unfairly acquire high rankings for their customers. Even more prevalent are those who play upon the inherent ambiguity of the system to sell entirely inaccurate information to unknowing individuals for their own personal gain. These unsavory types have combined to disseminate information throughout the marketplace that is often inaccurate, out-of-date, and just plain wrong.

The good news is that while there is no specific formula you can just plug into that will guarantee you 100% success with your search engine marketing endeavors, there are fundamental principles you can implement and consistently rely on that will serve you well and provide you with useful, targeted website traffic.

Websites Are Poorly Coded

Search engine optimization (or SEO) is defined as the set of actions you can implement structurally within the code of your website to boost your organic search engine rankings. SEO focuses on the on-page characteristics that affect your organic rankings in the SERPs. Simply put, there are a lot of poorly coded websites out there from an SEO perspective, and many are websites that organizations have paid substantial sums of money for.

---

[1] It says something about Google's ubiquitousness that searching for information online has come to be accepted as simply "googling."

While very beautiful to look at with sleek, creative navigation favored by many, Flash-based websites are obvious examples of poorly coded sites from an SEO standpoint because they almost always have their content locked into a single file with no hope of anything being indexed by engines. However, with Flash sites becoming less popular due to the lack of Flash support on many mobile devices, websites that instead simply lack the proper coding elements implemented in a systematic way have become the more common issue. What's sad is that, aside from lack of education, there's really no excuse to be delivering websites that are not suitably optimized, and yet it's more often the rule than the exception. Luckily for you, the bulk of this chapter will cover these on-page optimization principles.

There's a Difference Between SEO and SEM

Let's be honest here: much like graphic design, web development is a relatively easy field to enter for aspiring professionals. If you're looking to get started professionally in the industry, there are many tools available (WordPress being one of them) to help you with the more technical aspects of development. Clients, however, usually can't comprehend the difference between those just starting out and more seasoned professionals with a higher level of expertise; they just look to the developers they've hired to build the site and "ensure it ranks on the first page of Google."

This can lead to a situation where the client is leaning on a developer for expertise, and the developer simply doesn't know what they don't know. It's for this reason that the terms *search engine optimization* and *search engine marketing* are typically interchanged as if they are the same—but guess what … they aren't!

While search engine optimization handles the on-page aspects that relate to site rankings, **search engine marketing** (or SEM) can be defined as the set of techniques you can employ outside the context of your site to increase the ranking of a given web page. Search engine marketing is all about creating quality backlinks to websites, and employing Pay-Per-Click (PPC) and AdWords campaigns,[2] placing banner ads, employing remarketing services (where a site displays ads to users who've visited previously), and utilizing a score of other available techniques to drive traffic to a given page. Aside from recognizing that SEO and SEM are different sides of the same coin, the distinction is that while SEO is something you can simply do one time on your website (and quite effectively if you create a systematic approach for subsequent content to automatically be properly SEO'd while it's being added to a site), SEM is an ongoing marketing process which will have no definitive end and requires a decent budget to do well.

SEO and SEM Require a Team Effort

A healthy search engine marketing budget is all well and good, but many a frustrated business owner will tell you that they've spent far more money than they'd care to admit on PPC, AdWords, banner ads, and any number of techniques that have been promised to be the right solution. These

---

[2] http://www.google.com/adwords

business owners have probably even been patient—as many developers and marketers preach—but still see inadequate results, and find themselves hemorrhaging time, money, and sanity just by trying to coax people to their website. The reasons for these types of issues are varied: incomplete research, poor websites, inadequate search engine marketing campaigns, a lack of interest in the product or topic in general, or more usually a combination of these factors. However, when you initiate a search engine marketing campaign, it's crucial to recognize that its success or failure depends on the overall quality of the on-page SEO that you've set up throughout your website. Without these two distinct components coordinating to convey the same message, it's of little consequence how well each one is done; your website's rankings won't be going anywhere useful anytime soon.

To help explain the relationship between on-page and off-site optimization, let's examine a quick analogy to help us illustrate the interactions the two of them have. Visualize yourself standing on a beach with two kites, one of which is absolutely top-of-the-line, aerodynamic, light, and built to collect and utilize wind in the most efficient way possible, maximizing its potential for flight. The second kite, on the other hand, is literally a brick attached to a paper airplane that you tied a string around and proudly decided to attempt to fly. If we were to set both kites down on the sand and observe, we'd likely find that while we may not have much control as to the direction it's headed, the well-crafted kite would naturally be picked up by even a light wind and go somewhere on its own. The brick-on-a-string, however, would sit in the sand without a hope of meaningful flight.

It should be fairly obvious here that we're drawing a correlation between a kite's aerodynamic capacity with the quality of a web page's on-page SEO. Furthermore, a web page with content that's actually in demand will be afforded a basic level of organic search engine ranking for relevant keyword searches—even if that doesn't necessarily place it on the first page of Google. So where does search engine marketing fit in? Well, if a kite's already up and flying on the wind that's naturally blowing in off the ocean, search engine marketing works to artificially crank that wind up a notch or two. When harnessed and wielded by a skilled search engine marketer, that kite can use the extra wind to fly higher and do all sorts of precise tricks to yield specific results. In this way, effective search engine marketing can enhance properly set-up websites, turning them into profit centers for business.

Sadly, our brick-on-a-string is still out of luck, and no amount of wind short of a hurricane is likely to move it so much as an inch. Even when it does, it's just as likely to become buried in the sand as it is to take flight in any reasonable way, and control is something that you can just forget about. The point here is that without solid on-page SEO, successful search engine marketing campaigns are inherently doomed from the start. In this way, WordPress itself won't win you rankings on the first page of Google, but when properly implemented will at least give you the aerodynamic kite you need to have a fighting chance.

What's it all about anyway?

The urgency that website developers and business owners feel in driving as much traffic to their websites as possible badly misses the point. Getting traffic is nice, and receiving a large quantity of traffic is to be proud of, but regardless of the amount of traffic you drive to your website, it's a high **goal conversion rate** that is genuinely sexy.

But doesn't everybody want millions of unique visitors on their website? Yes, but what's vital to understand is that when business owners say they want *traffic*, they usually mean they want *money*. After all, unless you are building a site for altruistic purposes, it's more useful to have only a few hundred people visit your site who actually do what you want them to do, than a few thousand show up who promptly leave without doing anything at all. This means that every page on your website has to have a concrete purpose, and not just a generalized "save-the-world" kind of purpose akin to corporate mission statements; it needs to be specific, measurable, and real. We'll call them goals.

A website with a high goal conversion rate is one that convinces its users to take the action it want them to take. It's the dirty little secret that so many professionals miss, which ultimately creates the defining difference between a successful and unsuccessful website development project.

We'll cover goal conversion further on in this chapter, but as this is a book about WordPress, we'll focus more on SEO as it relates to WordPress, rather than SEM and goal conversion in general. (For those interested in the latter, SitePoint has published *The SEO Business Guide,*[3] which gives a good overview of this subject.) Search engine marketing is a complex field whose best professionals are often not advanced programmers, in the same way that expert coders are not typically entirely up to speed with the intricacies of the latest Google algorithm updates and modifications. Let's focus on being the best WordPress developers that we can be.

The Big Three Fundamental SEO Components

Now that we have a basic understanding as to why generating search engine rankings and traffic is a little touch-and-go, let's see how we can tune up WordPress and make it a veritable search engine optimization workhorse for us. While there are lots of tweaks you can do to fine-tune your website's performance, there are what we'll refer to as the Big Three primary SEO components.

The Big Three fundamental SEO components are:

- semantic permalinking
- proper `<meta>` tag and `<title>` tag inclusion
- proper `<header>` tag structure and implementation

---

[3] http://www.sitepoint.com/kits/seo-business-guide/

As long as you pay attention to these Big Three SEO components and keep in mind that *absolutely nothing is a substitute for quality, relevant content that's actually of interest to your visitors*, you'll be sitting pretty regardless of what SEM strategy you choose to move forward with. We'll discuss the importance of relevant content further on in this chapter, but for the time being understand that it simply makes no difference how well you optimize your web page content if nobody is interested in reading it anyway. Therefore, it's vital that you make sure there's an audience who is genuinely interested in what you have to say on a particular topic before you invest any time authoring and optimizing it. With that said, let's now look at the Big Three in depth.

Semantic Permalinking

The importance of semantic permalinking cannot be overstated, and yet it is one of the most overlooked and underutilized aspects of basic search engine optimization. As we all know, each web page on the Internet has its own web address (or URL), and that URL can take a lot of different forms. The permanent form of this link is called a permalink. When we talk about semantic permalinking, we are talking about the extent to which that permalink is **semantic**; that is, the extent to which the permalink describes that content that exists on the page. To illustrate the point, let's look at a few examples of possible links to a page that discusses the biography and resume of Dr. Marco, a member of the antelope veterinarian team at a large animal hospital named Esquandolas. There are a lot of ways that the URL for this link could be constructed, some of which are more semantic than others.

Example 1: http://www.esquandolas.com/index.php?p=311

This link is not semantic at all. Sure, we have the name of the animal hospital in the domain name itself, but it gives us no indication as to what is actually on the page, and the domain itself gives no reference to an animal hospital. The domain issue is a common one and not that big of a deal, but you can rest assured that taken as a whole the URL lacks meaning for either a human reading it or a search engine spider looking to index it. Overall, it's a very poor choice for SEO purposes, providing almost no SEO value whatsoever.

Example 2: http://www.esquandolas.com/about.html

Although it's uncommon to use this type of a link with WordPress (although it is possible by using the permalink rule /%postname%.html), it's a typical format for many websites. While this link is a touch more semantic in that it tells us this is "about" whatever is on esquandolas.com, both humans and search engines are still left wondering exactly what that might be. After all, unless you happen to know that esquandolas.com is an animal hospital, this will mean little to you, and trust us—Google won't necessarily know by looking at the URL either.

Example 3: http://www.esquandolas.com/about-dr-marco

All right, this is more semantic, but still has much room for improvement. While we're yet to comprehend what esquandolas.com is all about, we do know that this page is designed to be some form of biography on a doctor named Dr. Marco. This is enough to give both humans and search engines some clue as to what's on the page, but we could still do better. Let's see how …

Example 4: http://www.esquandolas.com/veterinary-staff/antelope-specialists/about-dr-marco

Bingo! Here we have a very semantic link. We now can tell that esquandolas.com has veterinary staff, of which some are antelope specialists. It's easy then to deduce that we must be talking about a sizeable animal hospital of sorts, or some type of large animal breeding center. We also know that the page in question will be about Dr. Marco, an antelope specialist on the veterinary staff at esquandolas.com. In other words, both humans and search engines can reasonably infer what the content of the page in question is just by looking at the link. If you get this portion of your SEO correct, you have a great base to work with in your SEO endeavors.

We've already discussed actually setting up your semantic permalinking in WordPress, but to review, you can navigate to **Settings > Permalinks** to create the basic permalinking rules for the built-in posts and categories system, as well as tags. Managing these options will create the permalinking structures that your posts will ultimately be attached to, with each post being differentiated by their unique slug—which is appended to the end of the permalink structure. A **slug** is typically a URL-friendly version of a post's title, but you can customize it to be anything you like. Therefore, if the permalink structure on the site previous was /%category%/%postname%/ as in Figure 12.1, the permalink for a post entitled **What is a band without saxophone?** might look like http://www.esquandolas.com/featured-news/what-is-a-band-without-saxophone/, where featured-news is the category and what-is-a-band-without-saxophone is the post's slug. Again, slugs can be customized for SEO purposes on an individual basis, so if you decided that this post would be better served from an SEO perspective if the slug was the-importance-of-saxophones-in-bands, you could make that modification as well.

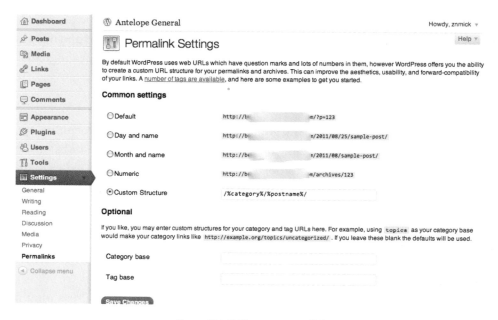

Figure 12.1. Setting your permalinks

Creating permalinks for your pages is easy. In WordPress, page permalinking is tied to parent-child relationships between pages. For instance, if we assumed that we were using pages in our example for http://www.esquandolas.com/veterinary-staff/antelope-specialists/about-dr-marco, there would be three pages tied to this permalink with slugs of veterinary-staff, antelope-specialists, and about-dr-marco. The page with the slug of veterinary-staff would have the page with the slug of antelope-specialists as its child page, which would in turn have the page with the slug of about-dr-marco as its child page. Again, easy stuff once you know how it works.

Finally, the mere fact that WordPress includes the ability to create custom taxonomies adds an entirely new, dynamic aspect to how you can bend WordPress to your SEO needs. Essentially, there's no limitation as to how you can utilize the system to generate linking structures for your content that makes intuitive sense to humans and search engines alike. Remember that the relevancy and consistency of your message is key, and for more information on using custom taxonomies, look back to Chapter 7 .

Proper `<meta>` and `<title>` Tag Inclusion

The next component of the Big Three is by far the oldest and most widely discussed aspect of search engine optimization: `<meta>` and `<title>` tags. Web developers and website owners have known about the importance of using these two tools correctly since the early days of the Web. Therefore, rather than beat the drum and go over in painstaking detail the basics of `<meta>` and `<title>` tags, we'll say simply that in a `<meta>` tag's `name` attribute, "`description`" refers to small text which talks about what is on the page, and "`keywords`" are essentially tags that describe what the basic topics of the page are. The `<title>` tag is just that—the title that is applied to the page, and in some

browsers is actually displayed on top of the browser window outside the viewable area. `<meta>` tags are important, cannot be overlooked, and need to be unique for each page on your site. Luckily, there are a pair of excellent WordPress plugins that you can download and use to manage these (and many other) aspects of your on-page SEO efforts in WordPress:

WordPress SEO by Yoast[4]

WordPress SEO by Yoast is probably the gold standard in on-page search engine optimization WordPress plugins. WordPress SEO lets you set templates for titles and `<meta>` `descriptions` and `keywords` for all types of pages and posts so that they automatically generate themselves when you initially post them. It also offers a handy **Snippet Preview** feature that shows you what your page will look like when it is found in Google SERPs. There's a bevy of other features that we'll talk about later on in this chapter including meta robots settings, canonical settings, and XML sitemaps, to name a few.

All in One SEO Pack[5]

The other trusted, time-tested favorite search engine optimization WordPress plugin is All in One SEO Pack. All in One is the most downloaded plugin of all time, and while it lacks the complete feature set that WordPress SEO has, it's sometimes better to go with a tool that does one task very well. When it comes to on-page SEO, All in One does one task *extremely* well—it generates unique `<meta>` `descriptions`, `keywords`, and `<title>` tags.

There are other plugins out there that also do a good job of handling `<meta>` and `<title>` tags, and you can find several themes that offer built-in support in this fashion as well. Whatever method you choose, the most important point is to make sure you address this aspect of your site's SEO efforts.

Proper Header Tag Structure and Implementation

The last but certainly not least component of the Big Three is proper header tag structure and implementation within the actual context of the page or post. This can only be automated to a certain extent, but getting it right is crucial to having a successful SEO experience on any given page. Header tags are sometimes referred to as `<h1>` or `<h2>` tags, and when used correctly serve to identify with more accuracy the important keywords and phrases within a given post or page. Search engines use these tags to sort out what you as the website owner believe are the central points of the content within the page, but they are often misused or not used at all because by default, header tags have formatting that makes the text within them appear bigger and bolder than regular text. For this reason, inexperienced users (both web developers and site owners) will sometimes use header tags to simply bold any given line, thinking of it as a visual formatting tool more than a content indexing tool. For the same reason, they may choose to not use them at all, which is a truly tragic choice. To better understand header tags, let's imagine a newspaper.

---

[4] http://wordpress.org/extend/plugins/wordpress-seo/
[5] http://wordpress.org/extend/plugins/all-in-one-seo-pack/

You might scan through a regular old newspaper by simply looking at the headlines. If you see something that catches your fancy, you might continue and will often see a subheadline. The main headline might read something like "Huge Storm Headed for the East Coast" with a subheadline in a smaller font that adds something pertinent to the basis of the story, like "Residents board up homes and evacuate to get out of storm's path." Following the two headlines, there would typically be a paragraph or two of text that discusses the central points of the story, reinforcing the main headline and the subheadline. Once those paragraphs are complete, there may be a new, smaller headline that talks about a more detailed aspect of the story with several paragraphs that follow, discussing the point. This pattern continues on and on to the end of the article, providing an organized, concise view of the information being presented. When implemented correctly, this same pattern holds true for how header tags should be used in the context of a post or page. Have a look at *The Mockingbird Gazette* in Figure 12.2.

Figure 12.2. The Mockingbird Gazette

We've taken a standard newspaper layout with various headlines and subheadlines, and superimposed their proper header tag equivalents. For instance, the main headline of any given page or post should always be an <h1> tag, denoting to search engines that this is the central thesis of the post, and that anything within the rest of the post will relate to it. The primary subheadline is noted as an <h2> tag, which keys to the search engines that the information therein is also important, but not necessarily the central topics of the post. After that we see two sets of <h3> tags that can be used to tip off search engines about what we as the website owners and authors find pertinent about the

subsequent paragraphs. We can continue using <h3> tags throughout the rest of the post until we finish it up.

Also important to note here is that while it's crucial to make use of header tags, it's even more so to ensure you actually make your header tags keyword-packed and entirely relevant. For instance, having an <h1> tag that is nothing more than the words "Home" or "Welcome to our website" may be syntactically correct, but it's not relevant in any way, shape or form and will not help you gain traffic. However, an <h1> tag that consists of "Huge storm headed for the East Coast" is extremely relevant and descriptive, and is a quality choice so long as the rest of the post discusses and supports the topic of the storm that is hitting the east coast.

Header tags can, to some degree, be systematically implemented in WordPress. Often, the post or page title is output in a theme as an <h1>, giving you an instant search engine anchor to describe what the page is about. However, further on-page SEO as it pertains to header tags really depends on the user entering in content from that point forward. Theme designers can (and should) create custom <h2>, <h3>, and <h4> styles to match content stylings inside their themes, but it is still up to the users to understand how to use them. Furthermore, because most WordPress sites are constantly being updated, it's not really something that you can do in one pass to officially "SEO a website," but rather a habit your authors and editors need to learn.

The Anatomy of a Typical Search Engine Spider Visit

Now that we've gone through each component of the Big Three, let's take a look at the decision-making process of a typical search engine spider as it views and indexes a given post or page on the site. Understand that this is a *very* simplified version of how your web pages are ranked and indexed; it's also not the entire story, as there are a number of off-page factors that contribute to any given page's ultimate ranking at a specific point in time. With that said, consider the following scenario:

At http://www.esquandolas.com/veterinary-staff/antelope-specialists/about-dr-marco, a search engine spider arrives and immediately logs the URL. Inside the URL, it sees that there are keywords it can understand and make associations with: veterinary staff, antelope specialists, and Dr. Marco. We'll assume that the <title> tags and <meta> tags that are built into the page back that information up. Then when the spider begins to parse the content on the page, it will hopefully find an <h1> tag that says something to the effect of "About Dr. Marco Pisgah, Antelope Veterinarian Extraordinaire". An <h2>-tagged line of text reading "World Famous Antelope Disease Researcher from Michigan State University" provides additional pertinent information about the central topic—Dr. Marco Pisgah. Assuming that the next few paragraphs of paragraph text support those two initial assumptions and then build upon the topic with subsequent header tags and paragraph text, we'll see that this page has a high base ranking which can be positively augmented by external search engine marketing efforts. In this way, all of the Big Three SEO components work together to drive traffic

when traffic is there to drive, which of course comes back to the notion of relevancy and demand for the targeted keyword and content area.

While these components are what you mainly need to pay attention to in order to have a chance at ranking well, there are a few caveats. First of all, the operative phrase in the previous sentence is "to have a chance at ranking well." As in life, there are never any guarantees other than you have to be in it to win it. Correctly making use of the Big Three merely gains you entry into the search engine game, giving you the opportunity to compete with everybody else. In many markets, the mere fact that you are set up correctly is enough to grab you traffic and rankings, but that's a phenomenon that will undoubtedly fade in effectiveness over time. Secondly, if you use any of these incorrectly (which is to say you mismatch the content on your site with your semantic permalinks and `<meta>` tags, etc) you run the risk of being slapped down in the search engines anyway. Keep in mind that search engines are not public but rather private entities, and they aim for relevancy. If your permalink indicates that a page is all about children's toys and in truth it is actually about trading stocks and bonds, your content mix will be off and your rankings likely will be too. The most important thing is to use your head, be relevant, and above all else do not try to game the system—ultimately, you'll lose every time.

Other Important SEO Aspects

What else can you do to really make the difference between a reasonably optimized site and a site that's akin to a race car cruising along in high gear? This is where the intricate changes in the search engine algorithms really come into play. The importance of any of the following tools and techniques will likely change over time with new techniques coming into play every week, so it's never a bad idea to consult with a reputable search engine marketing professional to find out about current trends. Paying attention to the following aspects of SEO will also help you quite a bit.

Image `alt` Attributes

A really easy way to increase any page's SEO is to properly optimize the images in the content of the page or post by setting descriptive `alt` attributes on your images (within the `<img>` tag). `alt` attributes are designed to provide a text-based alternative to describe what an image actually represents in situations where the image is unable to be displayed. For instance, in a situation where a search button that displays a magnifying glass is unable to be displayed, appropriate `alt` text might be `search` or `find`. Conversely, in a situation where an image displays a photo of a lighthouse in a story on coastal North Carolina, appropriate `alt` text might be `a coastal lighthouse in North Carolina`. The important point is that search engines can see that an image is supposed to be embedded on the page, but if it's without the benefit of `alt` attributes, they have absolutely no idea what that image is. Adding the `<img alt="…">` tag can give a search engine valuable information to better understand and create a relevancy ranking for any given post or page on your site.

In terms of actually implementing image `alt` attributes in WordPress, navigate to the Media Library and click on the **Edit** button of any given image to manage its characteristics. Underneath the **Title** field is the **Alternate Text** field. Simply fill in a value for the image in this field and click the **Update Media** button—you've added an `alt` attribute to your image.

Individual Page Privacy Settings

While usually you'll want to make an entire website readily visible and available to search engines, there are a variety of situations where it's desirable to have finer control over exactly how the engines treat your content. For times like this, the `noindex`, `nofollow`, and `noarchive` attribute values within the `<meta>` tag are available. These attribute values can be introduced in any combination with one another, and are used in the following situations:

`noindex` This attribute value is used in situations where you do not want a particular page indexed by a search engine in any way. This essentially makes the page invisible as far as search engines are concerned.

`nofollow` This attribute value is used when you want to have a certain page indexed, but you do not want search engine crawlers to follow any pages that may exist on a certain page.

`noarchive` This attribute value is used when you do not want a search engine to store a cached version of your page, and would prefer that users always go back to retrieve a fresh version of the page instead.

Your entire WordPress site will have `noindex` and `nofollow` values applied to it when you choose to make your website invisible to search engines in the WordPress administrative back end at **Settings > Privacy**. There is, however, a wide variety of plugins and themes that will give you greater control of these settings on individual pages and posts if you wish.

XML Sitemaps

XML Sitemaps are XML files that describe the complete, updated structure of your WordPress site at any given time. Each time search engines start indexing your site, they look for an XML Sitemap first to gain the overall lay of the land, to find out exactly what is on the site so that nothing is missed. In this way, XML Sitemaps are simple but crucial elements of SEO, and can be easily utilized to better improve the effectiveness of any search engine's indexing efforts.

There are several excellent XML Sitemap tools and plugins available for WordPress, one of which is the WordPress SEO by Yoast plugin we discussed in the section called "Proper `<meta>` and `<title>` Tag Inclusion". Quality WordPress XML Sitemap plugins generate a new copy of the Sitemap every time you make a content change to your site, as well as pay attention to the `noindex`, `nofollow`, and `noarchive` rules you set on any given page or post. Furthermore, quality plugins also notify all major search engines every time you create a new post or page.

Disclaimers, Terms and Conditions, and Privacy Pages

While this has little do to with SEO in particular, it has been repeatedly demonstrated that many search engines will tend to place a negative mark against websites that do not include pages which address their disclaimers, terms and conditions, and privacy policies. As a general rule, if you are running a commercial website that is collecting money, it's a good practice to maintain these pages and make them visible on your site and in your XML sitemap.

Proper Use of 301 Redirects and Avoidance of 404s

Finally, it's rather common to find people migrating from other content management systems or static HTML sites to WordPress. In just about any instance where you are migrating your website from one platform to another, your permalinks will usually change too. Since most pre-existing websites have some form of traction in search engines, the question of what to do about these old links often arises.

Simply put, if a web page has been indexed in a search engine and then ceases to exist, the entry in the search engine itself still remains. Subsequently, when visitors click on the old link, they'll receive a `404 page not found` error, an adverse consequence that may cause SEO traction issues on your site. While it's actually a rather hotly debated topic as to whether the mere existence of 404s negatively affects search engine rankings for a given site, almost all search engine marketing professionals will recommend the implementation of **301 redirects** in situations where you are migrating posts and pages from one permalinking structure to another. 301 redirects are permanent one-to-one relationships that are established between the URL of the old version of a web page and the new web page's URL. In this way, when a user clicks on a search engine result that yields an older, nonexistent page, the user is immediately directed to the new version of the page in a transparent way. You can either hardcode direct linear relationships from page to page when establishing 301 redirects, or you can use regular expressions to create dynamic patterns that automatically push old links to their newer counterparts.

There are two primary ways to add 301 redirects to your site in WordPress: by directly editing the **.htaccess** file to hardcode individual 301s or 301 patterns, or through the use of a plugin. A really great plugin to use that handles all your 301 WordPress—by directly editing the **.htaccess** file to hard code individual 301s or 301 patterns, or through the use of a plugin. A really great plugin to use which handles all of your 301 redirection needs is appropriately named Redirection[6]. In addition to handling 301 redirects, Redirection also keeps track of 404 errors, so you can see if and where you have recurring 404 issues on your site. It also allows you to handle all your manual 301 reductions right inside the plugin without the need to edit your **.htaccess** file. Overall, a very handy tool to have at your disposal.

---

[6] http://wordpress.org/extend/plugins/redirection/

It's about GOAL CONVERSIONS!

As we noted earlier, grabbing as much traffic as you can handle is nice, but the big boys will laugh at you when you assert that somehow generating a ton of traffic will make your website successful. The need many developers feel to generate as much traffic as possible misses the point of why we've brought our website to the party in the first place—to generate a specific result. As we've already described, this consists of the process of setting tangible, specific goals for your website's performance, and measuring the success of your website against how well you meet your goals on a consistent basis. If there's no goal in mind for your website, you've already wasted your time and financial resources.

Let's consider a simple example. Two separate window treatment companies are each running websites with the same goal: to generate a list of people who are interested in the different ways that window treatments can increase the value of their home and ultimately make their lives better. The list itself is extremely valuable, as it allows each company to develop relationships with qualified consumers who may be interested in purchasing their products; the end goal ultimately is to sell these qualified consumers services on a recurring basis. In other words, it's essentially Permission Marketing 101, and it's a common strategy employed as the primary goal on many authority-type websites.

If the first window treatment company manages to secure 50,000 visits in a single month, but only has a goal conversion success rate of 0.5%, they'll have netted just 250 people on their mailing list. If the second company manages only 20,000 visits in that same period, but has a higher goal conversion rate of 4% (which is still a very conservative number), they'll end up with 800 people on their mailing list. Therefore, the second company has more than tripled the success and effectiveness of their campaign compared to their competitor, doing it with less than half the traffic. This is a scenario that plays out in businesses around the world every day, with the main point being that it's not about the quantity of traffic you receive or not, but how well you *convert* the traffic you bring to your website. For this reason, organic ranking is usually enough, especially in unique, noncompetitive search keyword niches. If your organization is operating in one of these niches and you think you're doing everything right, but seeing a diminishing margin of results, consider working on your goal conversion techniques and rates, rather than attempting to drive more traffic.

The next natural question is: *how* can we increase our goal conversion rates? While this isn't a book on search engine marketing and goal conversion per se, it's important to be asking the right questions so you can dig deeper into the topic. Therefore, let's cover a few of the more important aspects of goal conversion and the tools you can use to tighten up your results.

Metrics and Split Testing

First and foremost, if we want to be looking for goal conversion rates, we need to keep track of them with metrics. **Metrics** is a generic term for using tools to track the number of times that people visit

any given page and take certain actions. Probably the most commonly used metrics system is Google Analytics, a free service that you can integrate into any website to track who is visiting a given page, where they are coming from, what their path is through the website, how long they stay on any given web page in particular as well as the website as a whole, and much more. Many other systems exist that assist you with tracking, compiling, and parsing web page usage statistics in useful ways; the trick is in figuring out which systems work for you, so that you can track your own website goal conversion pages in the way you'd prefer.

However you set up your metrics systems, your next step is to set up mechanisms to figure out which methods are more effective than others. The most common way to do this is through **split testing**. Also referred to as A/B testing, split testing is as easy as coming up with two different versions of a web page or web page component, serving them up randomly to a suitable number of people representing a reasonable sample of your audience, and seeing which one does better overall. By using split testing over and over again on the same page, you can refine your presentation factors, including your page's layout and written content, and optimally increase your goal conversion rates. It's as simple as asking a group of your potential buyers which one they like—option A or option B. And best of all, since the pages are being served up randomly, your visitors have no idea that they're being polled; they just react genuinely. Split testing is truly an elegant solution to finding out what works and what doesn't.

Now that we are numerically tracking things and understand how to test different concepts, what are the variables we can test to increase our goal conversion rates? In truth, there are as many variables as your imagination can come up with. After all, anything that could even remotely affect your users' experience while visiting your site is a potential location to split test something in order to create a more favorable outcome for yourself. However, there are a few common variables we can outline.

Keywords and Text

In marketing, the substance of an offer is rarely as important as the actual wording used to convey that offer. It's for this reason that the saying is "people don't buy the product, they buy the salesperson." As a whole, people tend to want make an emotional connection with an item before they are moved to take an action or make a purchase. For this reason, marketers often choose to split test different copy to see which performs better. For example, if you are split testing a web page selling a diet pill, you may choose to test whether the headline "Feel better about yourself in your bathing suit this summer" performs better than "We can help you squeeze back into your bathing suit in time for summer." Both headlines say essentially the same thing, but one of them will more than likely test out better than the other in split testing. Once you find out which one works better, you can split test that against another sample to further hone your presentation.

Making the Right Offer

To generate higher goal conversions, work out whether or not you are making the right offer to your target audience. Let's say you're attempting to boost membership on your website's mailing list. A simple test could be to look at whether or not people are more likely to subscribe to the list if you offer the option to join the list for free product updates and sales specials, or if conversion rates are higher when you also offer to give them a free downloadable ebook. If the ebook opt-in tends to do better, a follow-up test might be to see whether a free ebook creates higher conversion rates than a free mp3 of the same content, or even a package deal that contains the ebook and the mp3 in one zip file. The possibilities are limited only by your imagination.

Different Visual Layout

Another common test that often yields eye-popping results is to compare individual layouts of the same page with different combinations of visual elements. Does an opt-in convert at a higher rate when it's on the upper-left or on the upper-right corner of the screen? Does it help if there's a video that urges visitors to claim that free ebook by filling out their information in the opt-in? And does it make any difference if the video automatically begins playing when you reach the page, or if you have to actually click the **Play** button to make it start? The answers to these questions will almost always differ depending on who your target audience is, and it's a fabulous topic to split test to achieve better results.

Heatmaps

Finally, there are tools and services you can use that actually keep track of where people click their mouse on a web page. This information is then translated into **heatmaps**, a graphical format that shows where people are actually clicking to take some form of action on any given page. Heatmaps are excellent for gaining additional insight as to how your users understand the different pages on your website, and can reveal problems and trends that you simply can't extrapolate by merely looking at the raw numbers coming in from the site metrics.

Over to You

We've only just scratched the surface of the various types of techniques you can use to increase your goal conversion rates, but the most important aspect to keep in mind is that while traffic generation is an excellent topic to study and implement, high goal conversion levels will ultimately determine the success or failure of your website.

Search engine optimization has traditionally been one of those "black magic" type topics in web development that business owners are fiercely concerned about and many web developers routinely duck or provide far too simplistic a solution to. In this chapter, we defined the difference between SEO and SEM, explained the primary reasons why it's all a moving target that's really tough to master, and explained that ultimately there is absolutely no substitute for quality, relevant content.

Following our introductory discussion on SEO and SEM, we tackled the meat of on-page SEO and introduced the Big Three fundamental SEO components: semantic permalinking, proper `<meta>` and `<title>` tag inclusion, and proper header tag structure and implementation. Afterwards, we put all three components together and offered a simplified explanation as to how they work in tandem (or against one another) when a search engine spider pays a visit to any given page or post. Afterwards, we finished up our discussion on SEO by examining a few additional items that are worth paying attention to when tweaking our search engine rankings and performance.

Finally, we unveiled the dirty little secret that while search engine optimization is nice, it's hardly the most important aspect in creating a successful site—a myth that's been forged by almost two decades of bad information. Instead, the real holy grail of website success can be found through goal conversions, a topic that deals specifically with identifying concrete, tangible, measurable goals for any given web page, and seeking to increase them through trial-and-error testing techniques. We then went on to discuss some of these techniques, and offered a basic path forward in learning more about creating successful websites.

Folks, it's truly been a fun ride, and we hope you've enjoyed reading this book as much as we've enjoyed putting it together for you. Until next time, so long … and thanks for all the fish! Be well.

Index

X

Y

What's Next?

Web designers: Prepare to master the ways of the jQuery ninja!

JQUERY: NOVICE TO NINJA

By Earle Castledine & Craig Sharkie

jQuery has quickly become the JavaScript library of choice, and it's easy to see why.

In this easy-to-follow guide, you'll master all the major tricks and techniques that jQuery offers—within hours.

 This book has saved my life! I especially love the "excerpt" indications, to avoid getting lost. JQuery is easy to understand thanks to this book. It's a must-have for your development library, and you truly go from Novice to Ninja!

Amanda Rodriguez, USA

How About ...

Occasionally something seriously cool happens in web development. This is it!

HTML5 & CSS3
FOR THE REAL WORLD

By Alexis Goldstein, Louis Lazaris & Estelle Weyl

HTML5 & CSS3 for the Real World is the perfect book for those who are new to HTML5 and CSS3, as well as those who are familiar with these topics but want to dive in deeper.

Save 10% with this link:

 www.sitepoint.com/launch/customers-only-htmlcss1

Use this link to save 10% off the cover price of **HTML5 & CSS3 for the Real World,** compliments of the SitePoint publishing team.

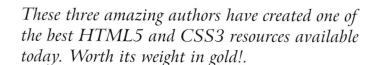

These three amazing authors have created one of the best HTML5 and CSS3 resources available today. Worth its weight in gold!.

Russ Weakley - maxdesign.com.au

How About ...

Start Building Web Sites Like a Pro!

Teach yourself SQL—the easy way

SIMPLY SQL

By Rudy Limeback

SQL is a simple, but high-level, language of tremendous power and elegance.

Believe it or not, a few lines of SQL can perform tasks that would take pages and pages of intricate PHP, ASP.NET, or Rails. This is true coder gold, as you can bring it with you, regardless of language or platform.

Save 10% with this link:

www.sitepoint.com/launch/customers-only-sql1

Use this link to save 10% off the cover price of **Simply SQL**, compliments of the SitePoint publishing team.

I had no clue SQL had t his much power! I love this book, (as) it's broken down very well and teaches you to fully understand what you're doing with every type of clause.

Jesse Boyer, USA

How About ...

Use your design skills to earn passive income with WordPress themes

BUILD YOUR OWN WICKED WORDPRESS THEMES

By Allan Cole, Raena Jackson Armitage, Brandon R. Jones & Jeffrey Way

Top WordPress theme designers earn a passive income of $10–25K per month! Read our new book and you, too, can grab a slice of that cake.

Save 10% with this link:

 www.sitepoint.com/launch/customers-only-wordpress1

Use this link to save 10% off the cover price of *Build Your Own Wicked Wordpress Themes,* compliments of the SitePoint publishing team.

It's refreshing to come across a book that shows how to build WordPress themes in a step by step, easy to understand format.

Liza Carey, Graphic Designer, Australia

Create mind-blowingly beautiful and functional forms with ease

FANCY FORM DESIGN

**By Jina Bolton, Tim Connell &
Derek Featherstone**

No longer do you need to worry at the thought of integrating a stylish form on your site.

Fancy Form Design is a complete guide to creating beautiful web forms that are aesthetically pleasing, highly functional, and compatible across all major browsers.

Save 10% with this link:

www.sitepoint.com/launch/customers-only-forms1

Use this link to save 10% off the cover price of *Fancy Form Design*, compliments of the SitePoint publishing team.

Overall it's a good book, entertaining, well-written, not overly long, (and) full of immediately practical examples that anyone familiar with form design and development can use.

Gary Barber, 17 Jan 2010

How About ...

HTML email simplified, seriously

CREATE STUNNING HTML EMAIL THAT JUST WORKS!

By Mathew Patterson

This step-by-step guide is perfect for front-end web designers looking to expand their range of services to clients. You'll be able to take your CSS and HTML skills, and deploy them to build beautiful, effective, and compatible HTML emails.

I have been searching for a book about HTML email design and have finally found it! I just read the entire thing in about 2 hours.

Russell , 6 May 2010

How About ...

By 2014, there will be more phones browsing the Internet than computers. Will you be building for them?

BUILD MOBILE
WEBSITES AND APPS FOR SMART DEVICES

By Earle Castledine, Myles Eftos & Max Wheeler

Grab hold of the most exciting and important development in computing since the Internet itself: The Mobile Web. It's a field brimming with possibility where you can bring your amazing ideas to life.

Save 10% with this link:

 www.sitepoint.com/launch/customers-only-mobile1

Use this link to save 10% off the cover price of *Build Mobile Websites and Apps For Smart Devices,* compliments of the SitePoint publishing team.

 FIVE BILLION apps were downloaded in 2010—up from 300 million in 2009

MobileFuture.org: Mobile Year in Review 2010

How About ...

Tired of making websites that work, but lack a certain spark?

THE PRINCIPLES OF BEAUTIFUL WEB DESIGN, 2nd Ed.

By Jason Beaird

Now in it's second edition, this gorgeous, full-color book will guide you through the complete design process, from getting inspiration and sketching ideas out, through to choosing a color scheme, designing the layout, and selecting effective imagery.

 Jason explains complex design principles in such a way that even those of us that lack a formal design background can apply these principles.

Jeffrey G. Allen